Platforms

Platforms

A Critical Introduction

Anne Helmond
Fernando van der Vlist

polity

First published in 2026 by Polity Press Ltd.

Polity Press Ltd.
65 Bridge Street
Cambridge CB2 1UR, UK

Polity Press Ltd.
111 River Street
Hoboken, NJ 07030, USA

ISBN-13: 978-1-5095-6810-9
ISBN-13: 978-1-5095-6811-6(pb)

A catalogue record for this book is available from the British Library.

Library of Congress Control Number: 2026930940

Typeset in 10.5 on 12pt Sabon
by Fakenham Prepress Solutions, Fakenham, Norfolk NR21 8NL
Printed and bound by Ashford Colour Ltd

The publisher has used its best endeavours to ensure that the URLs for external websites referred to in this book are correct and active at the time of going to press. However, the publisher has no responsibility for the websites and can make no guarantee that a site will remain live or that the content is or will remain appropriate.

Every effort has been made to trace all copyright holders, but if any have been overlooked the publisher will be pleased to include any necessary credits in any subsequent reprint or edition.

For further information on Polity, visit our website:
politybooks.com

Contents

Tables and Figures

Tables

Figures

Acknowledgements

This book reflects over a decade of collaborative and individual research into platforms and platformisation. It brings together our empirical, methodological, and theoretical engagements with the infrastructures, strategies, and power relations that define contemporary platform societies.

We are deeply grateful to our colleagues and collaborators over the years: their insights, joint effort, and critical dialogue have contributed to shaping the ideas presented here. We thank our editor, Mary Savigar, for her support and for guiding this book project with care and encouragement, and Manuela Tecusan for her careful copy-editing of the manuscript. We also thank the anonymous reviewers and José van Dijck and Thomas Poell, whose thoughtful feedback made us sharpen our arguments and strengthen the manuscript. Special thanks go to family and friends for their sustained support throughout our careers.

Our names as authors appear in alphabetical order; this is intended to reflect equal contributions. Parts of this work were supported by the Dutch Research Council (NWO) Spinoza Prize grant number SPI.2021.001 (awarded in 2021 to José van Dijck, Professor of Media and Digital Society at Utrecht University); and by the NWO Talent Programme | Veni project number VI.Veni.241C.001 (DOI: 10.61686/ AHWQW77464).

1

Introduction

Platforms in Culture and Society

Our world runs on platforms.

On X (formerly Twitter), now owned by billionaire Elon Musk, misinformation circulates widely around ongoing conflicts in Ukraine and Gaza. The platform's AI chatbot, Grok, has generated antisemitic content, prompting urgent questions among European regulators about compliance with the Digital Services Act (DSA) in a digital space where fact-checking has been deliberately dismantled. Simultaneously, TikTok faces scrutiny from European regulators concerning the role of its algorithm in shaping public opinion and influencing national elections, notably in Romania, which further highlights the geopolitical dimension of platforms today.

Artificial intelligence (AI), powered by models from OpenAI, Google, and Anthropic, is now deeply integrated into workflows across nearly every sector, from business to education and health. Designers use generative AI tools such as Midjourney and Adobe Firefly as their creative partners, while businesses rely on Microsoft's Azure AI as the backbone of their customer service operations and data analysis processes. Salesforce's 2-billion investment in Singapore to embed AI-driven tools across business processes in Southeast Asia further entrenches corporate dependency on AI infrastructures.

The reach of platforms extends well beyond technology into the world's most traditional sectors. In North America, farmers use John Deere's proprietary software to manage precision agriculture and optimise yields in response to intensifying droughts and heatwaves caused by climate change. In the US defence sector, companies such as Palantir provide big data analytics as well as AI-driven operational planning and decision-making systems for military logistics and intelligence, while in the United Kingdom they extend into healthcare and public administration. In universities, Dutch academics warn executive boards about the risks of depending on US big tech providers amid shifting geopolitical relationships between Europe and the United States. At the same time, gig economy workers protest against opaque platform algorithms that determine their pay, scheduling, and livelihoods. Uber drivers in Amsterdam and Lieferando couriers in Hamburg took to the streets and went on strike to demand better working conditions, while Didi drivers in China used bots to manipulate the platform's algorithm and secure better fares.

The material footprint of this platform-driven world is immense. To power growing AI demands, Amazon and Google acquire former nuclear sites and invest heavily in energy infrastructure. This expansion places severe strain on local resources and communities, prompting successful protests by citizens and farmers worldwide. In the Netherlands protests targeted a new Facebook data centre on account of its projected impacts on energy grids, water provision, and agricultural land.

At the heart of these diverse scenes lies a single dominant organisational form and business model: the platform. Over the past two decades, digital platforms have become the primary infrastructures through which modern life is lived, managed, contested, and governed.

Platforms: A critical concept and global phenomenon

This book treats 'platform' first and foremost as a powerful analytical concept that helps us to make sense of how a small number of highly influential companies have come to shape major parts of economic, social, and cultural life around the world. While platforms are often associated with familiar social media apps such as Instagram, TikTok, or YouTube, they also include cloud infrastructures, app stores, developer ecosystems, e-commerce marketplaces, food delivery services, on-demand labour, AI models, and recommendation engines. They are not just services or technologies but socio-technical systems, companies, and infrastructures that organise participation, orchestrate interactions, and govern digital environments.

Platforms are powerful convenors and shapers

As we argue throughout the book, platforms act as *powerful convenors and shapers*: they are digital entities that bring together different actors – end users (consumers), businesses, developers, advertisers, creators, and institutions – and structure their relationships and interactions through interfaces, algorithms, policies, architectures, and infrastructures. Platforms do not simply enable connections; they configure who can participate, under what conditions, and on what terms. Their power lies not only in what they enable but in how they structure, constrain, and condition the possibilities for social interaction, expression, exchange, and economic activity across sectors. Chapter 2 will unpack this initial definition in greater depth, examining how platforms function as services, as part of companies, and as technologies or infrastructures embedded in wider ecosystems.

The most powerful corporations are now platform companies. In the United States, the so-called Magnificent Seven – Alphabet (Google), Amazon, Apple, Meta (Facebook), Microsoft, NVIDIA, and Tesla – dominate fields that range from advertising and AI to streaming, e-commerce, and cloud infrastructure. With market capitalisations that often exceed the GDP of entire developed countries such as Italy, South Korea, or the Netherlands, they represent an historic consolidation of infrastructural and economic power. These are not simply private companies but global actors embedded in systems of finance, labour, governance, and everyday life, all operating on a platform business model (more on this in chapter 3).

In China, a different but equally significant platform ecosystem has emerged. Companies such as Tencent, Alibaba, Baidu, Xiaomi, and ByteDance operate vast domestic platforms that serve massive user bases and extend their influence globally, particularly through 'super apps' – that is, all-in-one services that bundle messaging, payments, transport, and commerce. These platforms, exemplified by WeChat, increasingly shape digital infrastructures beyond China, especially in Southeast Asia, Africa, and Latin America (van der Vlist, Helmond, Dieter et al., 2025). At the same time, the Chinese government has asserted greater control over its tech sector, turning platform governance into an instrument of geopolitical and economic strategy (see chapter 4). Since 2020, regulatory crackdowns have reshaped China's platform landscape, wiping out more than a trillion dollars in market value (Kwok and Murdoch, 2023) and reconfiguring the balance of corporate and state power.

Despite differences in origin, regulation, or scale, these companies share a common platform logic. While their services and strategies differ, they rely for the most part on similar mechanisms: attracting third parties, orchestrating interactions and data flows, integrating with existing infrastructures, creating dependencies, and extracting value from data, often through advertising (see chapter 3). Their economic dominance generates profound societal consequences: they influence elections, reorganise labour conditions, transform cultural production, and raise urgent questions about public oversight and democratic accountability around the world.

The platform paradigm

As platforms continue to get deeply woven into everyday life, gaining public acceptance while also sparking heated debates, both academic and societal attention to them has sharpened. Platforms now profoundly *shape* and are *shaped by* our broader media and cultural environment. Jean Burgess (2021: 22) captures this shift through the notion of an emerging 'platform paradigm' that emphasises the far-reaching influence of platforms and of their operations and values on culture and society at large, well beyond online digital media.

Platforms thus reveal something fundamental about our current digital condition: they operate across culture, economy, and politics, shaping life both online and offline. Since the mid-2000s, they have been transforming not only how we communicate and consume media but also how we work, organise, and interact with institutions.

The global COVID-19 pandemic (2020–2022) accelerated this transformation. As public life was disrupted, platforms became essential infrastructure for work, education, health, intimacy, and entertainment. This period normalised remote work through corporate platforms, while labour itself came to be mediated by platforms even to a higher degree. Consequently, big tech's dominance and profits surged so much that Ovide (2021) declared: 'Big Tech won the pandemic.'

Today platforms are among the most profitable and powerful companies in history. While their reach is global, their operations and effects are moulded by local cultural, infrastructural, and regulatory conditions. This tension between global expansion and local adaptation lies at the heart of platform power: platforms universalise their models while simultaneously embedding themselves within, and reshaping, the specific contexts in which they operate.

A critical introduction to platform studies

This book offers a critical introduction to *platforms* and the burgeoning interdisciplinary field of *platform studies*. Having emerged in the mid-2000s in the wake of the growing prominence of digital platforms in economy, culture, and society, platform studies scholarship examines how online digital platforms (re)organise social, economic, and techno-logical life. Rather than treating platforms merely as media or technologies, this research field understands them as complex socio-technical systems that structure participation, mediate relationships, govern data flows, and redesign insti-tutions, infrastructures, and power dynamics. Crucially, it approaches platforms not in isolation but as embedded in broader ecosystems that they both shape and depend upon. Platform studies brings together perspectives from communi-cation and media studies, sociology, political economy, law, and science and technology studies to analyse how platforms are built, governed, and embedded in everyday life (more on this in chapter 2).

Two research orientations

As internet scholars like Richard Rogers (2013; 2024) and Tim Highfield (2022) have argued, the broader field of internet studies is defined by two key research orientations. The first, *medium research*, analyses platforms as environments in their own right, focusing on how their affordances, policies, and technical architectures shape user behaviour and content. The second, *social research*, examines how platforms mediate broader societal, political, and economic issues and processes. Highfield (2022, n.p.) puts it like this: 'Are you studying, for instance, Instagram or TikTok as a specific cultural space and how this affects the content being presented (medium research), or are you studying a practice that happens to be mediated through Instagram or TikTok (social research)?'.

This distinction reflects broader disciplinary divergences between the humanities, social sciences, law, business, and computer science. It is useful not only for researchers as they frame their questions, but also for our understanding of how different fields approach platform analysis.

This book's approach

In this book we speak to both orientations. We analyse platforms as cultural and technological formations in their own right *and* as infrastructures through which social and economic life is increasingly organised and contested. Our work and this book have been informed from the outset by dialogue with neighbouring disciplines such as communication, sociology, political economy, business studies, law, and science and technology studies.

Our aim is to provide conceptual frameworks and research strategies for engaging with these perspectives, with particular emphasis on critical and material approaches. Moving beyond the early focus on social media, the book offers a more comprehensive understanding of what platforms are, how they operate, and how scholars have examined them empirically and critically. We equip readers with key concepts, theoretical and empirical insights, and research strategies for analysing platforms as companies, services, infrastructures, and ecosystems. The book traces how platforms have evolved, how they operate, and how they forge and remodel cultural, economic, and institutional structures.

Central to our discussion are the fundamental domains that underpin platform power: political economy, which examines how platforms create and extract value; governance and regulation, which explores how platforms govern, are governed, and get contested; and strategy, which analyses how platforms compete and expand. These forces will be introduced in detail in the next chapter.

Why platforms matter
We argue that platforms matter not only because of their unprecedented scale or profitability but because, in both visible and invisible ways, they increasingly mediate, organise, and condition the environments we inhabit. They structure how we communicate, consume, work, and govern and how we relate to one another, embedding themselves deep within the infrastructures, institutions, and everyday rhythms of contemporary life. Understanding how platforms operate – and how they wield and distribute power – is therefore essential to understanding the social, cultural, and economic dynamics of our time.

This book is written for students, scholars, journalists, policymakers, cultural producers, and others who seek to make sense of the growing significance of platforms. It provides a set of conceptual frameworks and analytical tools drawn from across disciplines and designed to help us investigate how platforms work, how they configure society, and how their influence might be understood and contested.

Emergence of the platform model

To understand how the platform emerged as a dominant model for organising culture and society, it may be helpful for us to trace several formative episodes in its historical evolution. The idea of the platform did not originate in a single domain but evolved through developments in computing, economics and management, and the media industries. These histories are discussed in greater detail in chapter 2; here we outline them briefly, to highlight how the model's meaning and scope have expanded over time.

Origins of the platform

The term 'platform' first appeared in computing, where it referred to hardware (such as the IBM System/360 or the Atari gaming consoles) or to software environments (such as the Microsoft Windows operating system) that support other applications. As Marc Steinberg (2019) shows in his extensive genealogy of the platform model, these early computational platforms were never purely technical foundations: they also operated as business models by creating and managing markets for developers and applications. Windows, for example, generated value by enabling software developers to create applications for consumers while maintaining control over their distribution.

Steinberg also traces how, in economics, especially after Rochet and Tirole (2003), platforms were reconceptualised as intermediaries between distinct user groups, such as cardholders and merchants within the Visa network. Their work formalised the platform model as an economic framework for creating and capturing value by facilitating transactions and mediating interactions. While this narrative often centres on the United States and Europe, Steinberg (2019) offers a crucial counter-genealogy by tracing the emergence of platform capitalism to Japan, where this computational and economic model of the platform emerged. He demonstrates how systems such as the Nintendo consoles and the NTT Docomo i-mode provided an early infrastructure for hosting and distributing third-party digital content (such as news and games) and for enabling micropayments, in anticipation of today's global platform economies. Such perspectives remind us that platform models are shaped by distinct cultural and economic contexts (chapter 5).

The participatory web: From blogs to Web 2.0

Another influential moment came with the rise of the blogosphere in the late 1990s and early 2000s. Blogging services such as Blogger, LiveJournal, and WordPress offered accessible tools for independent and personal web publishing, allowing users to bypass traditional media 'gatekeepers'

(Bruns, 2008). These new web services also exemplified early platforms in a technical sense: they provided configurable and customisable environments that hosted user-generated content and supported extensibility through plugins, themes, and other developer tools. Bloggers built distributed networks and communities through blogrolls, really simple syndication (RSS) feeds, and comment sections, creating a participatory web culture. Blogs were celebrated as important 'platforms' for self-expression, especially for marginalised voices, and became crucial spaces for alternative journalism and activist mobilisation during events like the Iraq War and the Arab Spring (Bruns, 2008; Walker Rettberg, 2014).

By the mid-2000s, a major shift occurred with the emergence of what is now known as Web 2.0. Popularised by internet business guru Tim O'Reilly in the wake of the dotcom crash, the industry term functioned as both strategic rebranding and expression of a new vision of the web's potential. Web 2.0 framed the web not merely as a medium for publishing information but as a programmable infrastructure for building services – an infrastructure that O'Reilly (2005) dubbed 'the web as platform'. This vision supported a post-dotcom crash recovery narrative, which was marketing the web as a robust environment for software development and business innovation.

Companies such as Amazon and Salesforce began offering application programming interfaces (APIs), which provide structured access to platform data and functionalities, enabling external developers to build on and integrate with their services. The 2007 launch of the Facebook Development Platform extended this logic to the social web, allowing developers to use Facebook's user data and functionalities within their own applications. APIs facilitate a platform's programmability and infrastructural expansion by decentralising its features while centralising data and control. This dynamic is central to the process of 'platformisation' (see chapter 3).

The Web 2.0 era was characterised by user-generated content, interactivity (liking, sharing, commenting), network effects (value that increased with the number of users), and openness through APIs and mashups. Mashups are applications that combine data or functionality from multiple sources into a single interface. They became a hallmark of this era, demonstrating how platforms invited external developers to build new services on top of their infrastructure via APIs. While these developments were celebrated as signalling a new era of user empowerment, the participatory rhetoric around them masked a deeper reorganisation of power. As platforms grew, they absorbed and enclosed the decentralised practices of the early web. Bloggers started to embed YouTube videos and Facebook buttons, and many moved their activities to social media platforms altogether. As both Esther Weltevrede and Anne Helmond (2012) and Jill Walker Rettberg (2014) show, this shift dismantled the blogosphere's decentralised infrastructure, replacing open standards such as hyperlinks and RSS with commodified activities and algorithmically curated feeds inside the 'walled gardens' of social media platforms.

Critical scholars argued that these platforms did not simply facilitate participation but defined its very 'conditions of possibility', structuring what could be seen, said, and done within their commercial infrastructures (Langlois et al., 2009). As Gillespie (2018a: 254) notes, platforms 'rose up out of the exquisite chaos of the web', positioning themselves as the new architects of order. In doing so, they became 'private governors' of online life, curating content and policing activity at scale (Klonick, 2018; see chapter 4).

Beyond social networks: Mobile apps, the internet of things, and AI

In 2008 the launch of Apple's iPhone OS (later iOS) and of Google's Android mobile operating systems – alongside their respective app stores, App Store and Android Market – marked a new phase in the platform model. These stores operated both as matchmakers, that is, as platforms that connected app developers and users, and as powerful gatekeepers that controlled software standards, monetisation models, and developer behaviour (Dieter et al., 2019; see chapter 2).

During the 2010s, platforms expanded further, going beyond social media and mobile devices into physical infrastructures and everyday environments. Through technologies such as augmented reality, virtual reality, and the internet of things (IoT), platforms began to integrate networks of connected devices that ranged from smart homes to industrial sensors, all tethered to cloud-based services for data collection, analytics, and remote control.

More recently, platforms have become central to the current AI boom. Companies such as OpenAI, Google (Vertex AI), Amazon (SageMaker), and Microsoft (Azure AI) offer AI platforms, APIs, pre-trained models, and cloud infrastructure to integrate machine learning into a growing array of services across industries. These platforms now serve as infrastructural backbones for a wide range of sectors, from customer services to logistics, finance, advertising, media production, and education. They exemplify what we have termed the industrialisation of AI: the rapid commercial embedding of AI technologies across sectors – a process underpinned by platform logic and shifting interdependencies (as we shall see in chapter 5).

These short key episodes in the history of online platforms demonstrate how the latter have become central to shaping online and physical life, impacting economies, cultures, and institutions around the world.

Our position in the field

We are not just observers of the field of platform studies; we have actively contributed to shaping its development since early days.

In previous research (Gerlitz and Helmond, 2013; Helmond, 2015a, 2015b; Weltevrede and Helmond, 2012), we examined the rise of platforms in the early 2000s and their development into the dominant infrastructural and economic model of the web. We first introduced, then further developed the concept of platformisation to describe how platforms expand beyond their original domains and to present the wider implications of this expansion. This concept captures the infrastructural and strategic dynamics that underpin the reach and power of platforms (see chapter 3).

Our critical work advocated a *material–infrastructural* perspective on platforms, combined with a *techno-economic* general outlook. In simple terms, this means studying platforms not only as digital services but also as concrete socio-technical systems that support a wide range of activities and as companies with specific business models and strategic objectives. This approach highlights how a platform's technical design is closely tied to its economic operations and strategies. It foregrounds the material conditions of platforms: how they are built, how they shape user practices, and how they enable platforms to scale, exert control, and extract economic value. This materiality is central to the analytical framework developed in chapter 2.

In our later work we turned to the political economy, governance, and histories of platforms and apps (e.g. Bucher and Helmond, 2017; Helmond and van der Vlist, 2019; Helmond et al., 2019; van der Vlist and Helmond, 2021; van der Vlist, 2022; van der Vlist, Helmond and Ferrari, 2024). We thoroughly examined the features, affordances, technological infrastructures, and evolutionary trajectories of platforms as they became dominant development and business models. This work revealed the political-economic dynamics that drive platformisation and the distinct material conditions that make platform power possible. Our research has shown how platforms *convene* actors from across vast ecosystems and actively *shape* their evolution through diverse strategies: by managing data and content, by enforcing policies, by developing infrastructures, by setting technical standards, and by pursuing partnerships, mergers, acquisitions, startup investments, and lobbying efforts. These strategies allow platforms to scale, create dependencies, and accumulate strategic and infrastructural power, as will be discussed in chapter 3.

Through our long-term collaborations within the Digital Methods Initiative (University of Amsterdam) and the App Studies Initiative, we have also investigated mobile platforms in detail. Our investigations include analysing the mobile ecosystems of Apple (App Store, iOS) and Google (Play Store, Android), their policies, their tracking infrastructures (Dieter et al., 2019; Gerlitz, Helmond, Nieborg et al., 2019), and platforms' growing roles in areas such as digital advertising, automobility, and AI (Hind et al., 2022; van der Vlist and Helmond, 2021; van der Vlist, Helmond and Ferrari, 2024).

Moreover, our work has brought together insights from diverse disciplinary traditions. We have synthesised research from media and cultural studies, communication, information systems, engineering, law, business, and management, fields that have often approached platforms in isolation. We argue that an integrated and interdisciplinary perspective is essential for understanding platforms both as complex objects of study and in their broader societal impact. The present book is shaped by this conviction. While it adopts a global perspective on platforms and platformisation, it is grounded in our knowledge and experience in the field, inhabits a European context, and has its roots in media studies.

Critical platform studies approaches

Online platforms mediate and configure everyday life at both individual and societal levels, across economic, cultural, political, and institutional domains. Across their diverse forms, platforms bring together different users, services, and institutions, providing the technical, organisational, and economic means for others to create, share, and transact online. In so doing they structure participation, visibility, and value, setting the very conditions of social and economic life.

Building on cross-disciplinary scholarship, we approach platforms in their full complexity: as digital services used by billions, as corporate entities with distinct business models and strategic goals, and as technologies or infrastructures that undergird and organise contemporary societies. Across these dimensions, platforms function as powerful convenors that configure relationships, practices, and possibilities throughout the digital environment.

Over the past two decades, scholars from diverse disciplines have developed distinct methodological approaches to studying platforms. As the editors of the scholarly journal *Platforms & Society* (launched in 2024) observe, this has created a 'fragmented landscape' of platform research, in which various disciplines and regions conduct their own studies. This is a concern, given the global scale of platform-related challenges (Chen et al., 2024). Others argue that the issue is not fragmentation but the lack of variety, as platform research is 'heavily concentrated around a handful of themes' that reflect disciplinary habits, such as the focus on social media predominant in media studies (Narayan, 2024: 1). Both views point to the need for a more consolidated and diverse research agenda, which should draw on cross-disciplinary approaches to address the complex and global dynamics of platforms and platformisation and 'their impacts on and embeddedness in economies, cultures, and institutions around the world' (Chen et al., 2024).

By way of introduction, the following sections trace the development of critical platform studies, identifying three key waves of scholarship that reflect major orientations within the field. Each wave corresponds to a particular moment in the evolution of digital platform studies and demonstrates shifting understandings of what platforms are, how they operate, and why they matter. Together, all three illustrate how the study of platforms has expanded from analysing individual services to interrogating the infrastructures, economies, and governance regimes that underpin the platform society. Chapter 2 provides a more in-depth discussion of the cross-disciplinary conceptualisations and core characteristics of platforms and platformisation.

Platforms as and within culture and society: Three waves of critical platform studies, 2000s–2010s

The societal significance of platforms can be understood from two interconnected perspectives: *platforms as culture and society* and *platforms within culture and society*. On the one hand, platforms are embedded in social and cultural life, being shaped by norms, values, and user practices. This perspective focuses on what happens *on* platforms or *within* platform environments – namely user interactions, content production, and cultural expression. For example, studies of TikTok's remix aesthetics or YouTube's creator communities analyse how users produce and negotiate meaning *on* the platform. On the other hand, platforms also shape and are shaped by economies, cultures, institutions, labour, and public discourse; they are *part of* culture and society itself. From this perspective, research explores how platforms restructure news industries, reorganise creative labour, or mediate public communication. This dual framing helps to explain why platforms have become such central objects of study – and not only in communication and media studies but also across the humanities and social sciences.

First wave (late 2000s): Platforms as cultural and communicative environments

The first wave emerged in the late 2000s, as scholars developed new approaches to the critical study of software and computational culture (known as software studies), online (natively digital) culture, and social media. Research in this area examined life on platforms, focusing on the material and technical conditions of digital media, for example on interfaces, algorithms, protocols, and standards, and especially on how these technical components shape everyday practices and culture online (e.g. Bucher, 2012; Bogost and Montfort, 2009; Fuller, 2008; Helmond, 2015b; Langlois et al., 2009; Rogers, 2013).

Much of this work centred on social media and specific platforms such as YouTube, Google, and Twitter. A key insight was that platforms are not neutral intermediaries but *actively convene and shape* the production, dissemination, and consumption of media and discourse. For example, Burgess and Green's (2018 [2009]) influential study of YouTube demonstrated how the platform shapes cultural norms, political debate, and the economic dynamics of media production.

The concept of 'platform politics' emerged as a core theme during this period. Tarleton Gillespie (2010) showed how platforms discursively position themselves as neutral facilitators while significantly moulding online interactions and public discourse. He argues that platforms strategically mobilise multiple meanings of the term 'platform' – technical, architectural, political, and metaphorical – to appeal to different stakeholders and legitimise their role.

Meanwhile, José van Dijck (2013) traced how social media platforms evolved from standalone services into an interconnected, commercialised platform ecosystem that profoundly influences social interactions and cultural norms. Her framework offers a systematic way of analysing platforms through six interrelated dimensions: technology, usage, content, ownership, governance, and business models. This approach emphasises that platforms must be understood as socio-technical assemblages that are embedded in wider economic and cultural systems.

These contributions established a foundational understanding of platforms as deeply social and cultural entities rather than merely technical infrastructures.

Second wave (early 2010s): Digital methods and infrastructural analysis

The second wave of platform studies emerged in the early 2010s and was characterised by a critical technical engagement with the material conditions of platforms and apps and by methodological exploration and innovation (e.g. Rogers, 2013; Dieter et al., 2019). A key development was the introduction of digital methods for web research, which involved repurposing online platforms such as Twitter, Facebook, and Google for medium-specific research and for examining social and political issues through the lens of platforms (Rogers, 2013).

This period also embraced API-based research in the (digital) humanities and social sciences (e.g. Borra and Rieder, 2014; Venturini and Rogers, 2019). By using platforms' APIs to access data about users, content, and interactions, researchers could study both the platforms themselves (i.e. do medium research) and the societal issues they mediate (i.e. do social research). These approaches took advantage of the medium-specific features of platforms, for example their data structures, infrastructures, and algorithmic systems, to analyse how they organise communication and represent social phenomena.

A good illustration of this kind of approach is the multi-contributor volume *Twitter and Society*, which explores Twitter's roles *in* society in order to investigate the interaction between Twitter *and* society (Weller et al., 2013: xxxi). The authors emphasise how platforms like Twitter are deeply embedded in culture and society. The volume foregrounds how medium-specific features such as the hashtag delineate the platform's societal roles. The concept of hashtag publics captures how users form ad-hoc communities around shared topics or events and at the same time highlights how platform algorithms determine which voices and issues gain visibility (Bruns and Burgess, 2015).

Subsequent studies have examined hashtags as tools for networked activism. In 2011, #ArabSpring facilitated the circulation of protest information beyond state-controlled media. In 2013, #BlackLivesMatter became a rallying cry against racialised police violence, and in 2017 #MeToo ignited a global movement for raising awareness about sexual abuse and gender inequality. In each case, platform features were instrumental in shaping who could speak, what was amplified, and how publics were formed and sustained around societal issues.

This critical engagement with platforms' material conditions also revealed the often invisible actors and processes – such as data intermediaries and back-end infrastructures – that enable online tracking and targeted advertising, the business model that sustains most platforms. The back-end operations raised urgent concerns around privacy, surveillance, and the commodification of personal data (discussed in chapter 3). Within platform studies, the corresponding insights led to extensive research on the political economy of platforms and on the rise of the surveillance advertising model, which is driven largely by platforms and is based on the continuous harvesting and monetising of user data (Crain, 2021; Zuboff, 2019).

Third wave (mid- to late 2010s): Platformisation and the political economy of digital capitalism

Starting in the mid- to late 2010s, a third wave of research increasingly focused on platforms' systemic roles *in* society. Scholars examined concepts such as platform economy, platform capitalism, platform labour, and platform society in order to analyse how platforms reorganise various (semi) public sectors – news, transportation, healthcare, education, cultural production, and the gig economy (Kenney and Zysman, 2020; Poell et al., 2021; Srnicek, 2016; Steinberg, 2019; van Dijck et al., 2018; van Doorn and Badger, 2020).

In particular, this wave brought heightened attention to platform power and platform governance. Key discussions have centred on the politics of content moderation exercised by social media and app store platforms (Dieter et al., 2021; Gillespie, 2018a; Gorwa, 2024; Nielsen and Ganter, 2022; Roberts, 2019), as well as on broader concerns about the control of digital infrastructures, monopolistic data regimes, regulation, and the influence of platforms on public opinion and democratic processes (see chapter 4). Scholars have explored the spread of fake news and misinformation on social media platforms and the societal impact of this phenomenon (Rogers, 2023b). They have also examined how platforms mediate labour processes in the on-demand (or 'gig') economy and how this mediation impacts workers' conditions and experiences (van Doorn and Badger, 2020).

In sum, research has looked at the ways in which platforms are restructuring entire sectors such as health, education, and transport (van Dijck et al., 2018), thereby becoming integral to the organisation and delivery of essential services. In the cultural industries, platforms transform traditional media production while enabling new practices such as livestreaming, influencing, and podcasting. Such developments have duly attracted research too, because they have redefined market dynamics, infrastructures, and labour relations across creative economies (Poell et al., 2021).

Platform studies today

The evolving perspectives associated with this scholarship increasingly emphasise the role of platforms *in culture and society*, rather than viewing them as inherently cultural and social phenomena. This distinction echoes Marshall McLuhan's (1994 [1964]) famous claim 'the medium is the message', which reminds us that media technologies do not merely deliver content but actively determine how communication and culture are organised. In a similar way, platform studies has expanded to include both what happens on platforms (e.g. the practices and interactions they host) and how platforms themselves structure and condition social and cultural life. Over the past two decades, platform research has thus evolved from conceptualising platforms *as* culture and society to examining them *in* culture and society.

As part of this broader shift, platform studies has developed into what Burgess calls 'an umbrella term for holistic approaches to those entities that are understood and represent themselves as digital media' (Burgess, 2021: 25–26). Such approaches, she notes, attend to 'the technologies, interfaces, and affordances, ownership structures, business models, media and self-representations, and governance of these entities, positioning these elements in a coevolutionary relationship with the platform's diverse cultures of use' (26). In this way platform studies has become an interdisciplinary field that informs a wide range of research agendas. These include studies of digital (sub)cultures, content monetisation, online advertising, and content moderation, as well as research into polarisation, misinformation, political economy, labour organisation, and the (in)articulation of public values.

As a result, insights from platform studies are increasingly applied to understanding many spheres of life and sectors of society: education, healthcare, energy, even defence. In addition, platforms now play central roles in fast-evolving domains such as the app economy, self-driving technologies, autonomous systems and robotics, military decision-making, virtual reality (VR) and augmented reality (AR), the metaverse, cloud computing, and AI.

Recognising the diversity of the contexts in which platforms operate and are studied, the present book advances a central analytical proposition: platforms are powerful convenors and shapers of online and physical life (see p. 3). As convenors, far from being mere intermediaries, they actively and strategically bring together different user groups – consumers, developers, businesses, institutions – each with its own goals, practices, and interests in shared digital environments. As shapers, they orchestrate these interactions through technological architectures, embedded governance mechanisms, and business strategies that influence how participation unfolds and what outcomes become possible. Companies such as Google, Meta (Facebook, Instagram), Bytedance (TikTok), Amazon, and Airbnb exemplify this dual role: they bring together diverse actors around their infrastructures and strategic visions while moulding the social, cultural, economic, and political processes that result. This proposition underpins the analytical framework developed throughout the book.

Our framework builds on, and extends, foundational contributions to platform studies. These include van Dijck's (2013) conceptualisation of platforms as socio-technical and socioeconomic structures, which she analyses across six dimensions: technology, usage, content, ownership, governance, and business models. It also draws on van Dijck et al.'s (2018) notion of platform society, which captures how platforms pattern and are patterned by society and how their corporate logic and expansion challenge public values and sectoral norms around the globe. We also build on Poell et al.'s (2021) political-economic framework, which examines how platforms drive institutional shifts across markets, infrastructures, and governance and understands power as an emergent property of the platforms' modus operandi inside and across these domains.

Building on these foundations, our book introduces a distinct emphasis on *ecosystems*, *infrastructure*, and *strategic orchestration* to explain how platforms consolidate influence across sectors and scales. This focus helps us to trace the mechanisms and dependencies through which platforms entrench themselves and govern participation and interaction.

To investigate platform dynamics, our book develops a comprehensive analytical framework, which integrates key traditions in platform studies while advancing a global and systemic view. It approaches platforms simultaneously as *services* (e.g. for social media, advertising, ride-hailing), as *companies* (i.e. entities that own and operate one or more platforms), and as *technologies or infrastructures*; and it examines how their power unfolds across these dimensions (chapter 2). Together, these perspectives reveal how platforms act as powerful convenors, shaping economies, cultures, and institutions worldwide.

Book overview

The present book offers a critical introduction to platforms and to the interdisciplinary field of platform studies. Across three main chapters and a conclusion, it develops a relational and materialist perspective on platforms, bringing together key concepts, empirical insights, and theoretical approaches. It focuses on three cross-cutting dimensions – or domains of analysis – that help to explain how platforms accumulate and exercise power: *political economy* (profit and power), *governance*, and *strategy*. Throughout, examples are drawn from a wide variety of platforms – social media, app stores, e-commerce marketplaces, gig economy and on-demand labour services, cloud infrastructures, AI platforms, and 'super apps' – to ground the discussion in concrete and diverse cases and social settings.

Chapter 2, 'Understanding Platforms', lays the conceptual groundwork by asking: What are platforms, and how do they work? It develops an analytical framework that approaches platforms simultaneously as services, as entities owned and operated by companies, and as programmable technologies or infrastructures. Drawing from economics, computing, and media studies, the chapter traces the historical understanding of platforms as multisided markets, software infrastructures, and non-neutral intermediaries. It discusses core characteristics of platforms and emphasises the importance of studying them as objects embedded in wider technical, organisational, and institutional environments. It also introduces the three intersecting dimensions already mentioned – political economy, governance, and strategy: these underpin the influence of platforms and guide the book's overall structure.

Chapter 3, 'Profit and Power', explores the ways in which platforms generate, organise, and consolidate economic and infrastructural power. It introduces critical political economy as a lens for analysing platforms not just as market actors but as entities that restructure value chains, coordinate ecosystems, and create dependencies. The chapter identifies key mechanisms of platform power – such as datafication, infrastructuralisation, conglomeration, and orchestration – and shows how platforms act as convenors that enrol and integrate third parties into their ecosystems, for example by providing developer tools. It introduces 'follow the money' and 'follow the data' imperatives and ecosystem mapping as empirical strategies for studying these dynamics; and it conceptualises platform power as an iterative process of convening, integration, and capture. This perspective anchors the book's view of platforms as powerful actors that do not merely operate within economies, cultures, and institutions but actively restructure them.

Chapter 4, 'Governance and Regulation', examines platforms as both *governors* and *governed* entities. It distinguishes between *internal governance* (platform rule-making, moderation, and enforcement) and *external regulation* (state oversight, policy interventions, and geopolitical tensions). The chapter shows how platforms govern through layered and opaque systems of rules, policies, and technical infrastructures that influence both the behaviour and the access of different user groups or stakeholders. It introduces key approaches to researching platform governance and compares competing global regulatory regimes, as represented by the United States, the European Union, and China). Governance is shown to be uneven, layered, dynamic, and deeply embedded in material artefacts such as APIs, monetisation policies, and ranking systems. The chapter concludes by highlighting the geopolitical and jurisdictional complexities of regulating global platforms and thereby positions governance and regulation as crucial sites of contestation in the platform society.

Strategy, the third cross-cutting dimension, runs as a central thread throughout chapters 3 and 4. It connects the political-economic and governance perspectives by focusing on how platforms operate to secure their position in the long term. This includes launching new products, expanding into new markets and sectors, integrating infrastructures, managing their ecosystems of users, developers, and partners, and responding to or anticipating regulation. In this sense, strategy explains how platforms maintain their central position in society and consolidate power even as they face changing markets, technologies, political conditions, and regulatory frameworks.

The final chapter, 'Conclusion and Outlook', synthesises the book's core insights and outlines an agenda for critical platform research in the future. It identifies three key orientations: (1) present focus: the continued critical investigation of dominant platforms, including those in non-western contexts and in overlooked sectors such as health, education, and defence, or the military; (2) the future: analysis of emerging platform formations such as AI platforms, 'super apps', and hybrid infrastructures; and (3) the past: historical and archival approaches to reconstructing platform histories and to tracing infrastructural integrations as they evolve over time. The book closes with a call for empirical, critical, and imaginative scholarship that foregrounds the political, material, and infrastructural dimensions of platforms, inviting readers to contribute to a field that remains open, in motion, and urgently needed.

Discussion questions

- **Platforms beyond social media** The chapter opening includes examples such as John Deere's agricultural software and Palantir's defence services. How do these examples challenge a common understanding of 'platforms' as primarily social media, and what do they reveal about the pervasiveness of the platform business model in traditional sectors?
- **The platform paradigm** The chapter discusses the shift from the decentralised blogosphere to the centralised walled gardens of Web 2.0 and to the current platform paradigm. What were the long-term consequences of this platformisation process in terms of data ownership, user control, and the transformation of digital spaces?
- **Bridging research traditions** The chapter distinguishes between medium research and social research in internet studies. Using a platform like TikTok or Uber as an example, formulate one research question that exemplifies the medium research approach and one that exemplifies the social research approach. Why is this distinction useful for critical platform analysis?

Further reading

Burgess, J. (2021) Platform studies. In S. Cunningham and D. Craig (eds), *Creator Culture: An Introduction to Global Social Media Entertainment*. New York University Press.

Steinberg, M. (2019) *The Platform Economy: How Japan Transformed the Consumer Internet*. University of Minnesota Press.

Helmond, A. (2015a) The platformization of the web: Making web data platform ready. *Social Media + Society* 1(2). DOI: 10.1177/2056305115603080.

2
Understanding Platforms

Introduction

Every day, billions of people communicate through WhatsApp, search with Google, shop on Amazon, watch videos on YouTube, and hail rides through Uber. Yet these familiar activities only scratch the surface of what platforms do. Behind consumer-facing services lie vast infrastructures that shape the way we work, learn, communicate, and govern. Platforms now underpin agriculture through John Deere's cloud-based Operations Center, which allows farmers to monitor crops and optimise yields remotely; they organise military intelligence through Palantir AI-driven analytics; they structure education through Google Classroom and Microsoft Teams; they facilitate live streaming and gaming through Twitch and Steam; they organise labour through ride-hailing and delivery services such as DiDi, Uber, and Gojek; they bring buyers and sellers together on e-commerce and marketplace services such as eBay and Temu; and they coordinate logistics and commerce through Amazon Web Services (AWS) and Alibaba Cloud. From social media and entertainment to finance, healthcare, and defence, platforms have become foundational to contemporary economic and social life.

What are platforms?

This chapter addresses a deceptively simple question: what are platforms? The challenge lies not only in their diversity – Instagram, AWS, and Uber operate very differently – but also in how deeply they are embedded in everyday life, integrated across sectors, and understood differently by users, companies, scholars, and regulators. While platforms are ubiquitous, the term 'platform' itself remains analytically challenging precisely because of this breadth.

Across disciplines and fields, scholars converge on a core insight: platforms facilitate relationships between different user groups and entangle both people and things. They act as powerful convenors and shapers of relationships and inter-actions – to use our own formula, established in chapter 1 and deliberately repeated a few times throughout the book; and they do so through an object, system, space, or (digital) architecture commonly referred to as 'the platform'. For instance, as media scholar Steinberg (2019: 92) suggests, platforms are 'structures of relation, or the formalisation of relations in varying degree of technological means'. Similarly, Srnicek, (2016: 43) and van Dijck et al. (2018: 4) define platforms as 'digital infrastructures' or 'programmable architectures' that act as intermediaries, enabling interactions between multiple user groups – customers, advertisers, businesses, and public actors – while offering tools for others to build services and applications on top. Yet, because platforms operate across so many domains and have different functions, these definitions also expose key analytical challenges for studying them critically.

First, platforms are multiple things at once. As we will suggest later in this chapter (pp. 55–60), they may be approached as services (e.g. TikTok or Google Search) used by billions of consumers globally, as entities owned and operated by companies with strategic goals and business models (companies such as Bytedance or Alphabet), and as technologies or infrastructures that others build upon through application programming interfaces (APIs), software development kits (SDKs), and cloud services. Most users experience only the consumer-facing interface, while much of a platform's power resides in what remains unseen: its underlying infrastructures, algorithmic systems, moderation tools, and developer ecosystems. Moreover, platforms bring together diverse groups (they are multisided) and assume different roles, depending on who interacts with them. End users may primarily experience them as services; businesses, advertisers, and creators – as marketplaces; developers – as technologies or infrastructures; and companies or institutions – as partners or regulators. Actors can occupy multiple roles simultaneously and encounter distinct interfaces and user experiences tailored to each role.

Second, platforms are not standalone digital entities but layered and relational systems that both summon and depend on larger *ecosystems*. They mediate relationships between people, institutions, infrastructures, and markets. They assemble and coordinate networks of third parties – consumers, developers, businesses, and institutions – while operating within wider social, economic, and infrastructural environments that we understand as dynamic ecosystems. Their power lies in determining the way these connections are structured and sustained, and this makes it difficult to study platforms in isolation.

Third, platforms are dynamic and expansionary. They evolve continuously. What began in 2004 as Facebook.com, an online social network for students, rebranded as Meta Platforms in 2021 and by 2025 had turned into a sprawling conglomerate that spans social media, VR, and AI. This ongoing expansion into new domains is often described as platformisation, a process that unfolds over time and extends platform logics into the sectors and domains the platform enters (chapter 3).

Fourth, platforms are politically charged. The label 'platform' is not neutral or apolitical; it has legal and strategic implications. Companies exploit its ambiguity to present themselves as neutral intermediaries and thereby avoid responsibility, while regulators, especially in the European Union, have begun defining dominant platforms as 'gatekeepers' because they control access to markets, users, and data. How a platform is defined depends on who is doing the defining and for what purpose.

Defining platforms

This chapter argues that platforms are best understood as socio-technical systems: digital entities owned and operated by companies that enable and organise interaction, exchange, and creation between diverse actors. In their design and operation, they function as convenors of digital and physical life by bringing together users, developers, businesses, and institutions and by structuring their interactions through interfaces, algorithms, and infrastructures. In this way platforms operate simultaneously as digital services used daily for communication, consumption, and coordination, as corporate entities that pursue strategic and economic objectives, and as technologies or infrastructures upon which others build and depend, which embeds them in wider ecosystems.

Across these roles, platforms share a set of core characteristics and should be studied relationally, within the ecosystems they both sustain and depend on. Platforms cultivate and govern such ecosystems by positioning themselves as intermediaries and orchestrators between different user groups and by providing tools, products, and services that structure participation and value creation. Through their architectures, rules, and economic models, they shape the conditions under which users, developers, advertisers, and institutions interact and rely on one another.

Platform studies, then, seeks to understand not only *what* platforms are (which varies from case to case) but *how* they summon and influence – and are influenced by – the wider economic, cultural, and political environments in which they operate.

Chapter overview

This chapter develops a framework for analysing platforms through a relational and multidimensional lens. It proceeds in three steps. In the next section we identify four core characteristics of platforms and show why they must be understood relationally, as socio-technical systems embedded in ecosystems. The section on complementary traditions, which follows it (pp. 43–54), traces the various manners in which platforms have been conceptualised across three broad disciplinary traditions: as multisided markets in economics and business; as programmable systems in computing, engineering, and information systems; and as non-neutral intermediaries in communication and media studies. The section titled 'Analytical framework' (pp. 55–63) synthesises these perspectives into an analytical framework that views platforms simultaneously as services, as entities owned and operated by companies, and as technologies or infrastructures and introduces the three cross-cutting dimensions that structure their power: political economy, governance, and strategy. This framework underpins the chapters that follow.

Understanding platforms: A layered and relational perspective

Platform scholars such as Marc Steinberg (2019: 1) have noted that 'almost anything can become a platform if one merely calls it as such' (and Tarleton Gillespie, 2010, makes a similar point). Indeed, in both popular discourse and industry rhetoric, the term 'platform' is applied expansively to social media services, online marketplaces, cloud infrastructures, software frameworks, and nearly any digital system that facilitates interaction, transaction, or content creation. Used as a metaphor, it carries many different meanings and associations, many of which evoke natural or biological imagery.

For most people, however, platforms are primarily associated with social media: spaces where users share, comment, follow, and engage with content from friends, celebrities, creators, or brands on services such as Instagram, WhatsApp, Facebook, TikTok, RedNote, or QQ. In everyday usage, 'platform' is often used interchangeably with 'app', 'site', or 'service'.

Yet such views obscure the broader role platforms play in structuring relationships across diverse social, economic, and institutional domains. Platforms do not simply facilitate interactions; they actively shape them through design choices, monetisation mechanisms, algorithmic systems, and strategic decisions. Moreover, these relationships are not external to the platform but constitutive of its form and function. Platforms are shaped by and embedded in wider contexts – economic competition, cultural norms, technical standards, legal frameworks, and regulatory environments – that influence how they evolve and operate.

Consider how multiple forces configure platform development. Business pressures drive platforms to mimic competitors, integrate new functionalities, or acquire rivals. Snapchat's success with Stories, a series of photos or videos that disappear after twenty-four hours, was copied and popularised by Meta with Instagram Stories and, later, by YouTube with Shorts. Reward structures influence what creators produce, as seen in Twitch's incentive schemes, which encourage longer streaming hours, or in the algorithmic amplification of videos that contain trending audio on TikTok's For You page. Technical changes can disrupt entire industries: Apple's introduction of the App Tracking Transparency framework in 2021 reshaped the digital advertising ecosystem, reducing Meta's ad revenue while benefiting Apple's own services. Interface tweaks alter news exposure and political expression, as when changes to Facebook's 2018 News Feed prioritised personal posts over news, weakening traffic to publishers and altering information flows during elections. Policy interventions trigger lobbying, self-regulation, or product redesign; for example, the EU Digital Markets Act compelled Apple to open iOS to alternative app stores. Grassroots campaigns likewise challenge platform power through boycotts or collective action: creators organised the 2018 YouTube Adpocalypse backlash against new demonetisation policies, while activists launched the #StopHateForProfit campaign to pressure Facebook, Reddit, TikTok, and others to improve content moderation and to stop generating profit from hate speech, disinformation, and bigotry on their platforms.

For platform studies, then, the object of inquiry is not the platform in isolation, but the evolving web of relationships, dependencies, and infrastructural integrations through which platforms both shape and are shaped by society.

Platforms' core characteristics

No two platforms are the same, and all are in continuous evolution. To identify and analyse platforms comparatively across different sectors and scales, we identify four core characteristics that at once define them and underpin how they create, structure, and govern their ecosystems: multi-sidedness, programmability, layering, and materiality. These dimensions are not fixed or universally present. They vary in degree and configuration across different kinds of platforms, for example social media, e-commerce, ride-hailing, cloud services, and AI systems. They are primarily analytical tools for comparison, not necessary and sufficient conditions. They serve as flexible analytical lenses for understanding how platforms attract other actors, enable participation, consolidate control, and accumulate power.

First, platforms are *multisided*, essentially acting as match-makers that bring together various user groups – end users, developers, advertisers, content creators, institutions, and so on – within a shared interface or infrastructure. This ability to mediate across 'sides' allows platforms to generate powerful network effects: the more participants from one group join (e.g. Uber drivers), the more valuable the platform becomes to others (e.g. ride hailers). As more actors are drawn into the ecosystem, the platform's centrality and influence grow, often extending into adjacent sectors such as news, education, or health.

Second, platforms are *programmable and extensible*. They offer technical interfaces and resources (e.g. APIs, SDKs) that invite external actors to build on top of them. This programmability encourages the development of apps, services, content, and integrations with other platforms and facilitates expansion into new sectors and domains. OpenAI's APIs allow developers to integrate ChatGPT into AI companion apps that build on AI models, or into the online grocery delivery platform Instacart, which is available as an app within the ChatGPT store – in other words into apps or services of their own. Programmability also leads to a layered architecture, often theorised as a 'stack', where platform owners typically control the lower infrastructural layers (e.g. APIs, SDKs, data protocols), while inviting contributions at the upper layers of applications and content. This layered structure gives rise to new, often asymmetrical dependencies across the ecosystem. For instance, when Facebook restricted its API access after the data scandal with Cambridge Analytica, thousands of third-party apps and businesses lost access to data they had relied upon for their services.

Third, this *layering* is not merely technical but is also economic, cultural, and institutional. Most of a platform's inner workings remain invisible to users and even to many third-party partners. Different actors experience and access different views of the platform, depending on their role: on TikTok an end user sees a personalised For You feed, a content creator sees analytics dashboards and monetisation tools, an advertiser finds its audiences using targeting interfaces, developers work with the API to upload content from their app to TikTok, and a researcher interacts with the Research API to examine the circulation of misinformation. These differentiated access points illustrate how control is unevenly distributed, platform owners managing access, visibility, and integration possibilities.

Finally, platforms are *materially* constituted and embedded in material circumstances that leave tangible traces in the world. Despite often being perceived as abstract or immaterial, they are made up of concrete, observable components such as code, documentation, developer and user interfaces, design patterns, legal frameworks, and business strategies. Certain material components, which we later define as 'ecosystem resources' (pp. 40–1), both facilitate participation and govern relationships within the ecosystem. Examining this materiality offers rich empirical entry points for research, from technical artefacts like APIs and changelogs to product and developer documentation, privacy policies, community guidelines, monetisation policies, and multisided user interfaces. Understanding platform materiality is essential for analysing how platforms are designed, work, are used and repurposed, or gain their power and for reconstructing their histories and strategic evolution.

Consider Facebook (Meta) as an example. It brings together multiple user groups – users, creators, advertisers, businesses, and developers – in a shared digital environment. It offers tools and interfaces such as APIs, which allow others to build apps and services on top of itself (programmability or extensibility). Its operations span several layers, from vast data centres and machine-learning systems to end user interfaces and mobile apps (layering). And all this rests on a material foundation of software code, infrastructural integrations, and monetisation policies that make the platform's functioning both tangible and governable (materiality).

Together, these four dimensions form the conceptual backbone of our analytical framework; it will be further developed in the following sections. They enable researchers to compare platforms across different types and scales, revealing both family resemblances and key divergences in how they operate, govern, and expand.

Platforms as socio-technical systems

Before delving deeper into these core characteristics and the manner of their study, we will examine the conceptual underpinnings of our relational perspective. Platform studies draws on decades of scholarship in science and technology studies (STS) that examines the relationship between technology and society, extending intellectual traditions that partly predate the web.

The design, development, operation, and use of digital platforms are determined by social forces such as user behaviour, cultural norms, economic pressures, and regulation. This means that platforms are not isolated technological tools; they are deeply intertwined with the social contexts in which they operate. Two influential STS frameworks have been central to this understanding: the social construction of technology and society (SCOT) (e.g. Bijker et al., 2012 [1987]; Bijker and Law, 1994); and the social shaping of technology (SST) (e.g. MacKenzie and Wajcman, 1999 [1985]).

Both these frameworks challenge technological determinism – the idea (and the often implicit assumption) that technological development alone drives social change. SCOT emphasises that technologies develop through socially situated processes of negotiation and interpretation that take place between engineers, users, and policymakers. SST highlights the broader and continuous interplay between technological innovation and social institutions, norms, and power structures. From these two perspectives, digital entities such as platforms are neither purely technical nor social; they are socio-technical systems.

Platforms as and in culture and society

The traditions briefly reviewed here emphasise three key points that underpin the contemporary understanding of online digital platforms *as* and *in* culture and society.

First, technology and society have a formative influence on each other. Technology is inherently constituted by social forces and reflects the values, beliefs, and interests of those who create and use it (e.g. Bijker et al., 2012 [1987]; Bijker and Law, 1994; MacKenzie and Wajcman, 1999 [1985]). This means that platforms are not simply tools or systems created independently of society; they are deeply embedded within social, cultural, and economic contexts. For example, TikTok's algorithmic design and content moderation policies are heavily influenced by regional norms and regulations, a situation that produces markedly different versions of the app in China (Douyin) and abroad (Kaye et al., 2021). These contexts orient the development and use of platforms, which in turn reorient those very contexts. This reciprocal relationship, often termed 'co-construction', highlights the fact that platforms are both products of social forces and active formative agents in society.

Second, both human actors and non-human, material ones have agency and forge outcomes (Callon, 2021; Latour, 2007 [2005]). This perspective challenges the traditional view that only humans have agency and recognises that material objects, including platforms, embody political and power relations in their design. These power relations have material consequences: platform algorithms, for instance, may reinforce existing biases and social inequalities, steer behaviour, shape public discourse, determine what information users see, shape labour relations and working conditions, or create new power dynamics. On ride-hailing platforms such as Uber and DiDi, for example, algorithmic management determines driver routes, pay rates, and performance evaluations, often with little transparency (see p. 145).

Third, just like society at large and the markets extensively studied by sociologists (e.g. Callon, 2021), platforms are always evolving, always in the making. They are not static structures but dynamic systems continuously assembled and reassembled through the interactions of technical, economic, and social actors. Their constant state of flux is driven by technological innovation, shifting user practices, and changing regulatory or market conditions. For instance, Spotify's transformation from a music-streaming service into a multifaceted audio ecosystem that integrates music, podcasts, audiobooks, and creator tools exemplifies how platforms are continually reconfigured through market pressures. In this sense they are performative, just as the markets are: they are enacted and stabilised through ongoing practices and negotiations rather than existing as fixed digital objects.

Approaching platforms as ecosystems

Building on the idea that platforms are socio-technical systems, we now introduce a central outlook of this book: platforms must be understood within their ecosystems. From a relational perspective, they are inseparable from their wider environments, which are made up of technological components and embedded in organisational relationships, socioeconomic arrangements, and regulatory environments. Analysing platforms through this lens denaturalises their dominance by showing that they are not isolated entities but are deeply embedded in, and dependent on, broader configurations of interconnected actors, infrastructures, and institutions.

Early scholarship, particularly in media and communication studies, often analysed individual platforms in isolation, through Facebook studies or Twitter studies. While such research remains important, our approach shifts from platform-specific analysis to a more integrated framework, which considers how platforms are embedded within, and co-constituted by, larger economic, technical, cultural, and institutional environments.

The ecosystem concept offers a powerful lens for this. Borrowed from biology and systems theory and adopted across a wide range of disciplines – from management and innovation studies to platform and media studies (e.g. Gawer, 2021; Helmond and van der Vlist, 2024; Jacobides et al., 2018; Poell et al., 2021; de Reuver et al., 2018; Tiwana, 2014; van der Vlist, 2022; van Dijck, 2013; van Dijck et al., 2018) – it directs attention beyond the platform itself, to the wider networks of users, developers, advertisers, content creators, regulators, and infrastructures that sustain it and are fashioned by it. Although biological metaphors can risk naturalising platform dynamics as organic or inevitable, we use the term critically, by following existing academic scholarship on platform ecosystems that emphasises the interactions, interdependencies, and adaptive pressures between platforms, their many types of users, and their environments. These ecosystems are dynamic networks on which platforms depend and through which they exert influence and consolidate power.

Ecosystem actors, dependencies, and spheres of influence

A central aspect of platform ecosystems is the diversity of actors whom platforms convene. While often reduced to the catch-all term 'users', these actors in fact include end users (consumers), advertisers, developers, creators, institutional partners, and others, each with distinct roles, stakes, and relationships to the platform. Understanding this multi-sidedness is essential for analysing how platforms structure participation and control. In this book we employ 'user' as an umbrella term, and 'end user' specifically for consumers. In practice, each side of a platform is addressed, governed, and shaped through distinct tools, product strategies, and material infrastructures, a point we return to in the following section, on platform materiality.

Importantly, platform ecosystems operate at multiple levels. They include actors operating *within* the platform (e.g. users, creators, advertisers on Instagram) as well as actors building *on top* of the platform, through technical integrations (e.g. third-party apps that connect via Instagram APIs). These internal and external ecosystem dynamics often coexist and interact.

Here the platform represents the technical and organisational *core* (e.g. the Apple iOS or Google Android platforms), while the ecosystem refers to the broader constellation of *external* actors (often called users or complementors) along with their tools, apps, and services, which complement (i.e. interact with or build upon) that core. Large platforms such as Meta, Alphabet, or Amazon act as convenors and orchestrators of their respective ecosystems, setting the terms of participation. For instance, the Apple iOS ecosystem depends on thousands of app developers, accessory makers, advertisers, and users, but Apple maintains control by defining the interface standards, pricing models, and data policies that regulate these actors' participation.

This intermediary and orchestrating role is central to the processes by which platforms create value. They assemble multiple user groups and provide the means for others to create and share content, run marketing campaigns, or build new services. In doing so, platforms foster networks and generate mutual dependencies between users, developers, businesses, and institutions within their broader spheres of influence, the platform ecosystem (van der Vlist, 2022: 252). Understanding this distinction between platform and ecosystem and the interdependencies that flow from it is critical for analysing platform use, innovation, competition, control, and governance.

Van Dijck (2013: 21) describes how individual platforms operate as 'microsystems' that, collectively, form an 'ecosystem of connective media', so that each microsystem reacts to changes in the wider ecosystem. For example, when TikTok's rapid rise popularised the short-form video, other competing platforms such as Instagram (Reels), YouTube (Shorts), and Snapchat (Spotlight) quickly introduced similar formats. These shifts ripple outward, compelling creators, advertisers, and audiences to adapt their production practices and monetisation strategies.

In our approach, ecosystems are not only descriptive metaphors but analytical tools. Echoing influential notions from STS such as those of Latour's assemblage or Callon's *agencement* ('arrangement'), they make it possible to trace how human and non-human actors – including technical artefacts, institutional practices, people, and business models – become interwoven with relational structures that change over time. Platforms are embedded in these evolving relational structures – their ecosystems – which, to repeat, they bring together and mould.

So, whenever we study a platform, we must simultaneously consider its broader ecosystem. This is particularly important for understanding how platforms embed themselves across different domains and reorganise relationships, norms, and power structures in the process. By attending to platform ecosystems, we can uncover the often invisible interdependencies and infrastructures that underpin platform power. To study these interdependencies in practice, we turn next to the materiality of platforms, focusing on the concrete, observable forms through which ecosystems are structured, maintained, and made knowable.

Platform materiality

Although often perceived as abstract or black-boxed, platforms are in fact thoroughly material and leave traces everywhere. Their materiality is crucial for understanding the mechanisms by which they operate as intermediaries and connect people, technologies, and industries across diverse sectors and spheres of life. Platforms are designed and engineered by teams of developers, employed by end users, advertisers, creators, and politicians, funded by investors, and regulated by authorities. This web of production, maintenance, use, and governance leaves material residues in the form of code, documentation, changelogs, legal filings, prototypes, meeting notes, policy revisions, and endless beta versions, which together document and reveal how platforms function and evolve.

We refer to this as platforms' *dual materiality*. First there is their immediate, tangible constitution: interfaces, features, code, APIs, documentation, policies, developer tools, and data infrastructures. Platforms are not neutral or purely technical systems but are envisioned and engineered socio-technical constructs that embed power in their material design and operations. Second, there are the broader material, institutional, infrastructural, and economic conditions under which platforms are produced, maintained, and circulated. As Kirschenbaum (2007: 15) observed regarding software – an observation that we have extended to platforms (Helmond and van der Vlist, 2019: 11–12) – '[t]hese are material circumstances that leave material traces – in corporate archives, on whiteboards and legal pads, in countless iterations of alpha versions and beta versions and patches and upgrades, in focus groups and user communities, in expense accounts, in licensing agreements, in stock options and IPOs, in carpal tunnel braces, in the Bay Area and New Delhi real-estate markets, in PowerPoint vaporware and proofs of concept binaries locked in time-stamped limbo on a server where all the user accounts but root have been disabled and the domain name is eighteen months expired'.

The material components of platforms, such as 'like' buttons, content sorting and ranking algorithms, moderation mechanisms, privacy policies, and software developer kits, actively shape how different user groups connect and interact. This materiality not only enables interaction but structures and governs it, generating asymmetrical dependencies that are central to platform ecosystems.

While recognising the discursive power of platforms – a feature that accounts for their narratives, branding, and policy rhetoric – our focus here is on their technical and material work, namely the interfaces, architectures, and infrastructures through which they enact and stabilise power. Attending to this materiality is crucial if we want to analyse platforms' political economy and power (chapter 3) and their governing and being governed (chapter 4), excavate their past, write their histories, and trace emerging configurations (chapter 5). To illustrate this statement further, we highlight two key dimensions of platform materiality: the designed interfaces and affordances that mediate user experience; and the resources and documentation that structure participation within the ecosystem.

Interface features and affordances

Interface features and affordances are the immediate material components through which users engage with a platform. Affordances refer to the possibilities for action that these features enable or constrain; they suggest how users interact with the platform and with each other (Bucher and Helmond, 2017). They are socio-technical because they are structured by platform design but interpreted and enacted through user practices.

Importantly, affordances are not static. They can be reappropriated in ways that deviate from their intended functions, revealing the mutual shaping and socio-technical relationship between platform design and user agency. For example, Tinder's swiping mechanics facilitate rapid profile sorting, effectively gamifying the dating experience. Yet, as Stefanie Duguay's (2019) research shows, users have adapted Tinder's features for political activism, demonstrating how affordances can be reimagined for purposes that go beyond dating. Our own research similarly shows that app developers work with and around platform affordances and data to create new tools and services. The Google Play store, for instance, features many third-party apps that extend or modify Instagram's affordances. These include video downloaders for saving Stories and Reels – a functionality often unsupported or restricted by the platform itself – and creative editing tools for producing content. This practice of 'regramming' the platform illustrates how new apps and cultures of production emerge through the appropriation of platform affordances by third-party actors (Gerlitz, Helmond, van der Vlist et al., 2019).

Platforms also tailor their interfaces and affordances to specific user groups. Instagram, for example, provides the consumer-facing app for end users; analytics dashboards such as Instagram Insights for advertisers; creator tools such as Reels Edit and the Creator Marketplace for influencers and creators to find branded content partnerships; and APIs for (business) developers to manage content, connect with users, and integrate external services. These differentiated interfaces and affordances reflect the platform's multisided or multi-faceted nature (p. 30), which makes each group interact with a distinct material layer of the system.

Affordances can also evolve over time, as platforms adjust their priorities or respond to external pressures. For instance, the heart button of X (formerly Twitter) originally served as a bookmarking tool but came to signify endorsement for users even as it functioned as a performance metric for advertisers. A single feature thus carries multiple, shifting affordances depending on context and type of user type.

A key methodological approach for studying platforms and apps in this way is the walkthrough method, initially proposed by Light et al. (2016) and later extended by Duguay and Gold-Apel (2023: 2) to account for 'newer, highly personalized and algorithmically driven function-alities' associated with apps like TikTok. This approach examines affordances 'at multiple levels of scale' (2023: 4) by systematically navigating the platform interface from a user's point of view. Researchers engage directly with the interface, working through screens, tapping buttons, and exploring menus while they analyse the associated documentation that outlines the platform's vision, operating model, and modes of governance. This method contributes to uncovering the intended functions, cultural meanings, and idealised users built into design. In doing so, it offers a grounded and material way to study how platform affordances shape user behaviour, relations, and interactions.

Ecosystem resources and documentation

Beyond a platform's interface lies a vast and often overlooked material dimension: the developer tools, documentation, algorithms, and other artefacts that enable and structure inter-actions. We refer to these as *ecosystem resources*, building on the concept of boundary resources in management and information systems research (Ghazawneh and Henfridsson, 2013; van der Vlist, 2022). These resources include the technical, legal, and informational materials that platforms provide in order to engage and coordinate different stake-holders in their ecosystems.

Ecosystem resources play a dual role. On the one hand, they facilitate integration and participation by enabling developers, advertisers, creators, and other actors to connect with the platform and build upon it. On the other hand, they act as instruments of strategic control and governance, defining what actors can do, how they can do it, and under what conditions.

Platforms tailor these resources for users on their different sides or facets. For end users, these resources include help pages, privacy policies, community guidelines, and terms of service. Such materials outline what end users can and cannot do on the platform. For developers, they include APIs, SDKs, developer documentation, and changelogs. These document how developers can build on the platform, which data and functionalities they can access, and under which conditions. For businesses and advertisers, platforms provide marketing dashboards, analytics, and advertising tools with detailed documentation about how advertisers can target users. For creators, they offer monetisation and content management tools, along with policies that govern modalities for creators to earn money from their content. In each case, these resources formalise relationships within the ecosystem and guide behaviour through a mix of technical tools and written documentation and policies.

Ecosystem resources therefore provide valuable empirical entry points for studying how platforms attract, incentivise, and control complementary actors across industries and sectors. They articulate not only a platform's technical and economic modes of operation but also its vision, values, and norms: what forms of participation are encouraged and what forms are restricted or penalised. Terms of service, developer policies, and community standards, for example, explicitly define desirable and undesirable behaviour, embedding social and moral expectations into the material design and governance mechanisms of platforms.

Beyond shaping participation, ecosystem resources are also key primary resources for platform research itself. Materials such as developer blog posts, financial filings, interface snapshots, and regulatory documents form the archival backbone for studying the operations and evolution of platforms. They allow researchers to reconstruct platform histories and analyse the development of business models, technical architectures, and governance strategies over time (as we will see in chapters 4 and 5). Through these materials we can trace platforms' styles of managing data and privacy, designing and implementing monetisation and moderation mechanisms, targeting specific industries, and embedding strategic goals into their technologies.

Technography

Platforms generate and make publicly available very diverse materials, which range from technical tools and services to documentation, developer portals, partner programmes, help pages, and financial reports. By examining them we can better understand how platforms operate, govern relationships with stakeholders, embed themselves across industries, and configure broader societal outcomes. One methodological approach that directly engages with these materials is *technography*.

Technography is a descriptive and interpretive approach that critically analyses the structural and operational dimensions of technical systems. It focuses on the material and technical specificities that underpin a system's functioning, paying particular attention to how the system in question is configured, documented, and governed. As developed in our own work and in that of others (e.g. Bucher, 2012; Burkhardt and Rieder, 2024; Helmond and van der Vlist, 2019; Luitse, 2024; Mackenzie, 2018; van der Vlist et al., 2022; van der Vlist, Helmond and Ferrari, 2024), technographic research systematically studies, sometimes through archived sources, the documents, artefacts, and interfaces produced by or related to digital platforms. These materials, which are often publicly accessible but underused, reveal design logics, affordances, and strategic functions and goals that might otherwise remain hidden.

This material-based approach enables researchers to examine platforms not just as abstract or black-boxed entities but as concrete socio-technical systems. Through technography we can map the methods by which platforms construct and maintain ecosystems, create dependencies, and exert power through their interfaces, architecture, tools, and evolving documentation. While our own work often combines technography with digital methods, network analysis, infrastructural analysis, and visualisation techniques, other platform studies approaches also employ methods such as ethnography, content analysis, discourse analysis, or interviews.

However, this book – and platform studies generally – does not advocate for a single method or theoretical stance. Instead it provides a flexible toolkit of empirical strategies and conceptual perspectives that enable one to follow platforms as they evolve, adapt, and reconfigure over time. The works discussed throughout this book operate across multiple registers: they offer empirical insights into platform dynamics, advance conceptual frameworks, and demonstrate how such insights can be translated into research strategies and methods. Our aim is to equip students, scholars, and practitioners with adaptable approaches, concepts, strategies, and techniques for critically investigating the evolving role of platforms across sectors and societies.

An exploratory and creative engagement with platforms' dual materiality supports this aim. Yet opening up the black box of platforms increasingly requires a combination of technical literacy and methodological inventiveness. As platforms become more opaque and more complex, cultivating these twin capacities through collaborative, cross-disciplinary, or experimental research is essential for anyone who aims to examine platform ecosystems critically and to inform public debate, regulation, and user interests.

The next section traces the historical emergence and evolving understandings of the platform concept and its core characteristics across disciplines.

Platform studies across disciplines: Three complementary traditions

Platform studies is a highly interdisciplinary field. Its conceptual lineages have developed across several disciplines, most prominently in economics, business, and management (which are also concerned with non-digital platforms) and in computing, engineering, and information systems (which are focused on technical platforms). In the humanities and social sciences, critical scholars in communication and media studies have built on these traditions to examine how platforms influence culture, labour, politics, and society. Each tradition foregrounds different aspects of platform operation (economic, technical, and socio-cultural) and provides the historical background to the core characteristics that define platforms today.

Multisided markets and matchmakers: Platforms in economics, business, and management

Not all platforms are digital. In the 1970s–1980s, firms in automotive, electronics, and manufacturing industries began using the term 'platform' to describe modular product architectures composed of a shared technological core and reusable elements that could be adapted across product lines (e.g. Baldwin and Woodard, 2009; Steinberg, 2019). In industrial innovation and product management, Baldwin and Woodard argued that platforms share an architectural principle common across these contexts: a stable core that provides reusable components and sets interface standards for complementary products and services. This modular structure balances stability with innovation, allowing firms to scale production while encouraging variation and differentiation.

Over time, this idea expanded into industrial economics to describe companies that mediate interactions between distinct user groups. In the 1990s, economists studying US credit card antitrust cases observed that companies such as Visa and Mastercard were not simply selling products but acting as intermediaries between two groups: cardholders, who wanted convenient payment methods, and merchants, who wanted access to customers. Building on these insights, economists Rochet and Tirole (2003) developed the influential theory of multisided platforms or multisided markets. They argued that platforms create value by bringing together (or 'matching') distinct user groups (or 'sides') and generating 'network effects': the more participants (e.g. cardholders) join one side, the more valuable the platform becomes to the other side (e.g. merchants), which creates a reinforcing cycle of growth.

By the 2000s, multisided market theory extended to digital platforms: online video platforms connect content creators and viewers (YouTube, Twitch); e-commerce marketplaces connect buyers and sellers (Amazon, eBay, Temu); app stores connect developers and consumers (Apple's App Store, Google Play, Tencent Appstore); and social media platforms connect users, content creators, advertisers, and developers (Facebook, Instagram, RedNote). In each case, platforms act as intermediaries whose value lies not in producing goods or content themselves, but in facilitating and profiting from exchanges between others.

Economists Evans and Schmalensee (2016) describe such digital platforms as 'matchmakers' that operate according to a 'new economics', which distinguishes them from traditional firms. Companies like Amazon, Facebook (now Meta), Airbnb, and Uber have built business models around this matchmaking logic, earning revenue by facilitating exchanges rather than by selling products. For example, Uber does not own cars or employ drivers directly; instead it takes a commission on each ride and profits from the interaction it enables between riders and drivers. Some scholars describe this shift as a 'platform revolution' (Parker et al., 2016) that has fundamentally changed the modus operandi of markets and firms.

Orchestration and ecosystems in strategic management

Strategic management research builds on this economic view by showing that platforms do more than connect and match users. They also build and orchestrate entire ecosystems of complementary actors. Cusumano et al. (2019) demonstrate that companies like Amazon and Apple have moved from selling products to orchestrating networks of third-party sellers, app developers, and service providers. These external contributors generate complementary innovations that increase the value of the core platform. Network effects operate across this entire ecosystem: the more actors a platform convenes, the more central and valuable it becomes (Cusumano et al., 2019; Evans et al., 2006).

Two main analytical perspectives on ecosystems can be distinguished in this literature (de Reuver et al., 2018). *Technical* perspectives focus on the apps and services – the complements – built on top of a core technological platform such as iOS or Android, typically through the use of programming interfaces. *Organisational* perspectives, by contrast, emphasise the complementors – that is, the companies, organisations, and institutions that develop, sustain, or engage with these apps and services. While these perspectives often overlap in practice, both foreground questions of strategy and control.

While this body of work increasingly addresses digital platforms, its primary focus remains on the economic and organisational dynamics that distinguish platform companies from earlier business models, rather than on the specifics of their digital infrastructures. Nonetheless, such studies provide an important conceptual foundation for understanding the economic logics of platforms (more on this in chapter 3), which are key to understanding how platforms have transformed the contemporary platform economy and society.

Programmable systems: Platforms in computing, software engineering, and information systems

While economics highlights the multisided nature and matchmaking capacities of platforms, computing, software engineering, and information systems approaches emphasise their programmability and layered architectures. From this perspective, a platform is a type of system architecture, be it software or hardware, designed with a programmable and extensible codebase that enables others to build on it. The idea of modularity introduced in product design (p. 44) reappears here, as platforms provide a stable technical core with standardised interfaces that allow others to develop new tools, applications, and services.

A key historical milestone was the IBM System/360, introduced in 1964. This unified hardware architecture could run a wide range of software programs across compatible machines. By separating hardware from software, IBM created a stable foundation that external developers could build upon without changing the system's core. It also introduced the principle of *programmability*: the ability for external developers to build new applications on top of the platform.

This modular and extensible design became a model for later computing platforms such as Microsoft Windows, which provided a common software environment for thousands of independent applications, and for mobile operating systems like iOS and Android, which today are key platforms hosting vast app ecosystems. This architecture and computing logic laid the foundations for the digital platform model (Evans et al., 2006; Steinberg, 2019).

Platforms as extensible codebases or programmable architectures

In contemporary digital platforms, programmability is typically enabled by application programming interfaces

(APIs). APIs are sets of tools that provide structured access to a platform's data and functionality, as will be further discussed in this chapter. They are the technical mechanism through which platforms become extensible, enabling others to build on them and to integrate them into their own products and services. Platforms thus act as extensible codebases or programmable architectures, supporting ecosystems of third-party apps and integrations (de Reuver et al., 2018). For example, in the ride-hailing app Uber, the map showing the driver's location is not built by Uber but uses Google Maps' API. Google provides Uber with structured access to its mapping functionality, but not with access to its own under-lying code or data infrastructure.

Another contemporary example is OpenAI's API platform, which gives developers access to powerful large language models such as GPT-5. Just by interacting with the platform through its API endpoints but without accessing the underlying model architecture or training data, developers can integrate OpenAI models into their own applications, which range from chatbots and writing assistants to customer support tools and health and educa-tional apps. This approach allows OpenAI to maintain control over the model's operation and updates, while enabling a broad ecosystem of external apps and services around it. At the same time, these integrations are crucial for OpenAI itself: they generate continuous data flows about usage patterns, queries, and performance that can be used to refine, retrain, and monetise its models, thereby reinforcing the feedback loops that underpin the platform's growth and learning.

Platforms and service-based business models

The layered model of programmability has since evolved into a dominant service-based business model in computing, especially cloud computing, and it is often referred to as an 'as-a-service' (*aaS) business model. It is typically organised across three interrelated layers. At the base is infrastructure-as-a-service (IaaS), which provides the essential computing resources such as servers, storage, and networking that other systems rely on. Above this is platform-as-a-service (PaaS), which offers developers the tools, frameworks, and runtime environments to create, test, and deploy their own applications without managing the underlying infrastructure. At the top is software-as-a-service (SaaS), which hosts applications for end users, for example Microsoft 365, Salesforce, or Adobe Creative Cloud.

These layers form an integrated platform stack that underpins much of today's digital economy. Major cloud providers such as AWS, Microsoft Azure, and Google Cloud increasingly offer these three layers as part of a single, integrated service. This creates strong dependencies: once data, tools, or applications are locked into these systems, it becomes difficult to move them elsewhere.

Another key development was the microprocessor revolution of the 1970s: it further accelerated the spread of programmable platforms from traditional computing to smaller, portable devices and new domains such as industrial automation and agriculture. For example, Siemens' Insights Hub – an internet of things (IoT) platform – connects industrial machines in order to collect and analyse operational data for optimising operations and predictive maintenance in industrial settings such as marine engineering, water industry, automotive engineering, and power utilities. Similarly, John Deere's Operations Center uses cloud-based analytics to optimise farming processes via mobile apps. In consumer technologies, mobile-specific platforms such as Google Android, Apple iOS, and Huawei HarmonyOS power function, alongside their app stores, as distribution platforms for millions of third-party apps, by powering their smartphones, smartwatches, and tablets. Emerging environments such as the Meta Horizon spatial computing platform aim to provide a new computational layer, so that developers who work in augmented, virtual, and mixed reality may produce immersive games and environments such as the metaverse.

As Evans et al. (2006) argue, software platforms have become the 'invisible engines' of modern industries. What began as a technical architecture for computing has turned into a general organisational and infrastructural model that configures the operations of entire sectors, from mobile phones and digital advertising to education, agriculture, and automotive manufacturing. By providing the underlying programmable foundations for these industries, Evans and colleagues show that software platforms have become foundational to the digital economy and to our society at large.

Non-neutral intermediaries: Platforms in media, communication, and information studies

Building on our exploration of platforms in economics and computing, we now turn to perspectives from our own field of communication and media studies (and we include related fields such as cultural and information studies). From these perspectives platforms are approached not just as technical or economic systems but as socio-cultural actors embedded in everyday life. While scholars in these areas often draw on economic and computational notions of platforms, for instance as multisided markets or programmable architectures, they bring a distinct critical lens to the broader societal consequences of platforms across sectors and institutions.

As media forms have become themselves increasingly mediated by software, communication and media studies researchers have focused on platforms' operations of shaping social and cultural objects, processes, and practices. Traditionally, these fields examined the mutual influence between media technologies and the creation, distribution, consumption, and interpretation of media content, viewing such technologies as socio-technical systems.

Software and platform studies foundations

In the digital age, media theorists such as Lev Manovich (2001) and Matthew Fuller (2008), prominent in software studies and computational culture, built on this legacy by examining software's configuration of culture and society. In his work, Manovich emphasised the relationship between the 'computer layer' and the 'media–cultural layer' of new media, showing how software influences both cultural production and reception. Software studies treats software as a material artefact that is deeply embedded in daily life, forms the material backbone of contemporary cultural phenomena, and acts as the lens through which we engage with the world.

Furthermore, Manovich (2001) argued that digital media are inherently *programmable*, meaning that they can be modified and adapted through code, which distinguishes them from traditional media forms. He therefore advocated moving from traditional media studies to 'software studies' and stated that software now operates as a fundamental material force that structures content creation, distribution, and consumption within our 'software culture' (48).

Building on the foundations of software studies, game studies scholars Ian Bogost and Nick Montfort made a significant early contribution to platform studies by calling for close attention to the technical and material foundations of new media, specifically platforms, and the ways in which these constrain and enable cultural production and expression (Montfort and Bogost, 2009). They proposed that platforms should be analysed as both technical systems and cultural forms and that platform studies should focus on 'the connection between technical specifics and culture' (4). Theirs is a humanities-based approach to platforms, treated as computational infrastructures.

In defining what it is that makes a platform, Bogost and Montfort refer to Marc Andreessen's (2007) influential industry definition, which reflects a distinctly computational understanding of the topic. For Andreessen, a major figure in the tech industry, the defining feature of a platform is its *programmability*: its capacity to be reprogrammed and extended by external developers, often in ways the original designers did not anticipate: 'If you can program it, then it's a platform. If you can't, then it's not' (Andreessen, cited in Bogost and Montfort, 2009: 3). Building on this idea, Bogost and Montfort propose that understanding platforms requires more than analysing their technical architecture: it also involves examining how developers perceive, engage with, and creatively adapt these systems. A platform's significance, they suggest, lies not only in what it technically enables but also in how it is taken up, used, and valued within developer communities: 'Something is a platform when a developers [*sic*] consider it as such and use it' (Bogost and Montfort, 2009: 4).

Programmability and platformisation

When considering programmability as a core platform characteristic, a key question arises: 'What makes platforms programmable?' As discussed earlier (pp. 46–7), program-mability is typically enabled by APIs and SDKs for mobile apps, which provide structured access to a platform's data and functionalities. These interfaces allow third-party devel-opers to build new services on top of a platform without directly accessing or modifying its core code. This makes websites and services programmable and enables platforms to expand into new domains. For instance, the Facebook Graph API enables access to the company's social graph, while the TikTok Content Posting API allows third parties to publish video content directly to the platform. These forms of structured access not only facilitate programmability but also embed platforms into wider digital ecosystems. This makes them crucial ecosystem resources (see pp. 40–1).

From a media studies perspective, APIs are therefore more than technical tools. While they certainly enable software systems to interact and exchange data, they are also key instruments of platformisation (on this, see chapter 3). By enabling integration with other services, APIs allow platforms to become foundational infrastructure for a wide range of applications and online interactions. They make it possible, for instance, to embed a Google Map in a ride-hailing app such as Uber, to use a TikTok login on a third-party service, or to display a Facebook 'like' button across the web. Indeed, APIs form the invisible backbone of our digital world, serving as the lingua franca for data and service exchange between platforms. They have become core elements of digital infrastructure, underpinning today's platform economy and society. In doing so, APIs inherently create infrastructural dependencies, drawing developers, content creators, publishers, and service providers into the platform ecosystem. APIs enable innovation but also create dependencies: developers build businesses on platforms that can change the rules at any time.

Furthermore, APIs also function as governance mecha-nisms (we will talk about this in chapter 4). They regulate who can access what data, under what conditions, and through what terms of service or rate limits. By controlling the design, scope, and availability of their APIs, platforms can steer the kinds of applications that flourish or fail, can set the rules for participation, and can govern their ecosystems.

For instance, Facebook's repeated changes to its Graph API – particularly after the Cambridge Analytica scandal – drastically curtailed third-party access to user data, and this fact reshaped the wider app ecosystem. Developers who had once relied on these data flows for analytics, social games, or media sharing suddenly found their integrations restricted or terminated.

Understanding APIs in this way is essential for analysing the social, economic, and political dynamics of contemporary platforms. As later chapters will show, APIs play a key role in the political economy of platforms by enabling platform-isation, infrastructuralisation, cross-sector integration, data circulation, and monetisation (see chapter 3). At the same time, they are central to platform governance, as they determine how participation is managed, restricted, or encouraged (see chapter 4). In this sense, programmability is not simply a technical property but a central modality of platform power.

The turn towards social media in platform studies

Bogost and Montfort's original call for platform studies was centred on video game (hardware) platforms such as Atari and Nintendo. With the rise of web-based services and social media, however, the focus in the field broadened significantly. The growth, discussed in chapter 1, of social networking services (SNSs) and user-generated content (UGC) platforms during the Web 2.0 era turned scholarly attention towards the analysis of online platforms and social media.

During the Web 2.0 period, Tarleton Gillespie (2010) identified a critical shift: companies such as Flickr (founded in 2004), Vimeo (founded in 2004), Tumblr (founded in 2007), SoundCloud (founded in 2007), and YouTube (founded in 2007) began calling themselves 'platforms'. In his influential analysis, Gillespie showed that 'platform' became a strategic and adaptable label, which internet companies adopted in order to frame their services in ways that appealed to different audiences. He identified several overlapping meanings of the term – meanings that companies mobilised strategically (2010: 349–350). First, the word 'platform' retained its original *computational* meaning: it referred to a base that supported software applications and positioned its referent as a technical infrastructure. Second, it carried an *architectural* connotation, describing an intermediary that supported various activities and conveyed a sense of neutrality and openness. Third, in a *figurative* sense, it represented an open space or a space of opportunity, framing its referent as a type of entity that enabled participation for creators, users, and developers. Finally, it carried a *political* meaning and extended the architectural metaphor to express ideological positions. These multiple and overlapping meanings made 'platform' a strategically useful label, since they allowed companies to appeal to diverse audiences and to align the interests of different stakeholders.

This strategic positioning is particularly relevant in the context of platform regulation. Companies have long exploited the ambiguity of the term 'platform' to cast themselves as neutral conduits and thus to minimise their legal responsibility; we will explore this aspect in chapter 4. Gillespie (2010) described it as the 'politics' of platforms, arguing that naming something a platform is itself a political act, which shapes public understanding, regulatory frameworks, and corporate accountability. The political dimension remains a central theme in critical platform studies, both rhetorically and materially, especially in relation to the role of platforms as convenors and shapers, as we describe them in this book.

Building on this dimension, scholars have turned their attention to the processes by which specific software elements, from interface features to algorithms, manage to have an active impact on social behaviour, cultural practices, and content production and circulation. Their studies show that platforms are not passive conduits but non-neutral intermediaries, whose material design structures participation and value creation (e.g. Bucher, 2013a; Burgess and Green, 2018 [2009]; Langlois and Elmer, 2019).

Taina Bucher (2012) introduced the concept of programmed sociality to describe how social interactions on Facebook are organised through technical features. She showed that online friendships are produced through a 'friendship assemblage' of human and non-human elements, mediated by affordances and features such as the News

Feed algorithm. Similarly, Ganaele Langlois and Greg Elmer (2013) argued that corporate social media platforms do not merely enable content creation but transform user interaction into data, translating likes, shares, and comments into economic value and thereby producing a 'techno-social world' (10).

Carolin Gerlitz and Anne Helmond (2013) further demonstrated that Facebook's influence extended across the web through social plugins such as the 'like' and 'share' buttons, widgets, and trackers embedded on third-party websites. These integrations facilitated new forms of continuous data capture and circulation, laying the groundwork for a data-intensive infrastructure they called 'the like economy', which supports the business models of many platforms (chapter 3).

In one of the earliest critical histories of social media, José van Dijck (2013) offered a framework for analysing platforms as techno-cultural and socio-economic formations. She traced the evolution of platforms such as Facebook, YouTube, Twitter, Wikipedia, and Flickr from amateur-driven communities to global corporations. Central to this process was the extraction and exploitation of user connectivity, which turned social interactions into economically productive resources.

Around the same time, scholars began investigating the natively digital features and cultures of specific social media platforms, as social life increasingly moved online (e.g. Rogers, 2013; Weller et al., 2013). The emergence of digital methods and API-based research reflects a broader epistemological change: researchers no longer study platforms alone; they study *with platforms*. While APIs enable analyses of what happens on platforms, they also define what can be accessed, extracted, and known. This became particularly obvious after the Facebook–Cambridge Analytica scandal and other controversies, when tightened data access policies significantly restricted the granular study of social media interactions once enabled by open APIs (e.g. van der Vlist et al., 2022; Venturini and Rogers, 2019). As a result, platform APIs create the very conditions of knowledge production. This means that digital methods are not neutral techniques; they are themselves determined by the logics of the platforms under study.

Analytical framework: Three lenses and forces in critical platform analysis

This section synthesises the preceding discussions on the characteristics of platforms and on their conceptualisations across disciplines into an integrated analytical framework for critical platform analysis. To dissect the complexity of entities such as Google, Meta, or TikTok, we propose examining platforms through three complementary lenses: services, companies, and technologies or infrastructures (see Table 2.1). Each lens foregrounds a distinct but interconnected dimension: platform services foreground user practices and content, companies foreground corporate strategy and

Table 2.1. Complementary analytical lenses: Platform services, companies, and technologies or infrastructures.

Lens	Focus	Questions	Examples
Platform services	User-facing products and experiences	How do interfaces structure interaction? How do affordances shape behaviour?	TikTok's For You page, Uber's rider app, Google Search results, Meta's Ad Manager
Platform companies	Corporate strategies, ownership structures, strategic investments and partnerships, and business models	How do companies generate revenue? How do they expand through acquisitions and partnerships?	Meta's consolidation strategies, Palentir's partnerships, RedNote's business ecosystem
Platform technologies or infrastructures	Programmable architectures that enable third-party development, software standards, data flows	How do APIs govern access? How do platforms create dependencies?	Google Maps API, AWS cloud services, iOS developer ecosystem

economic organisation, and technologies and infrastructures foreground technical architecture and programmability.

The lenses align with the representation of platforms in the interdisciplinary platform studies scholarship and provide a layered understanding of platforms' operation, scaling, and exercise of influence. They trace the interconnections and mutual reinforcement of a platform's user-facing services, business strategies, and technical infrastructures.

Platform services

The first analytical lens focuses on platform services: these are the digital products and experiences through which billions of consumers encounter platforms daily. Social networking, messaging, search engines, dating apps, music streaming, ride-hailing, food delivery, and AI chatbots all exemplify this service dimension. The focus here is on how platforms' interfaces and affordances shape everyday practices, content cultures, and social interactions through their user-facing designs.

Platforms typically present themselves as services available through websites or mobile apps, but they differ from both websites and apps in their scope and function. A website such as Facebook.com is primarily made up of interconnected web pages that give users access to social networking tools and content sharing. By contrast, Meta Platforms functions as a broader digital infrastructure that goes beyond simply hosting web pages. It hosts multiple services, facilitates interactions between diverse user groups, provides tools for developers to build on its systems, and governs these exchanges through its policies, algorithms, and interfaces.

Originally launched in 2004 as a single-purpose social networking website, Facebook has grown into a multi-service platform with a family of apps that includes Instagram, WhatsApp, and Messenger. Unlike standalone sites or apps, platforms such as Meta create and manage extensive, inter-connected ecosystems that support a whole range of services and interactions across their network, going beyond an individual user interface.

Platform services often operate as modular, reconfig-urable assemblages of (micro)services and features (Blanke and Pybus, 2020) that are moulded by platform strategies and external pressures. These (micro)services are 'created by platform companies: the technology companies that own and operate platforms' (Gorwa, 2024: 17), while the capture, analysis, and monetisation of data are central to the functioning and evolution of platforms as 'service ecosystems' (Alaimo et al., 2020).

This perspective reveals that platforms, when viewed as services, are not neutral conduits but, we repeat, powerful shapers of social and cultural dynamics (see Burgess, 2021; Gillespie, 2010: 357). Their interfaces and policies determine which content becomes visible, how users interact, and what behaviours are rewarded or punished.

This service-centred perspective is also central to contemporary platform regulation (chapter 4). The EU Digital Markets Act (DMA) designates large technology firms – Alphabet, Amazon, Apple, Booking, ByteDance, Meta and Microsoft – as gatekeepers because of their structural role in mediating access to key digital markets. Yet the DMA does not regulate these companies as a whole. Instead, it targets the specific core platform services they operate – Google Search, Google Maps, YouTube, Google Play, Android Mobile, Google Chrome, and Alphabet's advertising infrastructure – as distinct regulatory units. This approach illustrates that platforms are governed as collections of strategically significant services, not as monolithic firms.

At the same time, the rise of what is now called 'super apps' (e.g. WeChat, Gojek, Grab) reflects the fact that platforms increasingly bundle multiple services, such as messaging, travel, transport, payment, food delivery, and logistics, and more, into single environments (pp. 99–100). This bundling occurs both horizontally, across service types, and vertically, across infrastructural layers, as super apps connect to cloud infrastructures, payment systems, and data infrastructures to consolidate control and to extend their reach. This trend underscores the need for an ecosystem perspective that sees platforms as strategic coordinators of multiple services that operate across sectors.

Platform companies

The second lens considers platform companies: these are corporate actors with specific business models, ownership structures, and strategic goals that are oriented towards profit-making.[1] In this sense, 'platform' refers, not to an individual service, but to the corporate entities that own, operate, and interlink them and that are defined each by specific ownership models, revenue strategies, and market logics. Such entities range from single-platform firms (e.g. Spotify or TikTok) to large conglomerates like Alphabet, Meta, or Tencent, which orchestrate multiple platforms within broader ecosystems. This lens foregrounds platform companies as powerful corporations and as the 'emblematic organisational form of the digital age' – one that has far-reaching influence on markets, institutions, and societies (Gawer, 2021: 111; Narayan, 2024; Srnicek, 2016).

Understanding platforms as owned by companies involves analysing their operating as economic actors. This includes studying their mergers and acquisitions, partnerships, holding structures, cross-subsidisation strategies, and global investment flows. Parent firms such as Alphabet, Tencent, and Amazon organise vast business ecosystems that span multiple subsidiaries, services, and sectors, each combining different platforms and services under a single corporate umbrella. These conglomerates often combine platform-based business models with more traditional revenue streams: Apple pairs the App Store as a platform with income from hardware sales, while Amazon pairs its marketplace with revenues from cloud, logistics, and retail operations. Since they are conglomerates, their platform strategies rely, unsurprisingly, on conglomeration. Conglomerates also depend on integration, both vertical and horizontal, and on partnership orchestration to expand their reach and create dependencies among consumers, developers, businesses, governments, and civil society actors that rely on their infrastructures and services. All this will be discussed in chapter 3.

Nick Srnicek (2016: 49) provides a useful typology of platform models that is based on their primary economic functions: advertising platforms such as Google and Meta collect and monetise user data by selling targeted ads; cloud platforms such as AWS and Microsoft Azure provide computing power and digital services to other businesses; industrial platforms such as Siemens and Honeywell support connected manufacturing through data-driven automation;

product platforms such as Apple iOS and Spotify transform physical products or media into digital services; and lean platforms such as Uber and Airbnb act as intermediaries for services while minimising asset ownership. This typology highlights that platform companies employ different economic logics to extract value across industries – an important foundation for the political-economic analysis that is developed in chapter 3.

Marc Steinberg (2019: 69–93) adds a historical and global dimension to the typology by tracing the evolution of the platform model through distinct phases of corporate development in the United States and Japan. The first phase, that of product-technology platforms (late 1970s–1980s), was one of computing infrastructures built for third-party development (programmable platforms: see pp. 46–7). The second was the phase of content platforms, which emerged with Web 2.0 and social media; the focus at that point was on user-generated content. The third phase was one of transactional or mediation platforms, which facilitated exchanges between users; this is now the dominant business model, in which platforms as commonly framed as multi-sided markets (see p. 44). Steinberg highlights Japan's 1999 Docomo i-mode service as an early example of this trajectory – a commercially successful and curated mobile internet platform that combines infrastructure, content, and transactions into a single business model, now found in many of today's dominant mobile ecosystems.

Importantly, platform companies do not merely participate in markets but increasingly organise them. As private regulators (Gawer, 2021; see also chapter 4 in this book), they oversee the business relationships, data exchanges, and transactions that occur within their ecosystems, effectively governing these interactions as their own private domains. This perspective is essential for analysing issues like monopolisation and anti-competitive behaviour. In some cases platforms act as aggregators, in other words as companies that attract a vast user base and then exercise control of access to these audiences so as to gain bargaining power over suppliers – as seen in Netflix's ability to dictate terms to content producers, or in Amazon's influence over third-party sellers (Thompson, 2017).

Additionally, understanding platforms as companies is key to recognising their strategic roles in forming partnerships, acquiring startups or competitors, entering new markets, and influencing global economic structures – as well as to conceptualising their political effect and impact. Treated this way, platforms are hybrid actors: they are both market participants and market organisers, as will be further explored in chapters 3 and 4.

Platform technologies or infrastructures

The third analytical lens examines platform technologies or infrastructures: these are the technical architectures and material foundations that underpin services and enable third-party participation. From this perspective, platforms are not just interfaces or business models but programmable systems made up of software modules, APIs, SDKs, data infrastructures, and hardware dependencies. These components mediate participation, innovation, and control, allowing platforms to evolve, scale their operations, and extend their reach across sectors such as media, mobility, education, finance, and AI.

This perspective highlights that platforms operate through ecosystem resources and strategies – the technical, legal, and informational artefacts that enable platform expansion and integration – while also functioning as tools of governance and infrastructural control (on this point, see chapter 4). For example, APIs are not simply technical protocols for interacting with platform functionality and data but also gatekeeping devices that determine who can access what data, under what terms, and for what purposes. SDKs, content moderation guidelines, advertising dashboards, and cloud services perform similar dual roles: they facilitate participation while structuring dependence. These infrastructural arrangements form the backbone of platform ecosystems, which are the networks of interconnected actors and artefacts that rely on platforms for development, monetisation, and distribution.

As van Dijck et al. (2018) argue, platforms increasingly operate as infrastructural bases. The authors distinguish between what they call infrastructural platforms, which serve as foundational layers for other services and applications, and sectoral platforms, which cater to specific domains such as news, transport, food, education, healthcare, finance, or hospitality (12–13). This distinction reveals that some platforms function as critical underlying infrastructures that enable a broad range of services, such as cloud computing or payment platforms, while others provide targeted solutions in particular sectors, such as ride-hailing or video streaming platforms. Major platforms like Google, Amazon, or Microsoft combine both roles, functioning as both infrastructure and sector-specific providers. Through as-a-service business models that integrate cloud, analytics, and software, they consolidate power both vertically (within a sector) and horizontally (across services).

In education, for instance, the Microsoft ecosystem clearly illustrates this dual role. It provides the foundational infrastructural platform through its Azure cloud and AI services. Simultaneously, it acts as a sectoral platform by offering a stack of services tailored specifically for the education sector, such as Office 365 Education (office software), Teams for Education (collaboration and learning environment), 365 Copilot Chat (AI assistant), and Minecraft Education (digital skill building). These sectoral services are bundled and deeply integrated as a result of running on top of Microsoft's own Azure infrastructure.

Viewing platforms through an infrastructural lens also exposes the dependencies they create. Research shows that platform ecosystems engineer the autonomy, agency, and strategies of those who depend on them across a wide range of sectors. These include people who work in in software and mobile app development (Gerlitz, Helmond, Nieborg et al., 2019; Gerlitz, Helmond, van der Vlist et al., 2019; Pybus and Coté, 2024), in AI and cloud infrastructure (van der Vlist, Helmond and Ferrari, 2024), in journalism and the news production (e.g. Hartley et al., 2023; Nielsen and Ganter, 2022), in advertising (e.g. Crain, 2021; Joseph and Bishop, 2024; van der Vlist and Helmond, 2021), in education (Kerssens, 2024), in cultural production (Poell et al., 2021), and even in defence (i.e. the military) (Hoijtink and Planqué-van Hardeveld, 2022).

This infrastructural approach connects platform studies with app studies, data studies, and software studies, which examine how data infrastructures, SDK integrations, and app ecosystems generate new forms of dependency and control (e.g. Dieter et al., 2019; Flensburg and Lai, 2023; Gerlitz, Helmond, Nieborg et al., 2019; Gerlitz, Helmond, van der Vlist et al., 2019; Pybus and Coté, 2024; van der Vlist, 2022; van der Vlist, Helmond, Dieter et al., 2025; Weltevrede and Jansen, 2019). This will be further discussed in chapter 3. By focusing on infrastructures, the third lens makes it visible for us that power is built into technical architectures, algorithms, and standards that produce layered dependencies and systemic vulnerabilities.

Cross-cutting forces: Political economy, governance, and strategy

Three central forces cut across the three lenses that underpin platform power: political economy (or, more precisely, profit and power); governance and regulation; and strategy. As typologies by Srnicek and Steinberg acknowledge, these forces explain how platforms – from social media and streaming to AI and cloud services – function, evolve, and accumulate influence regardless of their specific type. They organise the relationships between platforms and the many actors in their ecosystems, which constitute the platforms' broader spheres of influence; and they form the analytical foundation for this book and for critical platform studies more widely.

The notions of profit and power – discussed in chapter 3 within the framework of political economy – examine platforms' accumulation and consolidation of influence and value through design, market positioning, infrastructural embedding, and business strategy. They explain why platforms have become such powerful economic and political actors. The area of governance and regulation, explored in chapter 4, addresses the internal, rule-making and gatekeeping functions through which platforms govern their users and the external regulatory frameworks imposed by governments, courts, and international bodies. This discussion illuminates the tensions between the self-regulation and the public accountability of platforms. Finally, the joint themes of strategy and evolution, which run through both chapters, focus on how platforms adapt and expand through vertical and horizontal integration, ecosystem coordination, infrastructural expansion, and

Table 2.2. Cross-cutting analytical dimensions: Political economy, governance, and strategy.

Domains or dimensions	Questions	Examples	Place of discussion
Political economy (profit and power)	How do platforms generate profit and consolidate power?	Network effects, data extraction, ecosystem dependencies, market concentration	Chapter 3
Governance (regulation)	How do platforms govern and get governed?	Terms of service, content moderation, API policies, external regulation (e.g. EU DMA/DSA)	Chapter 4
Strategy (evolution)	How do platforms and their ecosystems grow and adapt?	Vertical/horizontal integration, acquisitions, ecosystem evolution, regulatory responses	Chapters 3–5

strategic responses to regulation. We will see how platforms adjust to competition, regulation, and shifting political and social pressures.

Together, these three interrelated domains – political economy, governance, and strategy – constitute a powerful framework for analysing how platforms, whether viewed as services, as companies, or as technologies or infrastructures, exert and maintain influence across economic, cultural, and institutional domains. The combination of three lenses – services, companies, technologies or infrastructures – and three forces – political economy, governance, strategy – offers a systematic way to study platforms as complex systems and to trace the broader consequences of their power.

Summary

This chapter began with a deceptively simple question: what are platforms? The answer, as we have seen, is neither simple nor singular. Platforms are multiple things at once: digital services used by billions, companies in pursuit of profit through strategic business models, and programmable infrastructures that others build upon. Across these forms, while no two platforms are alike, many share several key characteristics. They are *multisided* or *multifaceted*, as they bring together different groups of users, from consumers to advertisers, creators, developers, and institutions, and govern their interactions. They are *programmable* and *extensible*, so that others can build on top of them. They are *layered*, composed of visible interfaces and layers of invisible infrastructures. And they are *material*, made up of code, features, documentation, and ecosystem resources that structure participation and control.

Yet understanding platforms requires more than identifying their traits. Such characteristics should be seen not as a checklist that every platform must satisfy but as analytical dimensions that vary in degree and combination from case to case. For this reason, empirical case studies are crucial. Some platforms may be multifaceted to a greater extent than they are programmable (e.g. Airbnb, which primarily facilitates interactions between hosts and guests) while others may be infrastructural more than they are service-oriented (e.g. AWS, which underpins a wide range of applications and businesses). Moreover, such variations are not merely technical but translate directly into the way our three domains – political economy, governance, and strategy – unfold.

Importantly, we have argued that platforms do not operate in isolation; they operate in wider social, economic, and infrastructural environments, namely their ecosystems, which consist of constellations of actors, artefacts, dependencies, and regulatory entanglements that platforms both sustain and depend on. Analysing platforms therefore requires a relational perspective or a view of platforms as sociotechnical systems embedded in, shaped by, and shaping broader economic, cultural, and political environments.

This chapter also traced the understanding of platforms and their characteristics across disciplines. Economists and management scholars conceptualise platforms as multisided markets; computing, engineering, and information systems approaches define them as programmable systems;

communication and media studies scholars analyse them as non-neutral intermediaries.

Bringing these ideas together, the chapter proposed a tripartite analytical framework for critical platform analysis. Platforms can be approached through three complementary lenses: as services, as companies, and as technologies or infrastructures. Across these lenses, three cross-cutting dimensions or fields of analysis structure platform power: political economy (which focuses on profit and power), governance (which focuses on regulation), and strategy (which focuses on evolution). This is the analytical foundation for the systematic study of platforms, as proposed here.

Equally importantly, our framework underscores that we must ask not only what platforms are but also what they are to whom, under what conditions, and with what consequences. Such questions encourage students and researchers to suspend judgement as they balance their empirical curiosity and sensitivity to specific contexts with the pursuit of generalised conceptual understanding.

The next chapter builds directly on these insights by turning to the political economy of platforms. It asks how platforms have become so economically and politically powerful and examines how they accumulate, organise, and exercise power and how this power is governed, challenged, and reimagined in contemporary society.

Discussion questions

- **Applying the analytical framework** The chapter proposes that platforms be analysed as services, companies, and technologies or infrastructures. Choose a major platform (e.g. Amazon, TikTok, Spotify) and discuss how looking at it through each of these three lenses reveals different aspects of its power and function that a single, everyday definition might miss.
- **Socio-technical shaping** The chapter argues that platforms are socio-technical systems where technology and society *mutually shape* each other. Can you provide an example from the text or from

a recent event (e.g. a regulatory decision, a user boycott, a new feature) that illustrates how social forces led to a significant change in a platform's design or policy?

* **Core characteristics and power**   The platforms' core characteristics are multisidedness, programmability, layering, and materiality. How do the principles of *layering* (which gives different actors different views of the platform) and of *programmability* (which makes APIs and SDKs available) contribute to an uneven distribution of power between the platform owner and its various users?

Further reading

van Dijck, J., Poell, T. and de Waal, M. (2018) *The Platform Society*. Oxford University Press.
Srnicek, N. (2016) *Platform Capitalism*. Polity.
Gillespie, T. (2010) The politics of 'platforms'. *New Media & Society* 12(3): 347–64. DOI: 10.1177/1461444809342738.

3
Profit and Power

Introduction

Today a handful of global tech companies dominate not only digital markets but also the infrastructures that underpin contemporary economic and social life. Their rise represents one of the most consequential shifts in economic power in recent history. In 2011, venture capitalist Marc Andreessen famously claimed that 'software is eating the world' (Andreessen, 2011). More than being a celebration of software, the statement captured a deeper transformation, in which entire industries were being reorganised around a new class of internet-native firms that had survived the dot-com crash of the early 2000s. Companies like Amazon, Google, and eBay emerged from that period as dominant players.

Andreessen's statement also carried a warning: to succeed in the digital economy, companies must dominate or risk being dominated. In his view, 'Silicon Valley–style entrepreneurial technology companies' were not just transforming industries; they were the new winners, replacing incumbent firms and reshaping markets.

Platforms have eaten the world

Fifteen years later, it is fair to say that big tech companies *have* indeed eaten the world. A small number of extraordinarily powerful companies – Google (Alphabet), Apple, Facebook (Meta Platforms), Amazon, and Microsoft – now dominate the global economy. Often grouped under acronyms such as GAFAM or fanciful names like the Magnificent Seven (a group that includes NVIDIA and Tesla), these publicly traded firms are among the largest and most profitable in history, be that measured in users, in market value, or in annual revenue.[1] As we will see, their growth has been driven by aggressive strategies of infrastructure development, cross-sectoral expansion and integration, and financialisation.

The scale of this transformation is striking. As of late 2025, each of these firms had a market valuation that ranged between 2.4 and 4.9 trillion, surpassing the GDP of most countries (CompaniesMarketCap.com, n.d.). Seven of the ten most valuable companies in the world are platform firms and, together, account for more than 30 per cent of the Standard and Poor's 500 (S&P 500) US stock index. These firms are no longer just tech companies; they operate as infrastructural powers at the heart of the global economy.

A similar, if somewhat distinct dynamic can be observed in China, where companies such as Baidu, Alibaba, Tencent, Xiaomi, (often grouped under acronyms of the form BAT or BATX) ByteDance,[2] Huawei, and Meituan hold dominant positions in domestic markets and increasingly shape digital infrastructures across Asia, as well as in Africa and Latin America. While on a smaller financial scale, these firms operate in a different institutional context, closely aligned with China's state-driven ambitions for technological expansion and geopolitical influence.

At the same time, big tech is not a monolith. These companies differ in their revenue models, business strategies, and infrastructural footprints. For instance, Apple remains rooted in consumer hardware, Google and Meta in digital advertising, Amazon in logistics, and Microsoft in cloud computing and enterprise software. All operate as platform companies, yet their power is shaped through different combinations of services, technical infrastructures, and strategic ecosystems.

Political economy as a cross-cutting dimension

Understanding how platforms have become powerful convenors and shapers of economic and social life requires more than isolated case studies or company-specific histories. As outlined in chapter 2, platforms should be analysed as socio-technical systems, embedded in and formed by wider institutional, infrastructural, and economic environments. One of the most important domains that exert this formative influence over platforms and their ecosystems is *political economy*, which holds the economic and political dynamics through which profit and power are produced, accumulated, distributed, and contested.

A political economy perspective directs attention to platforms as entities embedded in systems of value creation, labour, control, and governance. It raises fundamental questions. How do platforms generate and extract value? How do they control access to markets, infrastructure, and data? How do they determine, and how are they determined by, legal, political, and economic arrangements? The rise of big tech is not simply a story of technological innovation or market success. It is also a story of strategic accumulation, infrastructural control, and shifting relations of power that define the digital economy.

Chapter overview

This chapter examines the interrelated power and political economy of platforms. In the next section it introduces the platform business model and its key characteristics, before turning to look at how critical political economy, as a theoretical tradition, has been employed to analyse platforms. Then the section on strategies (pp. 78–87) outlines two complementary research strategies for tracing the mechanisms by which platform power operates in practice: follow the money and follow the data. The section after it, on insights (pp. 87–107), synthesises critical approaches, empirical insights, and theoretical perspectives in order to explore platforms' consolidation of power through a set of interlocking dynamics: datafication and surveillance, platformisation and infrastructuralisation, conglomeration and financialisation, and orchestration and evolution. Throughout the chapter we show that these dynamics can be traced, visualised, and made visible. Finally, the last section (pp. 108–16) identifies key dimensions of platform power and proposes a framework for analysing its broader significance and implications.

Understanding the political economy and power of platforms

To critically understand platforms today, we must examine them not only as technological innovations but also as strategic agents embedded in and actively transforming contemporary capitalism – which Srnicek (2016) terms 'platform capitalism'. Platforms have become central agents in an economy where access to digital infrastructures and control over them increasingly determine who can participate in, benefit from, or be excluded from economic and social life. Political economy provides a framework for analysing these power relations but, to apply it effectively, we must first understand the economic mechanisms through which platform power operates.

Understanding what platforms *do* at the level of the economy requires an examination of the distinctive business model that underpins their operations and profitability. It is essential to get a good grasp of this model because critical political economy does not simply critique platforms in the abstract; it analyses specific economic mechanisms as they generate power, create dependencies, and enable accumulation.

The platform business model

How did a small number of tech companies come to hold such disproportionate economic, infrastructural, and cultural power? While technological innovation certainly played a role, what made these firms dominant was their adoption of a new business model: the platform. Foundational works in the platform business and management literature (e.g. Cusumamo et al., 2019; Evans and Schmalensee, 2016; Gawer, 2021; Parker et al., 2016) identify several key characteristics that distinguish platform business models from traditional ones (see Table 3.1).

The first characteristic is *multisided or multifaceted value creation*. Platforms generate value by facilitating interactions or transactions between distinct user groups through their digital infrastructures, in other words by acting as intermediaries or matchmakers (chapter 2). Classic examples are buyers and sellers on e-commerce marketplaces (Amazon, Alibaba), drivers and passengers on ride-hailing apps (Uber, Bolt, BlaBlaCar), advertisers and audiences on social media platforms (Instagram, TikTok), hosts and guests on

Table 3.1. The traditional business model, compared with the platform business model.

Dimension	The traditional business model	The platform business model
Value creation	Produces and sells goods or services to customers	Facilitates interactions and exchanges between multiple user groups
Scale	Scaling requires additional physical resources (capital, labour)	Scaling is driven by network effects and digital infrastructure; there are low expansion costs
Ownership and control	Owns and controls the linear supply chain and production assets	Owns and manages digital infrastructure, sets rules, orchestrates ecosystem participation
Ecosystem governance	Coordinates suppliers and distributors along a linear chain	Structures, governs, and incentivises third-party participation via APIs, standards, and policy
Revenue	Earns revenue from the direct sale of products or services	Earns revenue from transaction fees, advertising, subscriptions, data monetisation, etc.

short-term rental platforms (Airbnb), and app developers and end users on app stores (Apple's App Store, Huawei AppGallery).

The second characteristic is *rapid scaling* through network effects and digital infrastructure. Platforms are designed to grow quickly by harnessing network effects: as more users join sides, the platform becomes more valuable to all. More riders attract more drivers to Uber; more sellers attract more buyers to Amazon. This positive feedback loop fuels rapid growth and market consolidation, often producing a winner-takes-all or winner-takes-most outcome, in which a few dominant players capture most of the value. At the same time digital infrastructures such as application programming interfaces (APIs) enable platforms to expand into new markets with relatively low additional costs.

The third characteristic is *infrastructure ownership and control*. Platforms enable interactions; they also own and manage the digital infrastructures that underpin these interactions. They control the means of connection and govern access, participation, and innovation within their ecosystems, which include app stores, APIs, payment systems, and cloud services. For example, Apple and Google determine the technical and financial terms that decide which mobile apps can reach users through their app stores and how these apps can be monetised.

The fourth characteristic is *ecosystem orchestration and governance*. Platforms actively structure and manage the interactions between their various user groups by setting rules, standards, and access conditions (chapter 4). YouTube's monetisation policies determine which creators can earn revenue; Amazon's algorithms decide which sellers gain visibility. Such orchestration is never neutral. It allows platforms to enable or constrain participation selectively, in ways that advance their strategic interests.

Finally, *data-driven value creation* often lies at the core of the platform business model. Platforms capture value through matching algorithms, trust systems, transaction tools, and continuous data extraction. This value is monetised through various revenue models: advertising (Google, Facebook, X), subscriptions (Netflix, Spotify), freemium services (Dropbox), transaction fees (Amazon, PayPal), commissions (App Store,

Airbnb, Uber), affiliate marketing (TripAdvisor), licensing (Microsoft), digital goods (LINE), e-commerce commissions (RedNote/Xiaohongshu), and direct data monetisation (Facebook, Acxiom). Central to these models is the platform's ability to collect, analyse, and leverage data so as to optimise services, target users, manage labour, and create new revenue streams, as the next sections further explore.

While much of the business and management literature locates the origins of this platform business model in Silicon Valley, scholars in media and platform studies such as Steinberg (2019) have complicated the narrative by identifying important precursors in Japan's mobile internet services of the late 1990s. NTT DoCoMo's i-mode ecosystem, for instance, anticipated many features of today's platform model. It operated as a multisided market that connected consumers, content providers, and handset manufacturers, generated revenue through transaction fees, leveraged network effects to scale its user base, and acted as a strict gatekeeper by deciding who could participate in its ecosystem.

As the following sections show, the rise of platforms as powerful political-economic actors has prompted communication and media studies scholars to develop critiques of the platform economy and its dynamics.

Critical political economy of platforms

The platform business model is not politically neutral. Each characteristic creates specific forms of power: powerful network effects drive winner-takes-most markets; data extraction enables surveillance; ecosystem orchestration generates interdependencies. Political economy reveals the functioning of these business model features as mechanisms of accumulation and control.

Political economy originated as a school of thought concerned with the study of how political forces shape economic systems and how those systems, in turn, affect politics. Broadly speaking, it explores the mechanisms through which economic and political relations intersect to determine media, technology, and society as a whole (Hardy, 2014; Mosco, 2009 [1996]). Within communication and media studies, this analytical tradition has been widely applied to examine the organisation, financing, and control of media systems under capitalism, with attention to issues of ownership, labour, finance, regulation, and corporate power.

The political economy of communication is 'the study of the social relations, particularly the power relations, that mutually constitute the production, distribution, and consumption of resources', as Vincent Mosco (2009: 25) famously defines it. Power here refers to both the accumulation of economic resources and the ability of media systems, including platforms, to organise and govern markets, ecosystems, and actors, while influencing wider social and political structures.

Extending this tradition, Jonathan Hardy (2014) argues that to understand the role of media requires examining how they are funded and organised. The critical political economy (CPE) of media analyses the forces or power relations that shape media systems: ownership structures, financial models, governance mechanisms, and labour conditions. These dynamics influence what kinds of content and services are produced, how they are distributed, and whose interests they serve. CPE is centrally concerned with the relationship between money (or profit) and power and its structuring of media systems, their content, and their societal consequences.

While not all platforms are media companies, many now serve as essential infrastructures for communication, interaction, and information exchange. They shape visibility and attention, structure digital labour, and influence public discourse. For this reason, the political economy of communication and media studies offers a valuable perspective for analysing platform power and its implications.

Within platform studies, political economy approaches foreground platforms' concentration of power, their extraction of value, and their reforming of markets through control over data, infrastructures, and user interactions (e.g. Fuchs, 2021 [2013]; Narayan, 2024; Poell et al., 2021; Srnicek, 2016). Scholars in this tradition examine platforms as powerful economic and political actors that commodify data, exploit users and labour, monetise engagement, and act as private regulators of digital ecosystems.

From the viewpoint of political economy, several key areas of enquiry emerge for studying platforms. First, *ownership*:

who owns and controls platforms, and how centralised is this control? Ownership affects not only competition and innovation but also media plurality and democratic account-ability. Second, *finance* is another critical area, as it raises questions about how platforms are funded and how their revenue models inform their strategies, priorities, and content. Third, *governance* concerns the internal workings of platforms through decision-making processes and the external modes of platform regulation (chapter 4). Finally, *labour* draws attention to (a) those who produce the content, code, and infrastructure of platforms and deliver their services; (b) the conditions under which they work; and (c) who benefits from their efforts.

To investigate such questions, Hardy (2014: 75) highlights the analytical value of publicly accessible corporate documents: annual reports, financial statements, the US Securities and Exchange Commission (SEC) filings, investor calls, policy statements, and legal documents. These documents, along with trade publications and industry materials aimed at advertisers, regulators, and investors, offer insight into how platforms frame their value, communicate strategy, and navigate multiple audiences. Such document-based enquiry aligns with the technographic approach introduced in chapter 2, which focuses on interpreting platform operations through their own materials and documentation.

Platforms' material political economy
An important perspective in political economy analysis draws on economic sociology, where recent work foregrounds the *material dimensions* of platform capitalism. This aligns with our own framework. For instance, Donald MacKenzie's (2018) concept of material political economy, developed in the context of high-frequency trading systems, demonstrates that economic power is exercised not only through ownership but also through technical design. More than supporting economic activity, technical infrastructures such as software interfaces, system architectures, data pipelines, and protocols actively give it a form. By privileging certain actors, actions, and strategies through their very configuration, these systems embed asymmetries of power.

Applied to platforms, this perspective makes it clear that economic or discursive platform power is also materially embedded in technical infrastructures. Control is exercised through design decisions about algorithms ranking content, APIs granting or restricting access to platform data or functionalities, or interfaces conditioning visibility and monetisation. These are not neutral technical choices but political decisions built into infrastructure itself.

Building on this material perspective, Çalışkan et al. (2025) argue that platforms are often misunderstood in two ways: they are taken either for simple multisided markets that connect buyers and sellers or for all-powerful surveillance machines. In reality, platforms operate through what these researchers call 'stacked economisation': the layering of multiple business models and value extraction mechanisms within the same infrastructure. For example, Facebook functions simultaneously as an advertising broker, a data extraction system, a content licensing platform, and a marketplace. These economic logics are not separate but *stacked and integrated* within Meta's infrastructure. Such a perspective reveals how platforms accumulate value not through a single mechanism but through coordinated layers of economic activity, each embedded in material arrangements.

Together, these perspectives call for a broader conception of political economy, one that, apart from ownership and revenue models, includes the material, infrastructural, and architectural arrangements through which platforms operate and enable layered forms of value accumulation and control.

Understanding the power of platforms

Understanding the political economy of platforms requires analysing how economic structures and material infrastructures jointly organise, concentrate, and operationalise power in digital environments. A political economy lens shows that platform power is not exercised exclusively through market position or ownership. It also operates through infrastructures that platforms design and that create relationships of dependency, control value creation, and structure governance within their ecosystems.

This raises a central question for political economy: how can platform power be conceptualised, empirically traced, and located? As argued in chapter 2 (pp. 30–2), platforms are multisided, programmable, layered, and material systems and these characteristics form the architecture through which power operates. Platforms govern different user groups through separate interfaces such as developer portals, creator studios, and advertising dashboards. They maintain control through technical dependencies such as APIs, cloud hosting, and distribution pipelines. They shape behaviour through layered arrangements that include backend infrastructures, data processing, ranking systems, and enforcement practices. Power is also embedded materially in artefacts such as algorithms, access rules, and terms of service.

Analysing platform power therefore means tracing these sides or facets, layers, and material arrangements. It is this distributed architecture, rather than any single component, that enables platforms and the companies behind them to organise, govern, and restructure their ecosystems.

A relational concept of platform power

This brings us to a *relational understanding* of platform power. It is a form of power exercised between platforms and other actors and manifest across technological, economic, and political registers. It arises from multiple sources – control over data flows, technical integrations with third parties, strategic partnerships with businesses or governments – giving an otherwise abstract concept a concrete, materially grounded form. Google's control over the Android operating system and app distribution channels determines how millions of developers reach global audiences, while Amazon's dominance in cloud infrastructure positions it as a gatekeeper for much of the internet's back-end services.

Critical political economists investigate these dynamics through empirical analysis, historical inquiry, and theoretical reflection, seeking to identify the dimensions and sources of power (pp. 110–12) and to map the structure, exercise, and experience of this power, in all their consequences. Aradau and Blanke (2022: 103) describe this relationality as a 'microphysics of platform power': power does not reside in a single actor but emerges from constantly shifting asymmetrical relations. As they put it, 'platforms raise political questions in that they "press us into relations with others", while enacting asymmetries of power' (93).

Users, whether consumers, creators, developers, or businesses, do not simply 'use' platforms. They enter into *relations* of use and dependence that tend to privilege the platform over time. Building on Microsoft's or Amazon's cloud services can generate technical and economic lock-in; news publishers reliant on Facebook or Google for traffic and advertising revenue become tied to algorithmic systems and policy changes.

While much scholarship highlights platforms' central-ising tendencies and monopolistic ambitions, it is equally important to recognise that that platform power is relational, dispersed, and negotiated between actors (van der Vlist and Helmond, 2021). It operates through technical infrastruc-tures, financial mechanisms, institutional arrangements, and everyday practices (e.g. Helmond et al., 2019; Nieborg and Poell, 2025; Nieborg et al., 2024; Nielsen and Ganter, 2022; Steinberg, 2019; van Dijck et al., 2018; van Dijck et al., 2019; van der Vlist et al., 2022).

This relational perspective has two main implications. First, platform companies must be understood as embedded in ecosystems: they are dynamic networks of interrelated actors, infrastructures, and business logics. Second, these ecosystems extend into platforms' broader 'spheres of influence' (van der Vlist, 2022: 252), changing technological, economic, and social domains through infrastructural, financial, and regulatory interventions. Apple's introduction of new privacy rules for data tracking on iOS, for example, forces adver-tising firms and data brokers to reconfigure their operations.

As we are going to see in the following sections, these spheres of influence constitute the terrain on which platform power is enacted, negotiated, and contested. But first let us turn to the empirical analysis of platform power.

Strategies for analysing power relations

Since platform power is relational and distributed, a central methodological principle involves tracing and mapping actor networks or what science and technology studies (STS) scholars describe as 'following the actors' (Latour,

2007 [2005]; Venturini and Munk, 2021). Within the STS framework of actor–network theory (ANT), power is not treated as something an actor or an institution possesses, but as an effect of relationships and alignments within a network. It emerges when human and non-human actors (users, algorithms, devices, policies, or interfaces) enrol each other – that is, define each other's roles and align their interests within a network – and stabilise associations that make certain actions or outcomes possible. Applied to platform studies, following the actors means tracing the participation and interaction of technical artefacts (e.g. APIs, software development kits (SDKs), data centres, algorithms), corporate actors (platform firms, advertisers, app developers), and institutional actors (regulators, civil society organisations) as they determine the evolution of platform ecosystems. In practice, this involves mapping connections, dependencies, and translations between actors: the ways a platform policy enrols developers, an API mediates data exchange, or governance arrangements stabilise power asymmetries.

These mappings are often complemented by *digital methods*, which, as Rogers (2013: 1) suggests, aim to 'follow the evolving methods of the medium' by using platform-native features such as hashtags, likes, filters, or algorithmic rankings. In this sense, digital methods can be understood as a means to follow the actors through their digital traces, both to investigate social phenomena and to analyse the technical principles of the platforms themselves. Extending this logic of tracing relations, two further analytical orientations have proven especially useful for studying the political economy of platforms: follow the money and follow the data. Following the money enables financial platform analysis, which studies the influence exercised on platforms by financial mechanisms, revenue models, business strategies, shareholder pressure, and investment flows (p. 80). Following the data supports infrastructural platform analysis. This is a strategy for understanding the control that platforms have over data infrastructures, their structuring of data flows, and their embedding in other systems and domains through infrastructural integrations (p. 85).

These empirical strategies do more than describe; they ground abstract theoretical claims about platforms and their political economy or power. As the following sections will show, such approaches help us to track the manifestations of platform power across different sectors, geographies, and institutional contexts. While follow the money and follow the data provide distinct perspectives, they are often interconnected and, together, offer a useful methodological orientation if we wish to dissect the intersections of economic and infrastructural forms of power.

Follow the money

The directive to follow the money offers a critical lens for analysing the financial foundations of platform power. This approach traces companies' generation of income by unpacking their revenue streams, monetisation models, and broader financial structures. Within platform and media studies, it reveals how platforms make money, who pays whom, and what economic incentives motivate their services, strategic priorities, and influence. For researchers, journalists, and policymakers, following the money can uncover the often hidden financial rationales – such as advertising dependencies or investor pressures – that guide platform decisions, determine user experiences, and drive expansion.

Over the past decade, big tech has dramatically expanded its economic footprint, contributing to an increasingly concentrated global economy. This raises a key political-economic question: how exactly do these companies make their billions? One powerful approach to answering this question is to tackle publicly available financial disclosures. In both technographic and critical political-economic research, platform documentation constitutes a valuable yet often underused empirical source; and this source includes financial documents. Publicly traded platform companies – for example Alphabet Inc., Meta Platforms Inc., Amazon.com Inc., Tencent Holdings Ltd, and Alibaba Group Holding Ltd – are legally required to file detailed quarterly and annual reports such as the US Securities and Exchange Commission (SEC) Form 10-K. These documents provide granular insight into a company's revenue sources, global operations, regulatory risks, and strategic outlook and are typically accessible through investor relations websites (e.g. investors.airbnb.com).

Major platforms' main revenue streams and geographic footprints

By following the money and reading these financial materials, we can show where value is generated and what activities or dependencies underpin profitability, thus tracing the structuring of platform power through revenue models. On the basis of our analysis of the 2024 10-K filings and annual reports from the Magnificent Seven, Alibaba, and Tencent, four dominant revenue streams stand out across these major platform companies: digital advertising; cloud infrastructure and AI services; hardware and devices; and retail and e-commerce. That said, each company has a distinct revenue profile and global footprint (Table 3.2).

Digital advertising remains the primary economic engine for several leading platforms. In 2024, Alphabet generated 75.6 per cent of its US$350 billion revenue from advertising across Google Search, YouTube, and its ad network. Meta's reliance is even more pronounced: 97.7 per cent of its US$264.5 billion income comes from advertising across its family of apps – Facebook, Instagram, WhatsApp, and Messenger. Tencent, best known for its messaging and content services, earned 18.4 per cent of its 2024 revenue from marketing services tied to its platform ecosystem. Even Amazon, which is widely recognised for e-commerce and cloud, has rapidly emerged as a key player in advertising, earning US$56 billion (or 8.8 per cent of its total revenue) from ads.

Cloud infrastructure and AI services represent some of the fastest-growing and most profitable revenue streams. Microsoft led in 2024, when it earned US$237.4 billion from cloud services; Azure alone was growing by 30 per cent each year. Amazon Web Services (AWS) contributed US$207.6 billion (16.9 per cent of total revenue), while Alphabet's Google Cloud brought in US$43.2 billion (12.4 per cent). In China, Tencent's cloud services are included in its FinTech and Business Services segment (32.1 per cent), and Alibaba Cloud contributed 8.1 per cent of company revenue. Across the board, cloud and AI infrastructure have become central to platform growth strategies.

Table 3.2. Revenue streams for the Magnificent Seven, Alibaba, and Tencent.

Company	Main revenue streams	Geography	2024 Total revenue in US$ (millions)
Amazon	online stores (38.7%), third-party seller services (24.5%), AWS (16.9%), advertising (8.8%), subscriptions (7.0%)	US-dominant (~70%)	637,959
Apple	iPhone (51.4%), services (24.6%), wearables and devices (9.5%), Mac (7.7%), iPad (6.8%)	US-dominant (>50%)	391,035
Alphabet (Google)	advertising (75.6%), Google Cloud (12.4%), subscriptions, platforms, and devices (11.5%), other (0.5%)	US (47%), EMEA (30%), APAC (15%)	350,018
Microsoft	server products and cloud services (40%), Office (22%), Windows (10%), gaming (9%), LinkedIn (7%)	US (~50%), international (~50%)	245,122
Meta (Facebook)	advertising (97.7%), Reality Labs (1.3%), other (1.0%)	US-dominant (>50%)	164,501
Alibaba	customer management services (China commerce retail) (41.1%), sales of goods (30.1%), logistics services (12.1%), cloud services (8.1%), membership and value-added services (4.5%)	China (>85%)	130,350
Tesla	automotive sales (74.2%), services and other (10.8%), energy (9.8%), regulatory credits (2.8%), leasing (1.9%)	US and international (US, Taiwan, China)	97,690
Tencent	value-added services (48.3%), fin-tech and business services (32.1%), marketing services (incl. advertising) (18.4%)	China (>85%)	91,900
NVIDIA	compute and networking (77.8%), graphics (22.2%)	US, Taiwan, China	60,922

Hardware and devices are central to platform companies that tightly integrate hardware, software, and services into a single ecosystem. Apple remains the most profitable hardware platform, the iPhone alone being responsible for 51.4 per cent of Apple's US$391 billion revenue. Its Services segment, which includes the App Store and licensing, added another 24.6 per cent. NVIDIA earned 77.8 per cent of its US$60.9 billion from Compute & Networking, which is largely driven by sales of graphics processing units (GPUs) for data centres and AI. Tesla generated 74.2 per cent of its US$97.7 billion from automotive sales, supplemented by services and energy. Meta's Reality Labs, focused on AR/VR, accounted for 2.3 per cent of revenue but remains central to the company's long-term metaverse vision.

E-commerce and transaction fees underpin the business models of firms that act as matchmakers by connecting buyers and sellers. Amazon's 2024 revenue included 38.7 per cent from its own online store and 24.5 per cent from third-party seller services. Alibaba's retail platform model generated 41.1 per cent of its revenue from merchant fees on Taobao and Tmall, 30.1 per cent from direct sales, and 12.1 per cent from logistics. Apple monetises digital marketplaces through the App Store and services, which together account for roughly 30 per cent of the company's total revenue. Tencent earned 48.3 per cent of revenue from value-added services (social media subscriptions and in-game sales) and 32.1 per cent from fin-tech and business services.

Despite their global scale, these companies vary widely in their geographic footprint. Amazon, Meta, and Apple continue to earn most of their income from the US market, which reflects the size and infrastructural coverage of their domestic base. Alphabet reports a more distributed income – 47 per cent from the United States, 30 per cent from EMEA, and 15 per cent from Asia-Pacific – while Microsoft earns roughly a half of its revenue from outside the United States. In contrast, Alibaba and Tencent remain largely domestic, over 85 per cent of their revenue coming from China. NVIDIA, as a global hardware supplier, has a diversified geographic footprint: it has major markets in the United States, Taiwan, and China that reflect its role in the international AI hardware supply chain.

In short, while the Magnificent Seven and their Chinese counterparts are often grouped together as big tech, they differ significantly in their business models, revenue structures, and strategic priorities. These are not global, generic monopolies but distinct firms with specific regional footholds and sectoral orientations. Recognising these differences is crucial to any political economy analysis that seeks to move beyond generalisation and understand how platform power is actually organised and exercised.

Financial disclosures, such as annual 10-K reports and S-1 registration filings, offer important empirical insight into these dynamics. Such documents go beyond reporting financial performance; they also reveal how firms articulate their strategic ambitions, assess competitive threats, and respond to regulatory pressures. While 10-K filings provide recurring detailed overviews of a company's finances, revenue composition operations, and risk exposure, S-1 registration filings, submitted to regulators in preparation of an initial public offering (IPO), are especially revealing because they frame the styles in which firms narrate their business models and justify their market position.

As Yuval Dror (2015) shows, Google's 2004 S-1 included a personal letter from its founders that articulates the company's broader mission and values. Similar founders' letters from Zynga, Groupon, and Facebook presented their IPOs not merely as financial events but as moral or cultural undertakings, inviting investors to buy into a vision of technological progress. Dror shows that such narratives offer precious insight into the values and ideological positioning of platforms, revealing how they seek to legitimise their business models.

In addition, Ronan Ó Fathaigh et al. (2019) demonstrate how financial disclosures can also expose the material consequences of regulatory change. Examining a range of filings and investor communications, they show that Apple's privacy reforms led Twitter to lose two million users via third-party apps and caused the ad-tech firm Criteo to report a US$25 million revenue drop. In this way financial documents make it visible that regulatory shifts transform platform dependencies, business models, and global markets (see chapter 4).

But, while the principle of following the money is a powerful means of uncovering financial dependencies and strategic priorities, it has its limitations. The approach works best for publicly traded firms that are subject to disclosure requirements. Privately held or opaque companies such as X Corp, Palantir, or Anduril operate with far less transparency, and this makes their financial structures and economic influence considerably harder to analyse.

Follow the data

Just as tracing revenue streams can reveal the financial structures of platform power, tracing data flows can uncover its infrastructure foundations. Follow the data is a strategy for investigating how data are collected, processed, circulated, and monetised within and across platforms (Flensburg and Lai, 2023). It asks what kinds of data are extracted, how they are used, who has access to them, and for what purposes. This approach shows that data flows underpin business models, structure governance, and produce dependencies and asymmetries between users, developers, advertisers, and platforms. It helps to expose the often invisible infrastructures and power dynamics that sustain the digital economy.

In tracing these movements, scholars such as Bates et al. (2016) have proposed the concept of data journeys to capture how data travel across different sites, systems, and practices. By tracing these journeys, researchers are able to follow data from the moment they are created and see where – in what specific organisational and material settings – they are processed, stored, and used. This makes it possible to understand, say, the transformations through which data become valuable or are sometimes withheld.

Following the data provides an empirical entry point into *infrastructural platform analysis*, which is the study of the technical and organisational systems that process data, transfer them across networks, and enable platforms to expand, enter new domains, and create value.

Infrastructural platform analysis, infrastructural inversion, and visualisation

Infrastructural platform analysis focuses on identifying, describing, and interpreting the infrastructural relationships and integrations that tie platforms to other actors. The aim is to understand the processes by which these connections allow platforms to function, scale, and generate value. Two complementary approaches can be distinguished.

An *externally focused* infrastructural analysis looks outwards, examining a core dynamic of platformisation, namely platforms' expansion into broader digital ecosystems. This includes their integration with third-party apps, services, and institutions. For instance, Google's advertising and analytics tools are embedded in millions of websites and apps; Meta's platform services are tightly linked with advertisers and developers; and Microsoft's products are interwoven with educational and public sector infrastructures. Central objects of analysis here are the ecosystem resources discussed in chapter 2, for example APIs and SDKs, which both enable and govern these technical connections.

One example of this approach is Gerlitz and Helmond's (2013) study, which repurposed privacy-focused browser plugins such as Ghostery and Disconnect in order to trace platforms' embedding of trackers in external websites for data collection. Analysing the top 1,000 most visited websites, the two authors mapped the presence of plugins such as Facebook's 'like' button and Google's login infrastructure, thereby unveiling the extensive spread of data collection systems across the web. Such approaches rely on procedures such as tracing trackers, mapping API connections, and analysing SDK integrations to demonstrate that platforms expand their data collection capacities far beyond their own properties. This pervasive data-intensive infrastructure forms the backbone of platforms' surveillance-based advertising model, which is further explored in this chapter.

By contrast, an *internally focused* infrastructural analysis looks inwards, at the architecture or underpinnings of a platform's internal ecosystem. The latter includes a wide range of products, tools, services, back-end systems, data structures, product integrations, internal APIs, and embedded third-party SDKs. Analysing this internal infrastructure can throw light on platforms' ways of managing data flows, optimising interactions, and coordinating technical services within their own stack.

For example, by using publicly available developer documentation, we traced the internal composition of Meta's platform ecosystem through its APIs (van der Vlist et al., 2022). Our analysis revealed distinct yet interconnected API clusters across the Meta family of apps (e.g. Facebook, Instagram, and WhatsApp). By examining which data fields were made available through these interfaces, we found that certain sensitive targeting categories, such as ethnic affinity, had been removed from public developer access but remained available to advertisers for commercial targeting purposes.

Underlying both the external approach and the internal one is a call to highlight the background systems and technologies that typically remain invisible unless they fail or break down. This is a tactic of infrastructural inversion (Bowker and Star, 1999: 34). Adapting it to the digital age redirects our attention from slick, surface-level user interfaces to the back-end infrastructures that outline social and economic life. Making these hidden systems visible through detailed description, mapping, and visualisation allows researchers to critically interrogate the technical foundations of platform power. Scholars often use software tools and visualisation techniques such as charts and network diagrams to trace and map networks of relationships, corporate structures, or platform architectures.[3] Such analyses not only make visible and expose how power operates and circulates within and across platform ecosystems but also provide valuable insights for regulators, policymakers, and civil society actors who seek to design interventions, craft or adjust legislation, and promote greater accountability in the digital economy.

Insights into the political economy of the platform ecosystem

The previous sections have shown how tracing financial flows and data infrastructures illuminates the relational and often invisible workings of platform power. Building on this foundation, the current section introduces four inter-related pairs of processes through which platforms extend their influence and consolidate control. While rooted in ownership, finance, production, labour, and generally the classical concerns of the political economy of media, these processes reflect the distinct dynamics of digital capitalism and the evolving structure of platform firms.

Recent scholarship in platform studies has identified several interconnected processes that drive the expansion, entrenchment, and consolidation of platform power. Scholars have studied these processes through the concepts of datafication and surveillance, platformisation and infrastructuralisation, conglomeration and financialisation, and orchestration and evolution. Each pair represents a core principle through which platforms reshape industries, economies, and societies by expanding across domains such as advertising, cultural production, journalism, education, healthcare, and the public sector.

The classical questions of political economy – who owns what, who controls what, and who benefits – continue to resonate throughout these processes. In the sections that follow we introduce each pair in turn. While analytically distinct, they often overlap in practice, highlighting that economic value creation within platform ecosystems is inseparable from broader questions of infrastructure, control, and power.

Datafication and surveillance

The paired concepts of datafication and surveillance describe how digital platforms turn everyday user activities – such as searches, clicks, messages, location data, or purchases – into structured, quantifiable data points (van Dijck et al., 2018). Datafication fuels processes of value generation and surveillance, that is, the continuous monitoring, analysis, and monetisation of data to classify, target, influence, and predict user behaviour, often at massive scale. Together, these processes form the backbone of the data-driven platform economy, transforming user behaviour into a central source of economic value while they reinforce power asymmetries through predictive and targeted control.

It is important to distinguish between *commercial* and *state* surveillance. Platform studies typically focus on corporate data extraction and surveillance. However, as Edward Snowden's mass surveillance revelations in 2013 made clear, state actors tap into big tech's data flows too, in the name of national security (van der Vlist, 2017).

Platform capitalism and data extraction

Critical political economy approaches examine datafication and surveillance not merely as technical operations but as processes foundational to platform power. Srnicek (2016) describes platform capitalism as a distinct phase of capitalist development characterised by the dot-com bust and the 2008 financial crisis. In this model, platforms are infrastructures designed for large-scale data extraction, processing, and monetisation. The data in question support personalisation, behavioural targeting, algorithmic matching, labour management, and AI training. For Srnicek, the strategic advantage of platforms lies in their capacity to extract, analyse, and capitalise on vast flows of user data; in other words, platforms position data as the new raw material of capitalism.

However, data extraction and commodification are only part of the story. Next, data must be structured and formatted to fit platform infrastructure and business models. After that, data become valuable only through the application of technical and economic processes that render them legible, useful, and valuable to particular actors; we have termed this process 'data marketisation' (Helmond and van der Vlist, 2023: 279). These operations require entire ecosystems of tools, practices, and intermediaries such as ad networks, analytics services, SDKs, and data brokers. Collectively, all these construct the form, function, and value of data.

Infrastructures and intermediaries in the audience economy

To grasp how data marketisation works, one needs to look beyond individual platforms and study the broader infrastructures and intermediaries that make up what we have called the global audience economy. This is an 'exceptionally complex, global, and interconnected marketplace of intermediaries involved in the creation, commodification, analysis, and circulation of data audiences for purposes including, but not limited to, digital advertising and marketing' (van der Vlist and Helmond, 2021: 1). Thousands of lesser known and often overlooked actors participate in this ecosystem, focusing on acquiring, exchanging, and monetising user data in a variety of ways.

We made this complexity visible through network analysis, using it as a form of externally focused infrastructural analysis (see p. 86). Drawing on publicly listed business and marketing partners from social media platforms, we mapped the partnerships that sustain the audience economy. Many of them are not only commercial relations but also technical integrations, facilitated by APIs that automate data exchange. Once these links were visualised as a network diagram, they pointed to the audience economy as a dense and interconnected ecosystem, highlighting central 'nodes' (companies with the most connections or partnerships) and showing that they hold infrastructural and strategic power (Figure 3.1).

This form of infrastructural analysis demonstrates that platform power is not concentrated in a single company – not even in giants like Google or Meta, which dominate digital advertising. It is instead distributed and reproduced through a complex network of partnerships, technical integrations, and data flows. Power in the audience economy is thus *relational* and often obscured within the infrastructures that enable targeted advertising as well as wider systems of digital surveillance and data-driven decision-making, from credit scoring to insurance risk assessment and employment screening.

From audience commodity to surveillance capitalism

At the heart of this economy lies what political economist Dallas Smythe (2012 [1981]) once called 'the audience commodity': the idea that commercial media generate profit not by selling content but by selling the attention and demographic profiles of their audiences to advertisers. In the now familiar 'free' model of digital platforms, users effectively become the product, paying not with money but with their data and attention. This dynamic is a mechanism of the modern attention economy, where user attention is treated as a primary resource, scarce and valuable.

Shoshana Zuboff's (2019) notion of surveillance capitalism describes this development as a new economic system, driven by the extraction of 'behavioural surplus' – that is, raw personal data generated through digital interactions, then

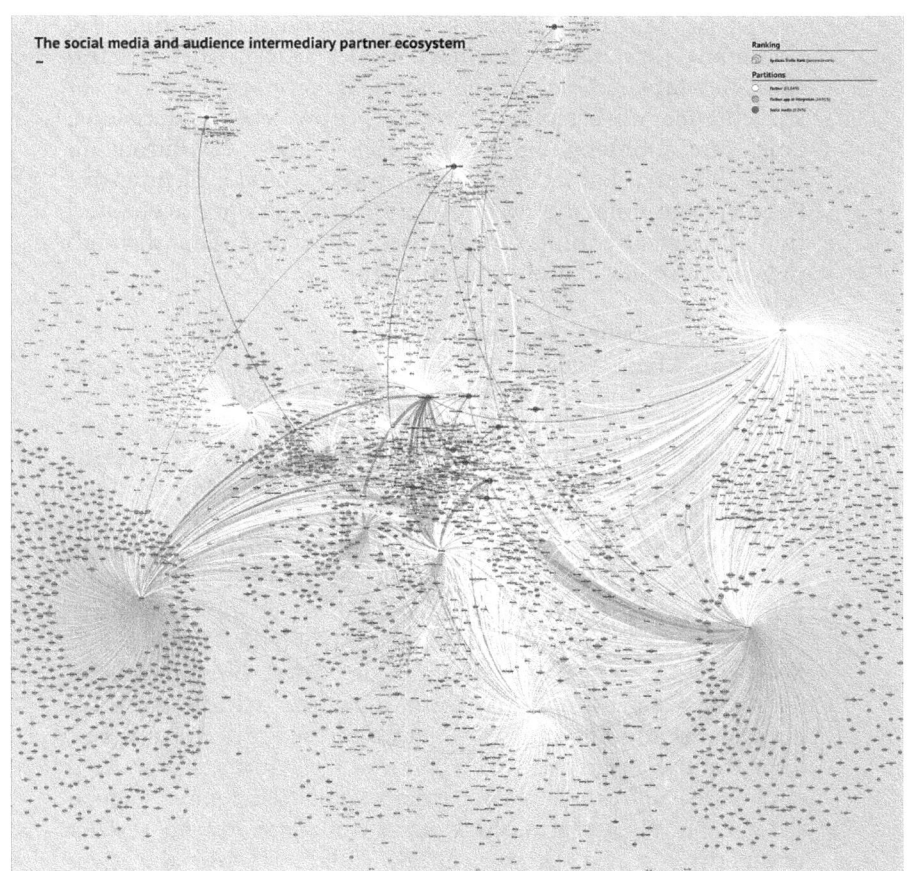

Figure 3.1. Global ecosystem of social media and audience intermediaries, interlinked through partnerships and API-based integrations. Source: van der Vlist and Helmond, 2021. https://osf.io/az76x.

transformed into products that forecast and influence user behaviour. Platforms like Google and Meta, she argues, have built 'extraction architectures' designed not only to monitor but also to modify user behaviour at scale. Lee McGuigan (2023) situates this within a longer 'calculative evolution' in capitalism that aims to render consumers more knowable, targetable, and predictable through increasingly sophisticated ad-tech tools developed to measure, construct, and commodify audiences.

Yet, as Matthew Crain (2021) demonstrates, this now dominant surveillance business model was neither natural nor inevitable. Tracing the political economy history of surveillance advertising, he shows how policy decisions, corporate lobbying, and favourable market conditions in the 1990s enabled its emergence. Today's model of intensive consumer monitoring by a few platforms was not accidental but strategically built, normalised, and defended through deliberate political and economic choices.

Capture, enclosure, and data as an asset

As Sarah Myers West (2019) and Kean Birch (2023) argue, platforms do not simply sell data; they control them. West's concept of data capitalism emphasises how commodifying behavioural data into audience profiles reorganises power, as platform companies gain disproportionate influence through their ability to amass data and exploit them, thus profiting from large-scale data collection, and ultimately reinforce existing asymmetries. Birch reinforces this set of ideas by portraying platforms as 'data enclaves' – proprietary infrastructures designed to capture and control data. While Myers West treats data as commodities to be traded, Birch sees them as an *asset*: a strategic resource enclosed within platform ecosystems and designed to generate future economic returns. This framing aligns with metaphors of platform capture and enclosure such as 'walled gardens' and 'data silos', which describe how platforms lock users and data in and restrict competitor access. Archer et al. (2025: 2) use the term 'platformed silos' to describe the infrastructures operated by platform companies that promise data connectivity and interoperability but in practice cause 'the further centralization and consolidation of data control'.

Understanding data as an asset helps explain how big tech consolidates its power: not by selling data directly, but by owning and controlling the infrastructures through which they are produced, stored, and monetised. Birch and Cochrane (2022: 47–53) describe this dynamic as 'digital rentiership', whereby one extracts value from one's ownership of or control over digital assets such as personal data rather than from labour or production. By creating and maintaining conditions of scarcity and exclusivity, platforms secure ongoing returns from their infrastructures. Digital rentiership thus reveals that platform capitalism depends on enclosing and governing data, which makes control itself the primary source of power and profit.

Platformisation and infrastructuralisation

The terms 'platformisation' and 'infrastructuralisation' capture platforms' expansion into new sectors and their transformation into essential intermediaries in social, economic, and technical systems. They indicate that platforms integrate themselves into new industries, which they then restructure around their own principles. Through these dynamics, platforms evolve from digital services into core organising (infra)structures of contemporary economic life with far-reaching consequences for the political economy.

The concept of platformisation was initially introduced to describe the fact that platforms extend beyond their original domains by embedding their infrastructure and economic rationale into new spaces (Helmond, 2015a). This process goes beyond technological expansion or market dominance; it involves the imposition of platform-specific practices such as data extraction, formatting, and monetisation on the environments they enter. Building on this, van Dijck et al. (2018) analysed how platformisation unfolds across key societal domains such as news, education, and healthcare, while Poell et al. (2021) examined its impact on cultural production and on the transformation of the cultural industries.

How platforms become infrastructures

We introduced the idea of platform infrastructure studies to set an agenda for the analysis of platform expansion and power consolidation. Platforms achieve both these goals by decentralising their own infrastructure to enable others to build on them, then recentralising their data collection and fostering infrastructural dependencies (Helmond, 2015b). Building on this idea, Plantin et al. (2018) create an important bridge between platform studies and infrastructure studies. They show that, as platforms scale, standardise, and gain widespread adoption, they begin to operate like infrastructures, offering back-end services that other actors rely on and often becoming essential to entire sectors. Unlike public infrastructures such as electricity or transport, these systems are privately owned and governed, which allows platforms to extract value and exert control without being subject to the same forms of accountability or regulation.

Van Dijck et al. (2018) use the term 'infrastructural platforms' to describe entities like Google, Facebook, or Amazon, which underpin key societal functions such as communication, information access, and service delivery across sectors. For these researchers, platformisation and infrastructuralisation are not merely technical processes but broad socio-economic transformations: they reorganise societal institutions, industries, and practices around corporate interests and commercial logics. This raises fundamental questions about the balance between public values and private power.

Further extending this argument, van Dijck (2021) identifies three strategies through which platforms expand their power. First, vertical integration links services across different layers of the digital stack. Second, infrastructuralisation enables platforms to become essential foundations for others. Third, cross-sectorisation allows them to enter and influence multiple societal domains. Through these combined dynamics, a small group of firms increasingly govern the digital ecosystem. According to van Dijck, platform power lies not simply in ownership or size, but in the capacity to organise and control the wider ecosystem (see van Dijck et al., 2019; van der Vlist, 2022).

Analysing platforms as infrastructure

Helmond et al. (2019) provide one of the most detailed empirical studies of infrastructuralisation in practice, tracing Facebook's transformation from a social networking site into what they call a 'platform as infrastructure'. They show that Facebook strategically used ecosystem resources such as APIs and SDKs, along with partnerships with developers, advertisers, and marketers, to make itself indispensable by embedding itself in the daily workflows of app and advertising industries. The professional tools Facebook offers developers, advertisers, marketers, media partners, and content creators further signal the places where it seeks infrastructural embeddedness and influence. The introduction of dedicated tools and partnership programs for influencers and creators in the late 2010s reflects a shift in strategic focus. Through analysis of archived materials from the Internet Archive Wayback Machine, Helmond and colleagues also mapped how dependencies evolved over time, demonstrating that platform power was built gradually, through the strategic introduction and discontinuation of tools and partnerships.

In related work, Nieborg and Helmond (2019) show that Facebook extended its infrastructural ambitions into the mobile ecosystem by transforming Messenger from a built-in feature on Facebook.com into a standalone app and, eventually, into a programmable platform. This evolution enabled third-party developers to build services within and on top of Messenger. By adopting similar strategies such as offering ecosystem resources and attracting business partners, Facebook enabled third parties to build services within and on top of Messenger. This development positioned Facebook as a gateway to mobile communication and commerce and advanced its ambition to make Messenger the core social infrastructure of the mobile web.

As discussed in the previous section, ecosystem resources such as APIs and organisational arrangements such as partnerships, together, form the infrastructure that connects advertisers, data brokers, and social media platforms in the audience economy. These technical and organisational connections enable the extraction, circulation, and activation of audience data across platforms and devices. Infrastructural power therefore emerges not only from technical integrations but also from the strategic partnerships and dependencies that structure the data infrastructure of digital advertising (van der Vlist and Helmond, 2021). As Flensburg and Lai (2023) argue, infrastructural power is a material and indirect form of power, rooted in the ability to shape and coordinate the activities of others through the infrastructures they depend on.

Complementing this research, Egliston and Carter (2022) analyse Meta Reality Labs and its infrastructural ambitions in spatial computing, virtual and augmented reality included. They identify three key mechanisms through which Meta seeks to expand its metaverse platform: acquiring third-party actors; capturing and collecting influence through partnerships; and expanding its developer ecosystem with developer tools. As these scholars collectively demonstrate, acquisitions, partnerships, and ecosystem resources are central to the processes through which platforms draw in third parties, deepen integrations, and entrench themselves across diverse sectors, enabling them to 'take on a central, infrastructural role in society' (Egliston and Carter, 2022: 7).

Technical dependencies and platforms as service assemblages

Other critical scholars have developed empirical and conceptual tools to study platform integration and dependency across the mobile and digital ecosystem (Blanke and Pybus, 2020; Gerlitz, Helmond, Nieborg et al., 2019; Pybus and Coté, 2024; van der Vlist et al., 2022; van der Vlist, 2022). Developers often embed SDKs from dominant platforms such as Facebook and Google into their mobile apps to provide core functionalities such as analytics, advertising, payments, and identity management. Blanke and Pybus (2020) therefore conceptualise platforms as 'service assemblages'. In their view, platforms decompose and recompose themselves through modular services and technical integrations, reflecting the dynamics of decentralisation and recentralisation discussed earlier. By embedding SDKs directly into the app source code, platforms aim 'to shift the economic dynamics of competition and monopolization in their favor' (Blanke and Pybus, 2020: 1). This creates forms of infrastructural dependency, such that the most powerful platforms are not necessarily the ones with the largest market share but often those other businesses rely on to operate and remain profitable. Pybus and Coté (2024) label these dominant platform companies 'super SDKs', to capture their infrastructural centrality and technical reach across the mobile ecosystem.

These observations align with the growing importance of platform strategy as infrastructure, particularly given recent developments such as the global rise of super apps. These all-in-one platforms mark a shift from traditional platform business models to ecosystem strategies that consolidate control across services and sectors. While platformisation typically refers to a single platform's extending into new domains, super apps expand infrastructurally by bundling services on a wide spectrum – from finance, health, and mobility to social media – into a single integrated ecosystem. This bundling increases platforms' embeddedness in everyday life and reinforces their role as a critical digital infrastructure.

Infrastructuralisation and cloud dependencies in AI
These dynamics are becoming even more pronounced with the ongoing platformisation and infrastructuralisation of AI. Van der Vlist, Helmond and Ferrari (2024) describe the commercialisation and 'industrialisation' of AI as a rapid shift from experimental research and development to practical applications across diverse sectors, accompanied by new dependencies and significant investments. The notion of big tech becoming big AI captures the structural convergence of AI and big tech, which is marked by AI's deep reliance on the hardware, software infrastructure, resources, and capital of tech giants. This reliance is most visible in the dominance of US-based cloud platforms (e.g. Microsoft Azure, AWS, and Google Cloud), which now underpin much of the global AI ecosystem. Against the backdrop of intensifying geopolitical and economic tensions, dependencies on such platforms have raised strategic concerns, particularly in Europe. Understanding the political economy of AI requires analysing the full 'cloud AI stack': the infrastructure, platforms, models, and applications on which contemporary AI systems depend and the companies that provide and control them.

This infrastructural dependency grants major platform companies substantial power; in fact Diewertje Luitse (2024) identifies three interrelated ways in which platforms exercise infrastructural power: vertical integration enables control over multiple technological layers; complementary innovation draws third-party developers, who integrate the platform into other sectors; and abstraction creates simplified interfaces that obscure the complexity of cloud-based AI services. Cecilia Rikap (2024) offers a related insight, arguing that dominance in AI is achieved not only through acquisitions or traditional economic power but through what she terms 'intellectual monopolisation': the control of data, knowledge, and talent, which are all disproportionately concentrated in the hands of big tech. Devika Narayan (2022) sees the scalability of cloud computing as a core 'infrastructural force' that is driving platform expansion. For her, the cloud is not merely a supportive or infrastructural technology but a precondition for contemporary platform capitalism, as it enables rapid operational scalability and economic reach across domains.

Situating and contesting platformisation

Yet platformisation and infrastructuralisation unfold differently across contexts. Van Doorn et al. (2020) introduce the notion of an 'actually existing platformisation' to highlight the situated, relational, and uneven nature of platform expansion. Rather than treating platformisation as a universal process, they draw attention to its different materialisations in specific institutional, social, and geographic settings. Kaye et al. (2021) use the concept of parallel platformisation to show that platformisation results from divergent regulatory and political environments. Their case study on ByteDance (the parent company of TikTok and Douyin) shows that the same underlying platform is developed and governed differently across jurisdictions. While TikTok (global) and Douyin (China) share a technical foundation, their infrastructures, affordances, governance regimes, and monetisation models are tailored to align with distinct user cultures, market logics, and state imperatives. Niels Kerssens (2024) offers a complementary case study from the Dutch primary education sector: here local platform partners helped to integrate Microsoft's educational tools into schools. He describes their contribution as a form of 'soft platform power' in which intermediary actors align public responsibilities for digital transformation with corporate interests, enabling Microsoft to consolidate infrastructural control as it navigates local institutional requirements.

Finally, Popiel and Vasudevan (2024) introduce the concept of friction to capture the visibility of platform power when it encounters resistance or infrastructural breakdown in context-specific settings. Frictions can arise from conflicts and protests against data centres, for example over energy and water use, or from incompatibilities with local norms and regulations. Such episodes expose the ongoing work of maintaining and expanding platform infrastructures and reveal the negotiations and contestations that underlie platform power on the ground.

Conglomeration and financialisation

The terms 'conglomeration' and 'financialisation' describe how platforms expand and consolidate economic power through broader corporate and financial strategies. Conglomeration refers to the growth of platform companies through the acquisition and integration of a diversity of businesses, services, and infrastructures that often span multiple sectors.[4] Financialisation points to the increasing influence of financial markets, shareholder value, and speculative investment on the strategies and priorities of these firms. These mechanisms can explain how platforms exert influence not only within their original markets but across entire sectors and even societies.

Platforms as multisectoral companies and service conglomerates

Returning to our framework, it is essential to recognise that platforms are no longer single-purpose digital services or companies but increasingly operate as *conglomerates*: they are multisectoral corporations that combine a variety of businesses, services, and infrastructures under a single corporate structure. Alphabet (Google), Meta (Facebook), Amazon, and Tencent exemplify this trend. These companies operate now across search, advertising, logistics, cloud computing, entertainment, education, AI, and even sectors such as defence and energy. Steinberg et al. (2022) revive the notion of the 'megacorp' to describe massive platform companies that cut across traditional sector boundaries, bringing together services from tech, finance, media, and logistics and amassing monopoly or oligopoly power in the process. As Srnicek (2024) argues, these developments require rethinking platform companies as organisational forms that are capable of integrating data and infrastructures across multiple domains.

A prominent example of this cross-sectoral expansion is the rise of super apps, especially in Asia (Steinberg et al., 2022; van der Vlist, Helmond, Dieter et al., 2025). Chinese platforms like WeChat or Alipay combine messaging, mobile payments, ride-hailing, e-commerce, and even access to government services within a single interface. More broadly, as emphasised in app studies scholarship, mobile apps have become the primary vehicles through which platforms embed their tools, services, and products into everyday life, economies, and institutions, especially in non-western contexts (Dieter et al., 2019; 2021; Gerlitz, Helmond, Nieborg et al., 2019; Morris and Murray, 2018; Steinberg et al., 2022; van der Vlist, Helmond, Dieter et al., 2025).

However, as van der Vlist, Helmond, Dieter et al. (2025) show, the super app model is not unique to China. Different varieties of super appification – which is an app-specific form of conglomeration – can be found in Southeast Asia, Africa, and beyond. These developments are shaped by various consolidation strategies: some platforms bundle their services within a single app while others expand them through subsidiaries, integrate third-party mini apps, or support broader external app ecosystems. WhatsApp, for example, has evolved into a super app in India and Brazil by integrating WhatsApp Pay and by partnering with local payment providers, whereas in regions such as Europe it remains primarily a messaging service. This illustrates how super appification, just like parallel platformisation, is informed by regional political economies and regulatory and technological environments and produces distinct platform constellations.

Such forms of conglomeration and cross-sectoral expansion raise new questions of power. As Gerbrandy and Phoa (2022) and, later, Srnicek (2024) note, traditional competition law typically assesses dominance within a single market, yet platform conglomerates operate across multiple domains simultaneously. This gives rise to new forms of structural influence, bargaining power, and gatekeeping that often fall outside existing legal frameworks. Recognising platforms as conglomerates shifts analytical attention from competition within markets to questions of infrastructural integration, control over data flows, and strategic sectoral alignment. In this way, conglomeration forms a key axis of contemporary platform power.

Financial strategies and market power

Conglomeration alone does not, however, explain how platform companies scale and maintain dominance. Platform operations are increasingly determined by financialisation, which encompasses the growing influence of financial markets, actors, and strategies on corporate decision-making. This influence is expressed in practices such as acquiring competitors, using debt to finance expansion, buying back shares, and investing in intangible assets to meet shareholder expectations and to solidify their market power (Jia and Winseck, 2018; Klinge et al., 2023; Nieborg and Poell, 2025; van Doorn and Badger, 2020).

Scholars have empirically documented this financialisation trend by following the money (see p. 80). Jia and Winseck (2018), for example, analyse the financial statements and corporate structures of China's Baidu, Alibaba, and Tencent (BAT) firms to demonstrate that ownership, board appointments, and capital flows reflect the growing influence of financial markets. Similarly, Klinge et al. (2023) have analysed the major global platforms (Alphabet, Apple, Meta, Microsoft, Amazon, Alibaba, and Tencent) and found that financialisation creates a 'self-reinforcing loop': it is both a result of platform growth and a strategy for entrenching and accelerating it.

Mergers and acquisitions are a central mechanism of financialisation (Jia and Winseck, 2018). Between 2019 and 2025, big tech companies acquired a new company roughly every eleven days, and only about 4 per cent of these deals were reviewed by competition authorities (Silva et al., 2025). Such acquisitions are not simply about expanding product offerings but also about securing infrastructural and reputational assets to enhance market position and respond to regulatory changes. A clear example comes from the audience economy: as consumer privacy regulations evolved, the data broker LiveRamp (which builds extensive consumer marketing profiles) acquired Faktor, a consent management platform. This strategic move allowed LiveRamp to secure the necessary tools to legally document user consent in an automated manner, thereby ensuring that its core data collection business could continue to comply with new privacy laws.

Regionally distinct platform capitalisms

Together, the processes of conglomeration and financialisation fundamentally shape the political economy of platforms by restructuring how they grow, operate, and exercise power. Conglomeration enables firms to extend their reach across domains, bundle services, and build infrastructural dominance, while financialisation drives them to prioritise valuation and investor sentiment. The result is a new configuration of platform power – a power rooted not only in digital intermediation (i.e. in the platform's role as matchmaker) but also in multisectoral reach, corporate consolidation, infrastructural control, and financial strategies.

At the same time, these processes unfold differently across institutional, economic, and geopolitical contexts. As Steinberg et al. (2022) note, developments like the rise of super apps in Asia challenge dominant, often western-centric models of platform capitalism and point to the emergence of regionally distinct corporate forms and configurations of power. They therefore talk of platform capitalisms, in the plural, in order to account for the diverse institutional configurations, cultural logics, and state-market relations that solidify platform power in different parts of the world. The central role of the state in China also figures in this discussion.

Take the global investment strategies of Chinese platform companies, for example. Alibaba's and TikTok's stakes in GoTo, the largest super app in Indonesia, signal that Chinese firms are increasingly investing in digital platforms that structure everyday life in the emerging markets. From a critical political economy perspective, these investments raise significant concerns, as they extend Chinese corporate and state influence over key layers of digital infrastructure in the Global South, for example fin-tech, communication, and everyday services.

These developments reinforce Narayan's (2024: 1) call for a more integrated approach to platform studies, one that brings together theoretical and empirical analysis of digital technologies, capitalist business models, and market dynamics: 'Retheorising the intersections between technologies, organisations and markets would not only better explain effects and discrete phenomena (datafication, surveillance, growth, monopolisation, etc.) but also widen and deepen our under-standing of "platform capitalism" at large.'

Orchestration and evolution

Building on the previous dynamics, the terms 'orchestration' and 'evolution' capture the fact that platforms consolidate and extend their power over time. They do so by actively managing their ecosystems and by continually adapting their interfaces, architectures, and strategies. These processes show that platform companies do not merely operate within existing markets but actively redesign them by drawing in new actors, setting standards, and redefining the conditions under which everyone must work.

Platform orchestrators and ecosystem management strategy

Orchestration refers to platforms' style of coordinating and influencing various actors – users, developers, advertisers, businesses, and even competitors – without owning them or controlling them directly. As Tiwana (2014) observes, platform orchestration resembles the coordination of a symphony under a conductor's baton. The platforms supply the instruments, set the tempo, and cue the various players. While allowing some autonomy, they ensure that the overall outcome serves the platform's broader vision.

This orchestration takes various forms and has been studied widely in economics, business, and management as well as in communication and media studies (e.g. Rikap, 2026; Tiwana, 2014, van der Vlist, 2022). Platforms use APIs, SDKs, training programs, and partner incentives to enrol third-parties such as developers, educators, and content creators into their ecosystems. Amazon's 2002 launch of its web services, AWS, exemplifies this strategy: by exposing its product data and shopping features to outside developers, Amazon invited thousands of actors to build on its infrastructure. Publicly framed as 'a welcome mat for developers' and 'a leap forward in the next-generation programmable internet' (Amazon Press Center, 2002), this was fundamentally a strategic effort to expand Amazon's online footprint while increasing traffic and transactions through its platform.

Other platforms have adopted similar approaches by setting technical standards. The Facebook Open Graph protocol and GraphQL query language enable developers to integrate more deeply with Facebook's infrastructure and social graph (i.e. the network of connections between users). By making GraphQL widely available, Facebook promoted its own model for organising data around relationships and interactions. The subsequent adoption of GraphQL by major platforms such as Reddit, GitHub, Shopify, Netflix, and Airbnb indicates that technical standards, once established, can structure the data themselves and configure their exchanges across entire industries.

In the AI sector, major platform companies pursue open-sourcing strategies designed to set industry standards and extend their influence. Frameworks such as Google TensorFlow and Meta PyTorch have become foundational tools for building AI applications. By releasing these as open source frameworks, companies attract developers and encourage widespread adoption. This turns them into '"on-ramps" to the proprietorial infrastructures of large AI companies' and determines the direction of future development (Dyer-Witheford et al., 2019: 55). Newer players such as Anthropic introduced the Model Context Protocol (MCP) to establish the next standard for integrating AI assistants into platforms, business tools, and data systems. As Nielsen and Ganter (2022: 157) argue, a central aspect of platform power lies precisely in this ability to set standards that others must follow if they wish to participate in the markets and ecosystems that platforms create.

Orchestration extends beyond developers, to end users themselves. Platforms guide user behaviour through interface design, specific features and affordances (as discussed in chapter 2), nudges, and default settings that are all calibrated to support engagement, monetisation, and strategic data capture. While users may appropriate or resist these affordances (Duguay, 2019), the material design and rules of the platform fundamentally shape the user experience and set the boundaries for action.

Platform envelopment, path dependence, and lock-in
While orchestration describes how platforms manage their ecosystems at any given moment, evolution focuses on

the longer-term processes through which platforms adapt, restructure, and entrench their position over time. This temporal dimension reveals that platform arrangements shift in response to internal strategies and external factors such as competition, regulation, and broader societal changes.

Several key dynamics affect platform evolution. Platforms often expand by leveraging their existing infrastructure and user base to enter adjacent markets, a process known as envelopment, or by absorbing successful third-party features into their core products and services – or coring (for short). Partin (2020) illustrates this with the livestreaming platform Twitch, demonstrating that platform capture drives evolution: platforms exploit power imbalances between themselves and third-party developers by incorporating the latter's innovations and redirecting their value back to themselves.

Path dependence is another crucial factor. Over time, early choices in design and governance become entrenched, render alternative paths costly and creating various forms of lock-in. Social media platforms exemplify this trajectory: network effects and the accumulation of content and relationships make it difficult to switch. As users build online identities, social networks, and content archives, migrating to a new or alternative platform becomes a major barrier. This explains why new competitors – the likes of BlueSky and BeReal – struggle to challenge established platforms – the likes of Instagram, YouTube, or X. The combination of path dependence, lock-in, and network effects limits the space for meaningful competition or alternative models.

Tracing platform evolution

Understanding these evolutionary dynamics requires historical and technographic analysis. Research on platform evolution (Helmond, 2015a; Helmond and van der Vlist, 2019; Helmond et al., 2019; Nieborg and Helmond, 2019; van der Vlist et al., 2022) demonstrates that platforms like Facebook (Meta) did not become powerful or infrastructural overnight. Rather than undergoing a sudden platform revolution (a topic we covered in chapter 2), Facebook developed gradually from being a social networking site to becoming an infrastructural backbone; and it achieved this change by expanding its own programmability through APIs and SDKs, by enrolling developers, marketers, and content creators, by forming asymmetric partnerships, and by embedding its services across external websites, apps, and industries.

Crucially, platform evolution is more than interface redesigns or new features. It also involves restructuring governance mechanisms and redefining access in response to external pressures. Using *externally focused* infrastructural analysis (3.2), van der Vlist et al. (2022) traced the evolution of Facebook's API architecture from being relatively open to becoming increasingly restrictive and tiered. Access to certain data fields was removed from the general Graph API but retained for commercial partners via the Marketing API. This change reflects strategic responses to regulatory interventions (e.g. to the EU General Data Protection Regulation), to public scrutiny (e.g. into Cambridge Analytica), and to shifting business priorities. Strikingly, sensitive user fields such as 'ethnic_affinity' and 'interested_in' were removed from general developer access, although they remained available to trusted advertising partners. These changes reveal that platforms govern developers and advertisers unequally (more on this in chapter 4).

Vendor lock-in, infrastructural control, and evolutive power
These evolutionary dynamics intensify in cloud computing and AI. Vendor lock-in and infrastructural control are defining features of platforms like AWS, Microsoft Azure, and Google Cloud. These platforms are designed as highly integrated services and, as such, create significant logistical challenges for those who migrate massive datasets. AI tools built on these platforms, for example Vertex AI, SageMaker, and Azure AI, require deep integration with proprietary infrastructure and services, which makes it difficult and costly to switch providers. As van der Vlist et al. (2024) and Luitse (2024: 27) argue, this lock-in is not incidental but a deliberate strategy to consolidate power through vertical integration, layered abstraction, and complementor innovation. In AI, platform power is therefore rooted not in any single product or application but in the interconnected infrastructures of software, hardware, and services

that develops all the time. This has major implications for governance: effective regulation cannot target individual AI systems alone; it must address the wider infrastructural dynamics through which platform power is operationalised.

The rise, then the evolution of super apps reflect distinct regional trajectories determined by local infrastructures, regulatory regimes, and user needs. In China, WeChat and Alipay emerged from communications and payment systems; in Africa, telecom firms drive the super app development, with a focus on financial services; and in Southeast Asia, ride-hailing platforms have expanded into finance and logistics. Mobile-first platforms like Gojek, Grab, and WeChat did not start out as 'do-everything apps'. They gradually expanded their services (e.g. ride-hailing, payments, food delivery, and e-commerce) through internal development, mergers and acquisitions, and cross-sector partnerships. In 2015, Gojek's was a ride-hailing service with four offerings; by 2023 it was a platform with twenty-three locally oriented services on offer. This journey exemplifies the incremental logic of super appification, understood as a gradual process of cross-sector expansion, service bundling, and consolidation (van der Vlist, Helmond, Dieter et al., 2025).

Together, orchestration and evolution offer a powerful perspective on how platform power is built and sustained over time. Platform dominance is rarely the result of a single disruptive breakthrough. Rather it emerges gradually, as platforms cultivate user bases and lock them in, build infrastructure, orchestrate users and ecosystems, and continually reconfigure interfaces, business models, and governance mechanisms in response to changing technological, regulatory, and societal conditions. These dynamics show that infrastructural power has a distinctly temporal and (in our terminology) 'evolutive' dimension, that is, the capacity to influence the evolutionary trajectory of an entire ecosystem (van der Vlist et al., 2022: 18; cf. Luitse, 2024).

Having outlined four interconnected processes through which platforms extend their influence and consolidate control, we now turn to the wider dimensions of platform power and introduce a framework that permits us to analyse how this power is structured and exercised.

The political economy of platforms and platformisation

So far, this chapter has shown that a critical political economy perspective is essential for understanding what platform businesses are today, how they operate, and how they consolidate power. Rather than relying solely on theoretical assumptions, this requires ongoing critical and empirical work that follows platform companies closely, as they continuously change and evolve.

Building on the methodological, empirical, and theoretical foundations outlined in this chapter, several observations can be made about the nature of power in the digital platform ecosystem. Platform power extends beyond the accumulation of users or economic resources. It also includes the ability to structure, both directly and indirectly, entire ecosystems, govern the behaviour of actors within them, and shape broader social, political, and institutional arrangements. These dynamics vary across sectors, regions, and regulatory environments, making it both challenging and necessary to examine the modalities in which platform power is configured, exercised, and contested in practice.

The layered and relational nature of platform power

Conceptualisations of platform power are grounded in detailed empirical and historical research, be it primary (i.e. original research) or secondary (i.e. work that draws on the former). These conceptualisations help us to understand platform power in its different dimensions and consequences, as introduced earlier in this chapter (pp. 87–107). Because this power is complex and context-specific, the approaches discussed in the previous main section ('Insights') have led to the development of middle-range concepts of power. These are not abstract, all-encompassing theories. They are focused, empirically informed concepts that explain the mechanisms through which power operates in specific situations. These concepts link broad theoretical perspectives to concrete empirical sources and channels, through which platforms accumulate, consolidate, and exercise power.

Understandings of power across political-economic scholarship

The research on datafication and surveillance presented earlier in this chapter (pp. 88–93) shows that platforms turn everyday user activities into quantifiable data assets; this way data become a primary source of power. Concepts such as platform capitalism, data capitalism, data enclaves, and surveillance capitalism capture the fact that platforms extract, process, store, and monetise vast data flows, which produce information and power asymmetries. Work on the audience commodity and the audience economy demonstrate that user attention and user data are commodified and traded, often through invisible infrastructures that are running between intermediaries. Here power is located not only in data ownership but also in control over the infrastructures and socio-technical systems that create, circulate, and valorise the data. This state of affairs creates new forms of 'digital rentiership' and enables different kinds of predictive governance, or what Zuboff (2019) calls 'instrumentarian power'.

Research on platformisation and infrastructuralisation illustrates how platforms extend their reach beyond their original domains and become essential intermediaries across various sectors. Concepts such as platform as infrastructure, infrastructural platform, and super SDK capture the process by which platforms accumulate power when they position themselves as indispensable back-end services for businesses, governments, developers, and users. They also shed light on the fact that platform power is both infrastructural and strategic. Tools like APIs create infrastructural dependencies, while strategic power emerges from exclusive partnerships and ecosystem integration. The ongoing platformisation and industrialisation of AI further deepen these dynamics, as cloud platforms increasingly serve as the foundational infrastructure for developing and deploying AI.

Studies of conglomeration and financialisation emphasise that platforms expand and consolidate economic power by expanding across sectors, acquiring competitors, and aligning with shareholder expectations. This often highlights corporate or market power. Terms such as 'conglomerate', 'megacorp', and 'super app' reflect the fact that Alphabet, Tencent, Meta, and their likes increasingly operate across different sectors, accumulating substantial monopoly or oligopoly power. The phenomenon of super appification illustrates that power derives from cross-sectoral operations rather than the dominance of a single market. At the same time, financialisation drives speculative growth and market influence, producing new forms of structural power and gatekeeping that often evade existing regulation.

Finally, research on orchestration and evolution reveals how platforms govern their ecosystems and adapt over time. This is a dimension of power that involves the capacity of platforms to actively structure and manage (or orchestrate) the interactions of a variety of user groups such as app developers, content creators, and advertisers. Through interface features, algorithms, moderation policies, and the strategic use and governance of APIs, platforms do not simply facilitate connections; they also direct and impose behaviour within their broader spheres of influence. The term 'evolution' captures the gradual and cumulative nature of this power, given that expansion, entrenchment, and consolidation unfold over time and iterative adjustments are made as a result of internal strategies and external pressures.

These dimensions carry significant implications for platform regulation. Power is not reducible to market share or ownership structures. It is embedded in infrastructural interdependencies, long-term forms of lock-in, and material arrangements that organise digital ecosystems. As platform infrastructures converge with the development and distribution of AI, an evolutionary perspective becomes even more important. AI platforms are not self-contained technologies but components of wider cloud infrastructures and developer ecosystems. Understanding how this power is gradually built – strategically, materially, and relationally – is essential for any future political economy analysis and regulatory response.

Analytical dimensions of platform power
The insights presented in this chapter disclose a set of interconnected sources and forms of platform power. These can

be broadly classified as technological, economic, social and political, infrastructural, ecosystemic, and temporal dimensions (see Table 3.3). While such dimensions are tightly interwoven in practice, distinguishing them analytically is useful if we wish to examine how power is structured,

Table 3.3. Broad picture of the analytical dimensions of platform power.

Dimension	Focus	Examples
Technological	Control over the technical tools and infrastructure through which interactions, data flows, and services are mediated.	APIs, SDKs, proprietary algorithms, app ecosystems (e.g. Apple App Store, Facebook SDK)
Economic	Ability to monetise user activity, extract value, and shape markets through business models.	advertising revenue (e.g. Meta, Google), platform fees (e.g. Apple, Amazon), data monetisation
Social and political	Influence over public discourse, policymaking, and regulation; private governance over ecosystems and users.	content moderation rules, lobbying efforts, terms of service enforcement
Infrastructural	Role as essential intermediaries in digital and physical systems; control over access, integration, and dependency.	cloud infrastructure (e.g. AWS, Azure), social login systems, SDKs embedded across mobile apps
Ecosystemic	Ability to orchestrate and govern multisided ecosystems of users, developers, advertisers, businesses, and institutions.	platform-partner programmes, family of apps (e.g. Meta), super app models (e.g. WeChat, Gojek)
Temporal	Capacity to create long-term dependencies, lock-in effects, and future trajectories of industries, technologies, and institutions.	standard-setting (e.g. AMP by Google), acquisitions meant to pre-empt competition (e.g. Instagram)

exercised, and contested in specific contexts. For instance, an API may serve as a form of technological control by acting as a governance mechanism; yet it also functions as infrastructure when it is used to interconnect systems, and as an economic instrument when it underpins monetisable services such as targeted advertising. This illustrates the claim that platform power is multisided and layered and operates simultaneously across different registers and scales.

Modern bigness: Beyond market power

While the next chapter explores governance and regulation in more detail, the multiple dimensions of platform power pose significant challenges for traditional governance frameworks. For instance, legal scholars Anna Gerbrandy and Pauline Phoa (2022) argue that current competition law (antitrust law in the United States) is ill equipped to grasp the full scope and complexity of contemporary platform power. They propose the concept of modern bigness to better capture the unique corporate power exercised by big tech platforms. They show how this power extends far beyond conventional market-based *instrumental* power to include *structural* and *discursive* forms of power that shape economic systems, political processes, social relations, and personal experiences. What makes platforms 'big', in other words, is not only their market share but their capacity to organise and influence multiple domains of social and economic life simultaneously.

Gerbrandy and Phoa call for expanding the focus of competition law to account for these broader forms of corporate power. Yet they also acknowledge that modern bigness remains a theoretical construct and that much empirical work is needed to map the operations of this power across specific sectors and settings. This reinforces the ongoing importance of detailed, case-based research for advancing both academic debates and public policy responses.

Shifting industry relations, dependencies, and the role of the state

The different dimensions of platform power are not just abstract concepts; they materialise in concrete infrastructures, standards, business models, and relationships across a growing number of industries and sectors, as shown throughout this chapter in areas such as cultural production (Poell et al., 2021), journalism and publishing (Nielsen and Ganter, 2022; Simon, 2022), marketing and advertising (Joseph and Bishop, 2024; Crain, 2021; MacKenzie and Çalışkan, 2025; Nieborg and Poell, 2025; van der Vlist and Helmond, 2021), primary education (Kerssens and van Dijck, 2021; van Dijck et al., 2018), automobility (Hind et al., 2022; Steinberg, 2021), and the military (Hoijtink and Planqué-van Hardeveld, 2022). In these sectors, general platform theory can be adapted to identify where power resides and how it is accumulated, operationalised, and contested.

Take the music industry, for example: Spotify's curated playlists are not neutral recommendation tools, but expressions of what Prey (2020) calls 'curatorial power'. Through decisions about what to organise, prioritise, or promote, Spotify directly moulds listener behaviour and artist visibility, reinforcing market conditions aligned with its own commercial goals. Yet even powerful companies within their own niche, such as Spotify, face infrastructural dependencies. The service relies entirely on Google Cloud Platform, after Spotify's 2019 decision to go all in by consolidating its infrastructure with a single cloud provider. The company framed this move as a strategic partnership designed to 'build a deeper working relationship that went beyond simply offloading infrastructure to a third party' (Gustavsson, 2019).

In journalism and the news industry, platforms such as Facebook and Google not only distribute news content but also restructure the way it is produced, discovered, and monetised (Nielsen and Ganter, 2022; Poell et al., 2022). As Poell et al. (2022: 1391) note, platformisation in the news industry is not a linear or one-sided process but unfolds through ongoing interactions between media organisations and platforms within 'spaces of negotiation' in which media organisations retain some agency but must adapt to platform principles and technical conditions. These interactions are not limited to publishers: they extend to marketers, developers, content creators, advertisers, researchers, and every other user group on the platform.

In the automotive sector, tech giants such as Alphabet, Apple, and Amazon are transforming the car into a digital platform. Through in-car operating systems, software services, and strategic partnerships with automakers, they are turning vehicles into nodes within broader digital ecosystems. As Hind et al. (2022) argue, these firms are making cars platform-ready, marking the deeper integration of hardware, software, and data flows in automobility and blurring the line between car and computer.

These cases show that, while the forms and consequences of platform power differ across industries and regions, they consistently reshape markets, redefine professional practices, and reorganise value flows in ways that serve platform interests. Even as platforms adapt to local conditions, their control over core infrastructures ensures that this power remains highly centralised.

While much scholarship has rightly focused on the corporate, economic, and societal dimensions of platform power, the role of the state must not be overlooked, especially in areas such as regulation, public service delivery, national security, and the militarisation of digital infrastructures. Charis Papaevangelou and Eugenia Siapera (2025) rightly argue that the growing entanglement between platform companies and state actors has become a defining feature of today's digital political economy. Their study of Microsoft's data centre construction in Greece shows that the state actively enabled infrastructural expansion, sometimes at the expense of environmental priorities and citizen interests. In such cases, state power directly contributes to the consolidation of platform power.

Convening, integration, and capture: A cyclical framework for platform power

To understand the evolving nature of platform power in the digital ecosystem, we conclude with a conceptual framework rooted in the political economy of platforms. Building on the empirical and theoretical insights from this chapter, especially the interconnected dimensions presented in the previous section (pp. 111 ff.), the framework identifies three interrelated dynamics that explain how platform companies expand their reach, consolidate control, and restructure economies and societies – in a nutshell, the concentration of power through platformisation. These three dynamics are *convening*, *integration*, and *capture*. They do not operate in isolation but as an iterative and mutually reinforcing cycle that drives platformisation.

The first dynamic, convening, is the most subtle yet fundamental. 'Convening power' refers to a platform's ability to bring together diverse stakeholders – developers, advertisers, content creators, educators, institutions – and align them around a shared technological vision or strategy (van der Vlist, Helmond, Luitse et al., 2025: 7; cf. Egliston and Carter, 2022; Helmond et al., 2019). This is about not just attracting end users but enrolling entire industries and communities into the platform's ecosystem. Platforms exercise convening power through a combination of financial incentives (grants, developer credits, startup funds), strategic partnerships, third-party marketplaces, and carefully crafted corporate narratives about technological futures. When companies such as Microsoft, Amazon, or Google release founders' letters, host developer summits, or launch new products, they do more than make announcements; they actively guide the others' vision of the future of technology, position themselves as central to it, and set the terms for participation.

This ability to set the stage and attract participation is a relational rather than coercive form of power, and is highly effective in cultivating long-term dependencies. Unlike traditional forms based on force or financial leverage, convening power is a form of 'soft power' (Kerssens, 2024) grounded in influence, reputation, trust, and the capacity to mobilise actors in pursuit of shared goals. While convening power has traditionally been exercised by states – for instance, to coordinate infrastructure projects, set policy standards, or initiate collective responses to societal challenges – it is now increasingly large technology platforms that perform this role. As Rikap (2026) similarly observes, this form of corporate power extends beyond direct control. It is exercised indirectly, through planning, coordination, and influence over value and knowledge chains, and increasingly reaches into entire societies via cloud infrastructures. Such diffuse and anticipatory forms of influence present serious challenges for existing regulatory frameworks that are more oriented towards direct intervention.

Once actors are convened, integration comes into play. Platforms embed themselves, sometimes with the help of others (e.g. developers or partners), into the products, services, and workflows of third-party actors through a wide array of ecosystem resources. Some of these are technical, such as APIs, SDKs, creator studio tools, business management suites, and dedicated developer portals; others are non-technical, such as documentation, information portals, training materials, sample code, blogs, and online communities that further support this integration. These resources enable external actors to build on top of the platform, effectively extending the platform's infrastructure, functionality, and reach. Over time, this integration deepens and becomes infrastructural. Cloud services such as AWS, Microsoft Azure, and Google Cloud offer not only tools but essential back-end services, including AI models and enterprise software, on which sectors such as education, journalism, or healthcare increasingly rely. Although local and sector-specific conditions determine these integrations, the integrations themselves consistently render the platform indispensable.

This leads to the third, and perhaps most consequential, dynamic: *capture*. As platforms become deeply embedded in the operations and infrastructures of others, dependencies grow. This often results in infrastructural lock-in, where switching becomes costly, technically difficult, or economically unviable. Capture creates deep power asymmetries, as platforms come to control access to essential tools, user data, or even entire markets. This dynamic is further intensified by strategic acquisitions and mergers that consolidate services into conglomerate platform structures or super apps, and the urgent need to capture diverse data sources as essential inputs for training AI models.

Crucially, convening, integration, and capture are not linear stages but overlapping and recursive processes. They reinforce one another and define the political economy of platforms today. Understanding how these dynamics unfold and how they vary across sectors and industries is essential for analysing the evolution of platform capitalism and the contemporary configuration of platform power.

Summary

This chapter has shown that a political economy perspective offers a powerful framework for analysing platforms and platformisation across the digital economy, culture, and institutions globally. While grounded in classical concerns such as ownership, control, labour, and value, the understanding of platform power today also requires attention to newer mechanisms: datafication, infrastructuralisation, conglomeration, financialisation, and the orchestration and evolution of platform ecosystems. Platforms do not simply operate within markets; they *reshape* them by structuring participation, competition, and dependency across sectors. In many cases, they *are* the market.

Platform power is not fixed or singular. It is *relational*, *layered*, and *distributed*. It emerges through interface design, technical design, governance practices, business models, and infrastructural positioning and is exercised across networks of users, developers, advertisers, institutions, and other platforms. Platforms derive their power not only from centralising control but also from bringing others into their ecosystem and making themselves indispensable. As shown throughout this chapter, this power manifests itself differently, depending on an actor's position within the ecosystem, and this feature highlights the need for grounded, contextual analysis.

To make sense of these dynamics, we introduced the conceptual framework of platform power, understood as *an iterative cycle of convening, integration, and capture*. Platforms attract external actors through resources such as APIs, SDKs, documentation, training programmes, and partnerships. These ecosystem resources facilitate third-party participation, but also function as instruments of strategic control. Through them, platforms embed themselves into diverse industries, creating dependencies that facilitate value extraction and ecosystem dominance.

Critically, platform power is also infrastructural. It operates through material artefacts, technical systems, and policy interfaces. Studying these systems requires methodological approaches capable of tracing how value, influence, and dependencies are organised. Political-economic research must therefore follow money flows, data structures, and strategic alignments across public financial filings, developer ecosystems, product architectures, and corporate networks. Technographic approaches, introduced in chapter 2, complement these strategies by offering accessible ways to examine platforms' material systems through documentation, interfaces, and code.

This chapter has also advocated for a *middle-range* approach that connects empirical research to broader questions about platform capitalism. Rather than treating platforms as abstract actors, we have opted for analysing them as embedded socio-technical systems that evolve over time, refashion practices, infrastructures, and whole industries, and reconfigure power.

The next chapter will turn to governing power: it will look at the way platforms regulate and are regulated. If this chapter examined platforms' accumulation of economic and infrastructural power, chapter 4 will explore the governing of that power via internal mechanisms and external regulatory regimes and its playing out across legal, political, and geopolitical domains.

Discussion questions

- **Platform power and monopoly** The chapter discusses the dominance of technology companies like GAFAM, BATX, or the Magnificent Seven. What are the most significant differences between the market power of contemporary big tech platforms and the monopolies of the twentieth century (e.g. in oil, steel, or telecommunications)?
- **Infrastructure control and governance** The platform business model is defined by infrastructure ownership and control. How does a platform's control over key digital infrastructures (e.g. app stores, APIs, cloud services) limit or enable innovation and participation by third-party actors in its ecosystem?
- **Data as a source of value and power** The chapter outlines a political economy perspective focused on

money and power. How should scholars or regulators understand the link between platforms' ability to extract value from data (profit) and their capacity to govern and shape markets (power)?

Further reading

Nielsen, R. K. and Ganter, S. A. (2022) *The Power of Platforms: Shaping Media and Society*. Oxford University Press.

Poell, T., Nieborg, D. B. and Duffy, B. E. (2021) *Platforms and Cultural Production*. Polity.

Mosco, V. (2009) *The Political Economy of Communication* (2nd edn). SAGE.

4

Governance and Regulation

Introduction

Platforms today are not just digital intermediaries or corporate actors but powerful *governing systems*. As their influence extends across societies, economies, and states, they have become key arenas in which questions of control, legitimacy, and public accountability are fiercely contested. Governance and regulation, both by and of platforms, have become central forces of the digital environment and reflect wider tensions around sovereignty, institutional power, and global order.

This chapter foregrounds *governance* as a core dimension through which platform power is exercised and contested and one of the three cross-cutting domains introduced in chapter 2. Through governance, platforms influence user behaviour, organise their ecosystems, negotiate or resist regulatory demands, and assert infrastructural control. Together with political-economic dynamics and a strategic evolution, governance and regulation are essential for understanding that platforms operate not only as companies but as rule makers, norm setters, and infrastructural stewards. Platforms increasingly govern others while being themselves governed, both formally, by states and regulators, and informally, through public scrutiny, industry norms, and geopolitical rivalries.

As discussed in chapter 3, the economic and infrastructural dominance of big tech is inseparable from its ability to set the terms of participation through interface design, terms of service, algorithmic decisions, data policies, and application programming interface (API) access. But understanding this power requires us to analyse both *platforms' governing* and their *being governed*. The dominance of platforms has prompted increasingly robust efforts from states and regulators to hold them accountable. Platforms are powerful actors that articulate public discourse, business models, and data flows, while simultaneously being subject to legal, political, and social oversight. They operate in a contested regulatory space where governments, civil society, and transnational institutions compete to define their boundaries.

Platform governance as a site of (geo)politics and contestation

Take the ongoing global disputes around TikTok. Concerns about Chinese state influence, algorithmic opacity, and privacy practices have led to societal anxieties, regulatory investigations, platform bans, and legal battles. Owned by Beijing-based ByteDance, TikTok has come under scrutiny from foreign governments worried about data privacy, algorithmic transparency, and foreign influence. In the 2024 Romanian presidential elections, a viral TikTok campaign helped an obscure far-right candidate, Călin Georgescu, win a surprise first-round victory. Amid accusations of Russian disinformation and algorithmic manipulation, the Romanian Constitutional Court annulled the election results. The European Commission then launched an investigation into TikTok's compliance with the EU Digital Services Act (DSA), which requires very large online platforms (VLOPs) and search engines to assess and mitigate systemic risks, including threats to democratic processes such as elections (European Commission, 2024).

Other governments have also acted against various platforms. India banned TikTok in 2020; the European Union restricted its use on official devices in 2023; South Korean regulators removed the Chinese AI-chatbot DeepSeek from app stores in early 2025 as a result of privacy violations; and in late 2025, TikTok agreed to divest its operations in the United States to a US-controlled entity, to avert a nationwide ban. These conflicts show that platform governance is no longer a technical or procedural issue but is directly entangled with national sovereignty, global regulation, and geopolitical power.

These tensions are not limited to social media. In the European Union and United States, Apple's control over its app store has repeatedly drawn antitrust scrutiny, particularly regarding its commission fees, restrictions on competitors, and influence over market access. As a global cloud infrastructure provider, Amazon Web Services (AWS) has faced criticism for its central role in both private enterprise and public infrastructure, igniting debates about dependency, autonomy, and digital sovereignty. Meta's Oversight Board, an experiment in quasi-independent self-regulation, exemplifies the complex governance models that platforms now develop to manage content, reputation, and legitimacy.

Meanwhile, platforms such as Uber, Glovo, and Deliveroo have become regulatory flashpoints in cities worldwide, generating disputes over labour classification, taxation, and local sovereignty. AI platforms such as OpenAI and Anthropic are also facing growing scrutiny over training data, copyright, data governance, model accountability, and compliance with emerging AI regulations.

These examples illustrate a central theme of the current chapter: platform governance is inseparable from broader struggles over political authority (who gets to make the rules), market access (who gets to compete in the economy), and institutional legitimacy (who has the right to be in charge).

Chapter overview

This chapter examines platform governance – that is, the governance and regulation of and by platforms

– distinguishing between the means by which platforms govern (the rules, policies, and enforcement systems they use to structure their ecosystems) and the means by which they are governed (the legal, social, and political efforts to regulate platform operations from the outside). As in the previous chapter, the next section will introduce key concepts and definitions, tracing the emergence of governance as a central platform function and its evolution, especially in relation to social media content moderation. After that, a section on strategies (pp. 130–4) will outline key strategies for studying how platforms govern and are governed. In the section on insights that follows it (pp. 134–46) we examine platform governance in practice, across different stakeholder groups (end users, developers, creators, advertisers, and gig workers), showing that each group is governed via distinct mechanisms and with different levels of power and visibility. Then a new section (pp. 146–55) will synthesise these insights and reflect on the layered nature of platform governance, its crisis-driven character, the shifting boundaries between platform and state power, and the challenges of studying governance as it evolves over time.

Together, these chapter sections contribute to a broader understanding of platforms as socio-technical systems embedded in complex regulatory environments. They show that governance, both as a tool of platform power and as a response to that power, is central to the ever-changing role of platforms in society. Platforms' governing power determines public debate, economic activity, cultural life, and institutional processes globally.

Understanding platform governance

Governance was a central concept in political science and international relations long before being taken up by platform studies. Media scholars Robert Gorwa (2019, 2024) and Terry Flew (2021) and legal scholar Kate Klonick (2018) trace how this broader intellectual history has informed various analyses of how governance operates in and through platforms. If in political science governance refers to the frameworks and mechanisms, both formal (e.g. governments and courts) and informal (e.g. norms and networks of influence), through which societies are organised and managed, in international relations it focuses on global issues and their being addressed in the absence of a central world government, often through cooperation among states, international organisations, and non-state actors.

Drawing on these established perspectives, platform governance refers to the fact that digital platforms act as powerful shapers of culture and society globally. There are two complementary facets to this role: on the one hand, platforms govern online interactions and exercise control over users, industries, and governments; on the other, they are in turn governed or regulated through legal frameworks and societal pressures.

How platforms govern and are governed

As Gorwa (2019), Flew (2021), and Klonick (2018) argue, today governance extends beyond traditional state institutions and increasingly involves powerful private actors such as digital platforms. Klonick (2018) describes platforms as self-regulating 'private governors' of online life; they reflect a departure from state-led regulation. Positioned between governments and individual users, platforms set their own rules for online expression, access to information, and acceptable behaviour. Yet their commercial interests often clash with public values, raising concerns about democratic accountability, transparency, and fair participation (Klonick, 2018; van Dijck et al., 2018; van Dijck et al., 2025).

Tarleton Gillespie (2018a; 2018b) situates platform governance in the context of user-generated content intermediaries such as social media. He stresses that governance consists not only of the legal frameworks that define platforms' liabilities but also of the role that platforms play in articulating digital activity. In his view, platforms are not neutral intermediaries but participants that 'intervene in myriad ways', for example through interface design, content curation, and algorithmic ranking (Gillespie 2018b: 257). At the same time, he argues, platforms construct narratives of neutrality, presenting themselves as impartial facilitators in order to avoid regulatory scrutiny while they appeal to ideals of openness and free expression. Gillespie's work highlights that platforms infuse everyday life not merely by enabling interactions but by actively structuring, filtering, and controlling them.

Incorporating governance into platform studies, Gorwa (2019) defines platform governance as the set of structures that regulate interactions between a diverse set of actors on and around platforms. His definition emphasises that governance operates at multiple levels. On the one hand, *internal* platform governance consists of the rules, policies, and technical systems that platforms impose on their various users: moderation guidelines, algorithmic curation, terms of service. On the other hand, *external* governance encompasses the broader legal, political, and societal forces that shape platform operations: regulation, judicial rulings, advocacy by civil society groups, economic incentives, public opinion.

Gillespie (2018b) and Gorwa (2019) usefully distinguish between governance *by* platforms and the governance (or regulation) *of* platforms. Governance by platforms refers to platforms' designing and enforcing their own rules and mechanisms for curating and moderating content, setting terms of use, and managing data and access. Governance over platforms refers to the external legal, social, and political pressures exerted on platforms by states, civil society groups, advertisers, users, and others, often in an attempt to steer platforms towards greater accountability or public responsibility.

Extending this distinction, scholars such as Gillespie (2018a; 2018b), Gorwa (2019), Flew (2021), and Poell et al. (2021) highlight the importance of differentiating governance from regulation. Governance covers the wider system, namely the control exercised by both state and non-state actors, including the platforms themselves. It encompasses formal and informal mechanisms such as content policies, interface design, and industry standards. Regulation, by contrast, involves legally binding rules imposed by governments and often enforced through sanctions or oversight.

Although distinct, governance and regulation are closely intertwined. Platforms adjust their governance practices in response to legal pressure, while regulators respond to platform actions and controversies. In essence, while regulation emphasises formal state authority and binding rules with legal consequences, governance is a more inclusive and flexible concept. It captures the mechanisms via which power is exercised and contested across a range of sites and actors. Such mechanisms include the internal control that platforms wield over their ecosystems and the external forces that seek to mould or constrain platforms. Table 4.1 summarises these distinctions and the key actors, mechanisms, and forms of authority involved.

The rise of platform governance

How did we arrive at a point where commercial actors determine the rules for many of the online spaces billions of people use every day? The early internet was often imagined as a decentralised space where individuals could communicate and bypass traditional publishers or media gatekeepers. In the early 2000s, the rise of the blogosphere was celebrated as a democratising event that enabled anyone to publish content without editorial oversight (see chapter 2). Early online communities such as the Well, Slashdot, Wikipedia, and Reddit relied heavily on voluntary moderation, as users and administrators enforced norms through ad-hoc peer evaluation (Bruns, 2008). However, as platforms scaled and their social and economic influence expanded, more structured governance mechanisms became necessary for managing user-generated content and behaviour.

A key legal foundation enabling platform governance is Section 230 of the Communications Decency Act, enacted in the United States in 1996. This section shields platforms from being held legally liable for practically all user-generated content by classifying them as intermediaries rather than publishers. At the same time it allows platforms to moderate content 'in good faith', without losing that immunity. This combination of legal protection and editorial freedom has fundamentally contoured the internet as we know it (Gillespie, 2018a; 2018b).

Yet Section 230 has become increasingly controversial. Critics argue that it grants platforms too much unchecked

Table 4.1. Governance and regulation by and over platforms: Key actors, authority sources, mechanisms, logic, and aims or outcomes.

Feature	Governance by platforms (internal)	Governance over platforms (external, broad)	Regulation (formal, legal)
Key actors	platform companies (e.g. Meta, Airbnb, TikTok)	civil society, users, journalists, NGOs, advertisers, trade associations	state institutions (e.g. EU, FTC, national regulators, local courts)
Authority sources	corporate power, technical or interface design, platform ownership	market dynamics, public pressure, platform dependency	law and formal state authority
Mechanisms	terms of service, community guidelines, APIs, algorithmic curation, moderation, data access control	civil society mobilisation, advertiser boycotts, reputation pressure	regulatory and legal frameworks, executive orders, judicial rulings, fines, licensing conditions
Logic	platforms write and enforce their own rules (e.g. social media content, APIs, and other tools and interfaces)	indirect steering, influence without legal compulsion	binding obligations with penalties for non-compliance
Examples	TikTok's community guidelines, Facebook's API restrictions, YouTube's monetisation policies	campaigns against hate speech, advertiser withdrawal from X	EU Digital Services Act, GDPR, COPPA, Germany's NetzDG
Aims/outcomes	to influence user and developer conduct	to pressure platforms to act in public interest or align with democratic norms	to enforce platform accountability legally and protect public interest

power: it either enables arbitrary takedowns or fails to prevent harmful content. However, the law's original aim was to safeguard online expression by limiting liability, not to protect platforms as such. Much of the problematic content, including hate speech and misinformation, is already protected under the US First Amendment. This means that, even without Section 230, most platforms would still not be legally accountable for such content. The situation complicates any attempts to regulate platforms solely on the basis of liability.

Klonick (2018) argues that platforms moderate content for two related reasons. First, moderation is framed as a corporate social responsibility; platforms aim to create safe environments by limiting the spread of hate speech, harassment, and misinformation. Second, moderation is central to platforms' business strategy. Because they depend on user engagement for advertising revenue, they must maintain environments that are both welcoming to users and acceptable to advertisers. This dual imperative, Klonick argues, forces platforms to navigate constant tensions between supporting open expression and sustaining profitable, brand-safe spaces. Gillespie (2018b) similarly argues that governance is inherent in platforms because they must manage competing interests, enforce their terms of service, comply with legal obligations, and remain economically viable.

These tensions became visible in late 2023, when major advertisers withdrew from X after learning that their ads had appeared alongside pro-Nazi and antisemitic content. The situation escalated after X owner Elon Musk publicly endorsed an antisemitic conspiracy theory, which prompted IBM, Apple, and Disney to pull their advertising (Mac et al., 2023). The episode emphasises that moderation decisions are inseparable from financial incentives and public relations pressures and that platforms must continuously balance content moderation with brand safety and advertiser trust.

Competing models of platform regulation

Although Section 230 is a US law, it has global consequences because many of the world's largest platforms – Meta,

Alphabet, Amazon, Microsoft, OpenAI, Uber, and X – are headquartered in the United States. As these companies expanded internationally, they exported a governance model created by Section 230, in which platforms bear limited legal responsibility for user-generated content. But platforms operating globally must also comply with national and local laws. This need creates overlapping and sometimes contradictory regulatory pressures. In Germany, for example, the Network Enforcement Act (NetzDG) mandates the removal of hate speech and Nazi symbols within twenty-four hours and imposes steep fines in case they are not removed. The EU DSA goes further: it requires platforms to assess and mitigate systemic risks related to illegal content and disinformation. These laws force platforms to continually adapt their moderation and governance strategies to local and regional contexts.

Asia offers a contrasting regulatory model, most notably in China, where platform governance is closely tied to state power. Legal scholar Anu Bradford (2023) argues that, unlike the United States and Europe, where platform governance often involves negotiation among states, industry, and civil society, China operates with a rather top-down model and treats platforms as tools of political control and ideological expansion. Domestic platforms such as WeChat, Weibo, Douyin, and RedNote (Xiaohongshu) must censor politically sensitive topics (e.g. the Tiananmen Square massacre, or criticism of the Communist Party) and must share user data with government agencies on request, while foreign platforms such as Google, Facebook, and X remain blocked behind China's Great Firewall. China's influence extends beyond its borders. The transition from mere scrutiny to active enforcement regarding TikTok – exemplified by India's permanent ban, the United States' implementation of a forced divesture, and the European Union's enforcement actions under the DSA – proves that platform governance is increasingly at the mercy of geopolitical power struggles.

Bradford characterises these diverging regulatory principles as reflections of the existence of three global digital empires: the United States, the European Union, and China, each shaped by its own political, economic, and cultural worldview. She interprets them as three forms of digital capitalism that combine market forces, state control, and individual rights in different ways. The US model prioritises market freedom and promotes self-regulation and innovation, but also enables surveillance capitalism and harmful content. The Chinese model is state-centric, closely linking platforms to censorship, surveillance, and political control. The EU model is rights-based and places a strong emphasis on consumer protection, data privacy, and regulatory intervention aimed at limiting corporate power and strengthening digital sovereignty.

These models, Bradford argues, do not remain confined to their regions of origin. They are actively promoted and exported, as governments attempt to embed their own priorities and norms into the global digital ecosystem. This competition plays out both horizontally, in struggles over international regulation, and vertically, as states manage the growing power of tech firms at home.

This global competition shows the fragmented and contested nature of platform governance today. Governance is no longer dictated by a single legal framework but is imposed by a patchwork of intersecting and sometimes conflicting laws, norms, and institutional arrangements that operate at local, national, and global scales.

Strategies for analysing platform governance

Building on the conceptual framework outlined earlier in this chapter as well as on the strategies discussed in chapter 3, this section offers empirical tools for analysing the two complementary sides we outlined: external governance and societal pressures (being governed); internal rule-making and moderation practices (governing). We draw here on our analytical framework (presented in chapter 2), which emphasises the multisidedness, layering, and materiality of platforms.

The strategies can be applied to a single platform, across its multiple sides and users, or more widely, be it across platforms and jurisdictions, for example to draw comparisons between the United States, the European Union, and China, or across different national regulatory environments.

How platforms are governed: Analysing governance over platforms

Analysing how platforms are governed (what we call governance *over* platforms) involves examining the formative influence that legal, political, and societal forces exert on platform operations. One fruitful approach is doctrinal or regulatory framework analysis, which examines how laws such as the EU General Data Protection Regulation (GDPR), the DSA, the Digital Markets Act (DMA), and consumer protection laws function in practice and scrutinises their effectiveness, and societal impact. These frameworks often classify platforms as actors with specific obligations and require transparency, due diligence, and cooperation with regulators. For example, Paddy Leerssen's (2023) analysis of the DSA shows that the regulation's transparency requirements, which oblige platforms to inform users about the moderation actions taken in relation to their content, effectively limit shadow banning by demanding disclosure when content has been demoted or delisted.

The examination of platforms' responses, both discursive and technological, to such external pressures complements legal analysis. Studying them is important not only for assessing compliance but also for understanding that platforms interpret, negotiate, or resist regulatory demands in ways that affect users, markets, and public oversight. These responses are often articulated in public-facing materials such as company statements, blog posts, press releases, and audit reports, in which platforms frame their actions as responsible and transparent. For example, Amazon detailed how it introduced consent prompts, its own Data Portability tool, and new transparency measures in response to the DMA (Amazon News, 2024). Meta released independent audits, outlining its DSA compliance efforts (Meta Newsroom, 2024), while TikTok described EU-specific updates such as optional algorithmic personalisation, enhanced illegal content–reporting tools, and an API for researchers (TikTok, 2023). Platforms also react to civil society advocacy. For instance, Meta responded to concerns about algorithmic discrimination in targeted advertising for housing, employment, and credit by announcing the modification of relevant features and data access permissions (Sandberg, 2019).

These discursive responses are often accompanied by material changes to platform infrastructure whereby regulatory requirements and public concerns become embedded in technical systems and interface design. This material embedding can be studied through interface analysis and walkthrough methods (chapter 2), both of which involve documenting, interacting with, and analysing platform interfaces and features, including APIs, to trace how and where governance is operationalised. Examples include app stores adjusting their algorithmic curation to prioritise officially approved COVID-19 apps (p. 150); the insertion of misinformation warnings into posts and links to authoritative health sources such as the World Health Organisation (WHO), in user interfaces; the introduction of disclosure tools for influencers for sponsored content (p. 144); and the removal of sensitive data fields in APIs for the sake of complying with the GDPR or responding to societal pressures around algorithmic discrimination (p. 141).

In short, these analytical strategies make it clear to us that external governance translates into both discourse and material design, across the different layers of a platform. External pressures, be they from regulators or from civil society, can reconfigure platform operations and user experiences in concrete ways.

How platforms govern: Analysing governance by platforms

Analysing the way platforms govern requires a close examination of the materials and infrastructures by means of which platforms moderate user interactions. As a starting point, it is crucial to consider *who or what* is being governed. Since platforms are multifaceted and address distinct user groups – end users, developers, content creators, marketers, advertisers – governance takes different forms across these facets.

Each group is subject to specific rules, policies, and interfaces, and these may overlap or even conflict.

A key implication of our multisided perspective is the need to understand platform governance from an ecosystem viewpoint rather than limiting it to content moderation on social media – a topic that has traditionally dominated communication and media studies. Governance consists of interrelated tools and mechanisms through which platforms organise and control their ecosystems: decision-making structures and ownership models; transparency measures and developer-facing tools like APIs; rules and monitoring systems that regulate access, trust, and risk dynamics among participants; pricing and monetisation strategies; and the management of external dependencies and interoperability with other firms or services (van der Vlist, 2022: 43; cf. Schreieck et al., 2018). These tools and mechanisms indicate that platforms govern or moderate not only the content but also the infrastructures, practices, business models, and relationships that underpin their ecosystems – a state of affairs that connects governance to the political economy concerns introduced in chapter 3.

A productive way to study platforms governance is through technographic approaches, which treat platform materials as primary resources (see chapter 1). Technographic approaches analyse terms of service, developer policies, community guidelines, monetisation and advertising policies, and privacy policies. Such documents offer rich insights into a platform's intended uses, underlying norms and values, and explicit rules. Historical versions – available through the Internet Archive's Wayback Machine or through researcher-led repositories such as the Platform Governance Archive (p. 155) – allow researchers to trace the evolution of governance mechanisms and policies in the long run. Digital methods can further complement technographic analysis by systematically querying platforms for specific keywords, to uncover moderation patterns or platform responses to specific events or controversies (e.g. Gillespie, 2024; Rogers, 2023a).

Finally, qualitative methods such as the interview can capture users' experience of governance. Insights into such processes throw light on how moderation is felt and interpreted and, even more, on how rules are contested, weaponised, or circumvented by users themselves. Such perspectives are especially valuable if we want to understand the uneven distribution and experience of governance mechanisms.

In short, the analytical strategies presented here convey a clear sense of the interplay between platform governance mechanisms and external legal and societal forces. This combined approach presents platform governance as a layered, evolving, and contested process that unfolds differently across various user groups and infrastructural layers. Crucially, such strategies permit analysis of platform development in terms of their technical design, policies, and user practices – an essential step for legal oversight.

Insights and observations on the stakeholders of platform governance

Governance over and by platforms clearly involves more actors than just the platform companies themselves (Gorwa, 2019). A wide range of stakeholders – content creators, advertisers, developers, civil society groups, regulators, and governments – co-inhabit the platform ecosystem, each with its own interests and objectives. As a result, platform governance extends well beyond content moderation, into setting rules for community interaction, app development, advertising standards, and monetisation practices. Crucially, these stakeholders do not interact with platforms on equal terms. As we show in this section, they occupy different positions in a platform's hierarchy, are governed via distinct tools and mechanisms, and have oversight, access, and visibility to varying degrees.

The following subsections examine platforms' governance of key stakeholder groups – end users, developers, creators, marketers, advertisers, and gig workers – by analysing governance materials and identifying the tools and strategies that determine platform actions and participation. Other user groups are subject to platform governance as well, but the ones discussed here illustrate some of the most prominent and consequential regulatory relationships in platform ecosystems.

Governing end users

End users – platform users who consume or share content, interact with others, and generate data – are governed through a range of mechanisms. These include terms of service (ToS), community guidelines, and automated moderation systems that regulate content and behaviours such as hate speech, harassment, and copyright infringement. Governance is also embedded in platform infrastructure and interface design: at these levels it determines what users see, access, and can do. At the same time, users participate in it via reporting and flagging tools that feed into moderation processes.

ToS agreements outline the legal rights and responsibilities of users, while community guidelines articulate platform values and define acceptable and unacceptable content and behaviour. These guidelines present themselves as value-driven governance frameworks (Scharlach et al., 2023). For instance, Airbnb (n.d.) describes its guidelines as 'guiding behavior and codifying the values that underpin our global community', Uber (n.d.) emphasises 'safe, respectful, and positive' interactions, and Gojek (n.d.) promotes 'an enjoyable and safe environment for everyone'.

According to Rebecca Scharlach et al. (2023), these policies do more than set behavioural norms. They mediate platform values, balance multiple stakeholder interests, and serve as legal instruments that protect platforms from liability while demonstrating regulatory compliance. Their language often remains deliberately flexible, which allows for strategic interpretation and selective enforcement.

Governance is not only articulated in policy texts but also built into platform infrastructure. A key enforcement mechanism is content moderation, which operationalises platform policies. At the scale of platforms like YouTube, TikTok, or Facebook, which operate globally, moderation must accommodate a great variety of cultural and legal contexts. This has led to hybrid models, which combine automated moderation systems, human review, and localised enforcement to reflect jurisdiction-specific standards.

Automated and human content moderation

Automated moderation now underpins much of platform governance. Systems range from basic keyword detection to advanced applications of machine learning, deep learning, and natural language processing. These technologies process vast amounts of content in order to automatically identify and remove material that violates platform rules. While promising efficiency and scalability, such systems also introduce political and ethical concerns. As Gorwa et al. (2020) argue, automated moderation is often opaque, difficult to audit, and poorly understood, even by the platforms themselves. Rather than solving governance challenges, it can obscure accountability, reinforce existing biases, and hide the political nature of content decisions.

Despite the growth of automation, human labour and oversight remain essential. Sarah Roberts (2019) shows that people are still needed to define banned keywords, to label training data, and to review flagged content. Much of this labour is outsourced to commercial moderation firms in countries such as India, Kenya, and the Philippines, where workers are exposed to highly disturbing material – child abuse, executions, and live-streamed violence – with severe psychological consequences. Roberts concludes that moderation is, and will remain, a socio-technical process where human judgement, algorithmic systems, and legal frameworks intersect.

Platforms also enlist and mobilise users to enforce their rules. Reporting and flagging tools enable users to signal problematic content or behaviour for review by automated systems or human moderators. However, as Caroline Are (2025) argues, these mechanisms are often non-transparent: users rarely receive feedback on reports, and penalised users may not understand why their content was removed. Flagging mechanisms can also be abused; Caroline Are has documented that mass-reporting campaigns disproportionately target marginalised groups such as sex workers, which leads to content takedowns, shadow-banning, or deplatforming. These dynamics reveal asymmetries of power as a result of which participatory systems can be weaponised and become tools of exclusion.

Moreover, governance is rarely even-handed. Platforms may enforce their policies inconsistently or may fail to account for their infrastructure's reproducing social bias; and this would affect LGBTQ+, black, and other vulnerable communities. André Brock (2020) shows that platforms encode into their design and affordances cultural assumptions that can amplify some communities, as seen with Black Twitter, while constraining others. Duguay et al. (2020) similarly demonstrate that platform architectures articulate and sustain dominant techno-cultures and reduce the visibility and participation of LGBTQ+ users and other marginalised groups.

Finally, platforms govern end users not only as participants but also as data subjects. Platforms manage the collection, processing and monetisation of personal data and share these data with third parties (chapter 3). This mode of governance is formalised in privacy policies, which frame end users both as customers of services and as products to be profiled, targeted, and sold to advertisers. End-user governance is therefore determined by commercial imperatives embedded in advertising-based revenue models no less than it is by legal obligations or internal policies.

Deplatforming and deplatformisation as governance strategies

Platforms continuously navigate the tension between upholding free speech and enforcing content moderation, thereby making decisions about what content is allowed, what violates their policies, and how to sanction those who break the rules. This was starkly illustrated in the aftermath of the Capitol Hill riots in January 2021, when Facebook, Instagram, and Twitter (as they were then) suspended President Trump's accounts indefinitely, on the grounds that he had violated policies against inciting violence and promoting criminal activity. These decisions constituted an unprecedented intervention: platforms acting as private governors banned a sitting world leader.

This practice of suspending accounts for policy violations is commonly referred to as deplatforming (e.g. Rogers, 2020). As a governance tool, deplatforming raises important questions about the role of private platforms in regulating public speech and the mechanisms of accountability behind significant decisions. In the Capitol Hill January episode, deplatforming triggered a broader wave of enforcement. Numerous accounts, apps, and services linked to the Capitol riots were suspended. One of the most notable cases was the removal of Parler, a platform popular among US conservatives, including riot participants. Numerous tech companies reacted within twenty-four hours: Google and Apple removed Parler from their app stores for the violation of moderation and safety rules, while AWS ceased hosting it, citing ninety-eight posts that explicitly incited violence. The platform was rendered inoperable.

This incident exemplifies what van Dijck et al. (2021) call deplatformisation: a broader, systemic form of governance that targets not just individual users but entire platforms or services by cutting them off from essential digital infrastructures: cloud hosting, app stores, and payment systems. Without access to these layers, controversial platforms can be effectively excluded from the mainstream digital ecosystem. According to van Dijck et al. (2021), this process has contributed to the rise of fringe platforms. These are alternative services that position themselves outside dominant platform ecosystems and offer ideologically different governance models. Examples include Gab (n.d.), which calls itself 'the home of free speech online'; Rumble (n.d.), a video platform aimed at users 'who value freedom'; and AlignPay (n.d.), a payment provider that claims to be 'engineered to cancel "cancel culture"'.

The Parler case also illustrates that platform governance operates at multiple infrastructural layers. From platforms to app stores and cloud hosting providers, each actor at these layers enforces its own rules, and these rules may not align. Parler maintained that its users had not violated its internal guidelines, yet the app stores and AWS independently found violations of their respective policies, and this led to the platform's removal.

While public and scholarly attention has largely focused on end-user governance and content moderation, the following sections show that developers and creators are also governed through distinct mechanisms that shape what they can build, which data they can access, and how they can monetise their work.

Governing developers

Developers are platform users that build applications, services, and tools that connect with or run on platforms; they can be individuals, but more commonly are development or technology companies. Developers are governed through a combination of formal terms of service, technical constraints, and contractual agreements. Platforms publish developer policies, guidelines, and documentation that outline the data that developers can access, the kinds of applications they can build, and the rules they must follow.

Beyond these formal instruments, developer governance is also embedded in the material design of technical interfaces, especially through APIs, which serve as key gateways to platform data and functionality. APIs are not just neutral technical tools but function as 'material instantiations of regulatory instruments' (Puschmann and Burgess 2014: 45; see also Bucher 2013b), enforcing control through code. APIs determine who gets access, under what conditions, and with what limitations. By doing so they decide what services can be built, by whom, and how, and embed governance directly into platform infrastructure.

This mode of regulation, which displays the technicity of platform governance (van der Vlist et al., 2022), indicates that technical systems are used not only to enable third-party development but also to control it. Developer documentation, API references, and developer policies do more than provide technical guidance; they formalise and make visible the rules of participation. These materials decide what integrations are permitted and under what constraints, turning developer documentation into a central site where governance is made concrete and legible.

Developer governance is also dynamic. Platforms regularly update their API terms, limit or revoke data access, or change the availability of data fields in response to internal priorities and external factors – regulatory demands, societal pressures, or competitive threats.

Infrastructural access and control as governance strategies

Platform governance over developers includes determining what data and functionality are available, to whom, and under what conditions, and consequently what kinds of applications can exist. The management of API access displays this feature most clearly. Platforms can restrict access to specific data points, limit how often an API can be called, and block apps they view as competitive or as a risk to their business models.

In late 2024, Spotify and Strava introduced major API restrictions. Spotify revoked the ability of new third-party apps to access features such as music recommendations, curated playlists, and audio analysis. The company cited concerns about API abuse, though many developers regarded the new restrictions as an effort to block competitors from training AI-based recommendation systems on Spotify data (Zeff, 2024). Notably, these restrictions did not apply to Spotify's official business partners – an important indicator that API governance creates unequal access. Strava, too, changed its terms, banning the use of platform data for training AI models and limiting third-party visibility of user activity data. Although framed as privacy and security measures, these changes were also widely read as attempts to reduce competition.

Governance decisions such as these affect more than app developers. Civil society organisations, journalists, and academic researchers also rely on APIs in their study of platform effects, which can range from misinformation and hate speech to political advertising. The broader move towards closed APIs, sometimes referred to as the 'APIcalypse' (Bruns, 2019), has drastically reduced platform observability and hindered public interest research.

The Cambridge Analytica scandal of 2018 marked a major turning point. Facebook's Graph API allowed broad access to user data, which were exploited for political profiling. In response to widespread criticism and regulatory scrutiny, Facebook and other platforms substantially restricted data access. While presented as privacy reforms, these changes also limited independent research into platforms' methods of influencing public life.

Regulatory intervention further modified platform governance. In 2019, the US Federal Trade Commission (FTC) fined Facebook US$5 billion for misleading users about its data-sharing practices and mandated stricter privacy and governance protocols (FTC, 2019). In the European Union, the DSA, which came into effect in 2022, obliges VLOPs to give researchers and regulators access to data and thereby enable them to assess systemic risks. While this was a major step forward, Leerssen (2021) notes that effective researcher access remains a challenge: platforms can refuse requests on broad grounds, such as security or confidentiality, and access is usually limited to accredited academics rather than to journalists or NGOs. These shortcomings continue to hinder independent scrutiny. As a result, there are persistent tensions between privacy protections and the need for transparency and accountability.

Our own research confirms that platforms adjust the whole matter of API governance – that is, as we defined it, governance both *over* and *by* platform APIs – in response to internal strategies and external pressures (van der Vlist et al., 2022: 3). In our analysis of Facebook developer documentation and API reference materials, we observed the phased removal of the 'interested_in' field, which served to disclose users' sexual orientation, from the Marketing API for advertisers. The field was restricted for the first time in France in 2016, under the proviso 'due to local laws'. By 2017 'interested in' had been removed all across the EU, presumably in anticipation of GDRP restrictions on sensitive data categories, and by 2018 it was removed globally. The removal of Facebook's 'ethnic_affinity' targeting category followed a similar pattern. It was a consequence of civil society pressure over the use of this field in discriminatory advertising of housing, jobs, and credit (Merrill, 2020).

But not all external pressures lead to concessions. In 2023, Reddit imposed new API access fees, invoking concerns over data scraping by AI companies and the need to monetise its own data infrastructure. This led to the shutdown of popular third-party clients such as Apollo and triggered mass protest, including a temporary blackout by more than 7,000 subreddits. Reddit justified the new policy as essential for financial sustainability.

These examples support our argument that API governance functions as a form of infrastructural power. It determines not only who gets access to data but who can build, innovate, and participate in the digital economy. Developer governance is more than a technical issue; it is a central expression of platform power. As platforms face growing pressure from regulators, users, and the public, governance over infrastructure remains a central site of platform politics.

Governing creators, marketers and advertisers, and gig workers

As platforms have become more professionalised and commercialised, their governance structures have expanded to include creators, marketers, and advertisers, but also gig workers. This reflects the platform's growing role as marketplace and gatekeeper for gig work, creative labour, influencer economies, and digital advertising (Helmond et al., 2019; Joseph and Bishop, 2024; Poell et al., 2021; van der Vlist and Helmond, 2021; van Doorn and Shapiro, 2023).

As discussed in chapter 3, platforms' advertising-driven business models draw these stakeholders into their governance structures. Advertisers rely on platforms for audience access and brand visibility; marketers use platform tools to optimise their campaigns and targeting; and content creators, from influencers to professional media producers, depend on platforms for monetisation, visibility, reach, and income. These groups are governed through policies, guidelines, and technical features that regulate acceptable content, advertising formats, and monetisation conditions.

In this context governance is structured around economic imperatives. Monetisation policies, brand safety standards, and disclosure guidelines determine which content is appropriate, which ads are allowed, and how paid promotions must be signalled. These frameworks ensure compliance while creating the economic activities that platforms host. They align advertiser and creator behaviour with platform revenue models and reputational concerns.

Advertising and (de)monetisation as governance strategies

A central mechanism for governing creators is monetisation eligibility, whereby a creator gains the right to earn income from content through advertising, brand deals, or revenue-sharing programs. As Joseph and Bishop (2024) argue, advertisers play a key role here: they define the brand safety requirements that set the boundaries of acceptable – and thus monetisable – content. Platforms such as YouTube develop monetisation guidelines in close consultation with advertisers, translating the latter's preferences into enforceable platform policies. These rules dictate what content can generate revenue and under what conditions. Joseph and Bishop (2024) suggest that, by playing this role, advertisers become de facto governance actors and influence the economic terms under which creators operate.

This dynamic became visible during YouTube's 'adpocalypse' of 2017, when major advertisers threatened to pull their campaigns after discovering that their ads were appearing alongside extremist and hate content. YouTube responded by tightening its advertiser-friendly content policies and demonetising thousands of videos (Caplan and Gillespie, 2020). Many creators were left in the dark as to why their content had lost monetisation status. As Caplan and Gillespie note, 'demonetisation' is a distinctive governance tool for platforms with revenue-sharing models. It does not remove content but removes its capacity to generate income, effectively turning (de)monetisation into a form of content moderation.

This form of governance is especially opaque to smaller creators and marginalised communities, including LGBTQ+ content producers (Are, 2025). YouTube's 'tiered governance' strategy (Caplan and Gillespie, 2020) gives commercially valuable creators enhanced access to appeal processes, direct communication channels, and clearer policy guidance. Smaller creators, by contrast, must often interpret ambiguous rules on their own, which often leads to self-censorship and reduced visibility.

These asymmetries echo a broader pattern of layered and differentiated governance regimes. As we observed in our study of API governance (van der Vlist et al., 2022), platforms apply different rules to different actors, and even to the same actor across different platform services. After the Cambridge Analytica scandal, for example, Facebook tightened data access for developers via the Graph API, but continued to offer privileged access to approved advertisers through the Marketing API. This demonstrates that marketing and advertising developers are governed differently from general developers.

A similar structure applies to influencers. Taylor Annabell et al. (2024) show that the governance of influencer monetisation involves overlapping and sometimes conflicting rules, policies, interfaces, and legal obligations. Platforms like Instagram and TikTok distinguish between influencers and businesses, but the criteria for these classifications and the rules that apply to each category are not always clear. While EU consumer protection law mandates disclosure of any sponsored content, Annabell et al. (2024) found that platform-provided disclosure tools, monetisation policies, and legal requirements often do not align. This creates confusion, particularly for smaller or independent creators, who do not have platform support and must interpret these inconsistent signals on their own – a process with possible legal consequences.

Algorithmic management and interface steering as governance strategies

While creators and advertisers are governed through monetisation and content policies, gig workers such as ride-hailing drivers and delivery couriers on Grab, Gojek, Rappi, and similar platforms are primarily governed through algorithmic management and interface design. Niels van Doorn and Aaron Shapiro (2023) argue with good reason that the gig economy is built on low-wage service work, which is for the most part performed by independent contractors called gig workers, whose labour is mediated by digital platforms. These can be ride-hailing services (e.g. Uber, Lyft, DiDi), delivery apps (e.g. Grab, Gojek, DoorDash, Instacart), freelance marketplaces (e.g. Upwork, Fiverr, Freelancer), and (micro)task-based services (e.g. Amazon Mechanical Turk, TaskRabbit). All these platforms function as matchmakers: they connect workers with tasks, projects, or local services.

Although gig workers are typically self-employed, platforms very much structure their labour conditions and economic opportunities through data-driven systems that continuously evaluate, rank, reward, and discipline them (Rosenblat and Stark, 2016; van Doorn and Shapiro, 2023). Uber and Deliveroo, for instance, use algorithms to assign tasks, determine pay rates, and enforce performance standards through rating systems and customer feedback, both of which operate as instruments of algorithmic management. Dynamic pricing mechanisms such as Uber's surge pricing further govern the availability of labour by adjusting financial incentives in real time and by determining when, where, and how workers operate.

Alex Rosenblat and Luke Stark (2016) demonstrate that Uber's driver interface reinforces this control over drivers through heat maps, gamified incentives, and persistent notifications designed to steer behaviour by encouraging drivers to stay online during peak demand or by directing them toward high-demand areas. Grab's incentive zones operate in similar ways, using fluctuating bonuses and visual interface cues to influence driver mobility and availability. Rappi and other delivery platforms deploy comparable techniques, adjusting pay rates and penalties according to delivery speed and customer satisfaction. Like content creators, gig workers from marginalised groups are disproportionately penalised by these mechanisms, as customer ratings often reproduce social bias and discrimination (van Doorn and Shapiro, 2023).

Yet algorithmic management does not always result in compliance. As Julie Yujie Chen (2020) shows in her study of DiDi drivers in China, gig workers develop forms of algorithmic activism by using automated bot apps to manipulate a platform's algorithms, reject unprofitable rides, or secure higher-value ones. Rafael Grohmann et al. (2022) similarly demonstrate that algorithmic management often operates through dishonesty and uncertainty. On the basis of case studies in Brazil, they establish that opacity is embedded into surge pricing, pay systems, and user interfaces, creating environments in which workers are incentivised to develop workarounds and tactical misuses simply to make a living. Brazilian Uber drivers, for example, organise coordinated shutdowns to artificially trigger surge pricing, while microworkers on Amazon Mechanical Turk use multiple accounts or rely on informal economies to receive payments.

These examples from China and Brazil demonstrate that gig workers such as ride-hailing drivers and click workers do not simply submit to algorithmic governance. This form of control is continually contested, adapted, and negotiated across different contexts, which indicates to us that local gig worker communities mobilise in response to the control mechanisms of platform companies.

The governance and regulation of platforms

This section shifts the focus from how platforms govern specific user groups to how governance mechanisms intersect, overlap, and evolve within larger systems of power. Rather than a stable or unified model, platform governance (both *over* and *by* platforms) is best understood as layered, fragmented, and constantly evolving. It is shaped by a combination of technological developments, commercial imperatives, legal obligations, societal pressures, and geopolitical conflicts. This complexity also makes regulation and enforcement particularly challenging: as governance is distributed across technical systems, global corporate structures, and differing national jurisdictions, accountability is often diffuse and difficult to realise in practice.

The layered and relational nature of platform governance

As shown throughout this chapter, platform governance does not operate as a singular or consistent system. Instead, it unfolds through overlapping policies, infrastructures, and regulatory regimes that intersect in complex and sometimes conflicting ways. The governance of developers offers a clear example. Developers who build apps for Android rely on software development kits (SDKs), which provide functions such as analytics, ad integration, and login services. Each SDK comes with its own policies, which means that developers are governed not only by Google Play's app store rules but also by the policies of every third-party library they integrate.

Our research on app store governance and content moderation (Weltevrede et al., 2025) examined the ten most popular Android apps and found that every one of them contained multiple third-party development SDKs, each governed by its own policy documents (see Figure 4.1). This creates a

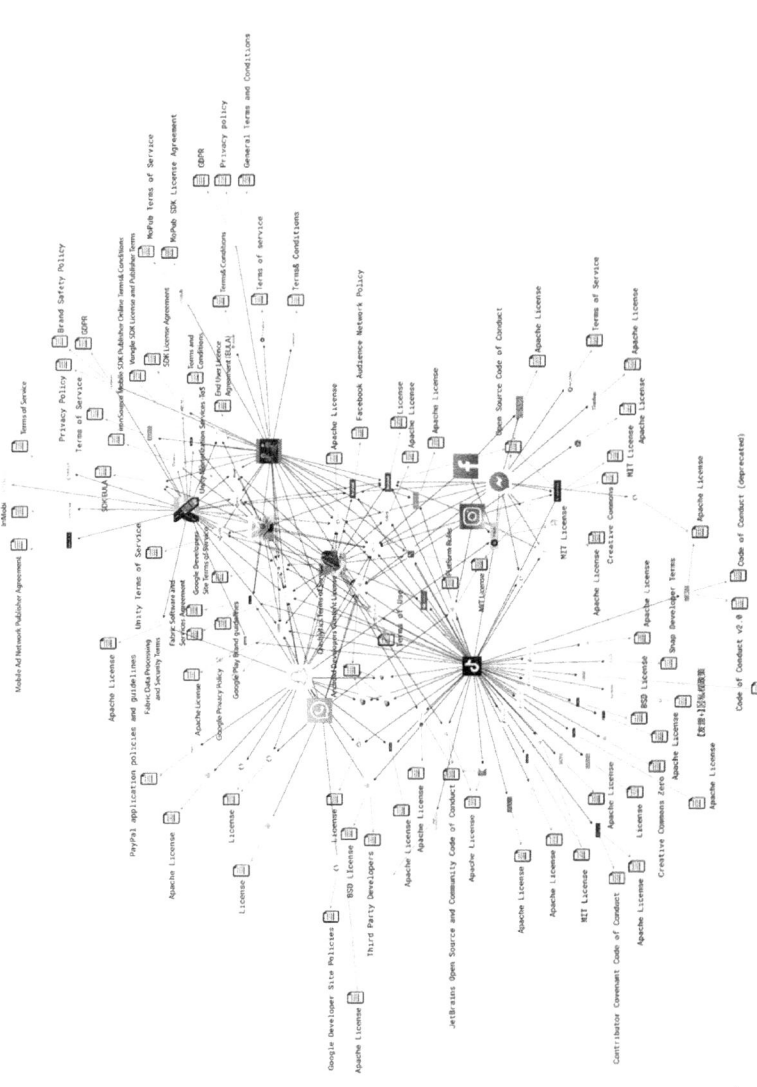

Figure 4.1. Ecosystem of third-party software development kits (SDKs) and policy dependencies in the top ten Android apps. Source: Helmond et al., 2019.

policy multiplication effect in which developers are subject to many interconnected governance regimes, enforced directly by Google and, indirectly, by SDK providers. The result is a layered and fragmented system of control that reflects the layered structure of platforms themselves – just as we encountered it in chapter 2.

This layering becomes even more complex in sensitive regulatory domains such as apps that target children. Developers targeting children must comply with Google Play Families Policy Requirements as well as with a range of external legal frameworks, including the US Children's Online Privacy Protection Act (COPPA), the EU GDPR, and the EU DSA. Google Play's documentation explicitly references and links to these external rules, integrating legal compliance into its governance framework. Apple's App Store, by contrast, mentions external regulations but does not link to them, leaving the responsibility for compliance more squarely with the developers.

Platform governance, then, is rarely unified or consistent. Duguay et al. (2020) describe this condition as 'patchwork platform governance': a messy, fragmented, and reactive mode of rule setting that emerges in response to scandals, legal obligations, public pressure, and shifting business priorities. They argue that this ad-hoc top-down approach prioritises formal policies while neglecting platform architectures' influence on user cultures (239). Thus governance is often reactive, inconsistently applied, and oriented towards immediate problems rather than systemic solutions.

This aligns with what Robyn Caplan and Tarleton Gillespie (2020) call a 'tiered governance strategy' and with the layered 'governance arrangements' that we identified in our work on Meta's API governance (van der Vlist et al., 2022). Across these accounts, platforms apply different rules and levels of access to different actors and adjust these arrangements to external pressures.

These fragmentations extend beyond platform boundaries, as countries and regions develop their own regulatory frameworks in response to the expanding power of platforms as global digital empires (Bradford, 2023). The clash between these competing frameworks is at the heart of current governance battles and is visible in the tensions between

US-based tech companies and the European Union. In April 2025, for instance, the European Commission ruled that Apple and Meta had violated the DMA (European Commission, 2025). Apple was fined €500 million for preventing app developers from telling users about cheaper offers or for restricting users' ability to complete transactions outside its app store. Meta was fined €200 million for its consent or pay system on Facebook and Instagram, a feature that forces users to choose between paying for an ad-free version and agreeing to having their data tracked for personalised ads. The Commission found that this model did not offer a genuinely less data-intensive alternative, as required by the DMA.

These actions intensified tensions between the European Union and the United States. American officials and industry groups criticised the decisions as unfair to US firms, while Donald Trump used the dispute to threaten new tariffs on EU exports, on the grounds that Europe was targeting American technology companies (Smialek and Satariano, 2025). These geopolitical conflicts once again indicate that platform governance influences global power struggles and is in turn influenced by them.

Crisis-driven platform governance

The fragmented character of platform governance becomes even more visible in times of crises, when platforms rapidly adjust their policies, infrastructures, and priorities to new threats, controversies, or emergencies. Crisis-driven governance responses reveal that platforms act increasingly as private emergency governors, taking on roles that would traditionally fall to the state.

A striking example is the COVID-19 pandemic, during which social media platforms and app stores, particularly Google Play and the Apple App Store, became central actors in global health governance (Dieter et al., 2021). Major platforms such as Facebook, YouTube, Twitter, Amazon, and the app stores collaborated with the World Health Organisation (WHO) and national health authorities to curate access to health information. They introduced COVID-19 information hubs, prioritised verified sources in search listings, demoted or removed flagged misinformation, and banned ads for unproven treatments, exploitative products, and anti-vaccine content.

App stores played a complementary governance role: they controlled which COVID-related apps could be developed, approved, and distributed. Apps in this category included contact tracing tools, exposure notification apps, public information platforms, and health monitoring apps. Apple and Google jointly created the Exposure Notification API, which set a global technical standard for contact-tracing apps and imposed strict privacy conditions, limiting governments' means of collecting and processing user data.

These interventions illustrate what Michael Dieter et al. (2021) call 'pandemic platform governance': a mode of governance where platforms balance corporate interests against emergency public health measures and assume state-like regulatory functions. A key mechanism in this process was algorithmic curation. In both app stores, search results for COVID-19-related queries were filtered to display only pre-approved government agency or official health organisation apps in the search results. By narrowing the field of visible results, platforms turned the search tool into a governance one, which directed users towards state-sanctioned health information while filtering out unauthorised apps.

The curation was locally adapted, too. On Google Play, the search results for 'COVID-19' were restricted by country, so users saw only the app approved by their national government. This procedure embedded national public health strategies into the global infrastructures of app stores. But these interventions were not politically neutral; they allowed platform gatekeepers to align the visibility of search with the shifting geopolitical stances of sovereign states, effectively moving the digital boundaries of public health information.

Platforms also regulated the commercial dimensions of these processes. Both Apple and Google prohibited the monetisation of COVID-19 apps, preventing developers from profiting directly from the crisis. Platforms governed not only the access to health information but also the economic terms of pandemic-related app development.

Such examples make it clear that platforms do not merely react to external pressures and crises; they give the responses themselves. Through their infrastructures, policies, and algorithmic systems, they coproduce public health governance alongside state actors and public health initiatives such as the WHO. Crisis moments like the COVID pandemic reveal that platform governance is never purely technical. It is fundamentally political.

Shifting platform–state relations

The growing entanglement between platforms and the state is not limited to moments of crisis; there is a broader shift in the mode of interaction between platforms and state institutions. Platforms are no longer simply private companies that host content or facilitate interactions. They have become political actors that influence elections, shape public debate, and increasingly participate in defining the very rules that govern them.

This shift is particularly visible in platforms' manner of relating to political figures and institutions. In November 2022, shortly after acquiring Twitter, Elon Musk dismantled many of its misinformation policies and reinstated thousands of banned accounts, Donald Trump's among them, framing this initiative as a restoration of free speech. A few months later, Meta lifted Trump's two-year suspension from Facebook and Instagram. Although Trump's accounts were initially placed under increased monitoring, these restrictions were quietly removed in July 2024, just before the Republican National Convention, where Trump was confirmed as the party's nominee. In fact Meta justified its action by invoking a commitment to equal treatment for presidential candidates.

Trump's earlier conflict with social media platforms had already escalated into legal confrontations. In 2021 he sued Meta and Twitter over his deplatforming. After his return to office in January 2025, the two companies settled: Meta paid US$25 million, X agreed to a US$20 million settlement. Around the same time, both platforms appeared to shift politically. Meta donated US$1 million to Trump's inaugural fund and subsequently its CEO, Mark Zuckerberg, dismantled the independent fact-checking program and relaxed the automated moderation of politically sensitive content. Elon Musk likewise used X to support Trump's campaign, donated financially, and amplified election-related disinformation. In Brazil, one of X's largest markets, the Supreme Court temporarily blocked access to the platform after Musk refused to remove accounts that spread disinformation about the 2022 presidential election. Access was restored only after Musk paid a US$5 million fine and complied with the court order. In Europe, Musk hosted on X a live interview with Alice Weidel, co-leader of Germany's far-right Alternative für Deutschland (AfD), a party he openly endorses.

This convergence between platform leadership and state power was made starkly visible at Trump's 2025 inauguration, where platform CEOs Zuckerberg (Meta), Musk (Tesla/X), Bezos (Amazon), and Pichai (Google) had front-row seats. Their presence drew criticism from regulators, particularly in view of ongoing investigations conducted by the US Federal Trade Commission (FTC). In March 2025 Trump unlawfully dismissed two Democratic FTC commissioners. This action intensified concerns about political interference in tech regulation.

Private sovereignty, lobbying, and regulatory capture

These developments highlight a deeper problem: as platforms determine what people see, say, and believe, particularly during elections, the boundary between private governance and state power becomes increasingly blurred. Legal scholar Julie Cohen (2019) has long argued that powerful platforms like Meta, Google, and X function as political entities in their own right, exercising private sovereignty – a type of political power that does not originate from the state but operates alongside it. She also notes that platforms pursue their own geopolitical interests, acting as diplomatic actors that send representatives around the world to negotiate over regulation, privacy, and data governance (236).

The platforms' extensive lobbying efforts and growing political clout illustrate precisely these pursuits and roles. *The Lobby Network*, a report by Corporate Europe Observatory and LobbyControl (Bank et al., 2021), draws on the EU Transparency Register – a database of 'interested representatives' that include organisations, associations, groups, and individuals – to document the scale and sophistication of big tech's lobbying activities in the European Union. It discloses to us that major tech companies engage policymakers, finance think tanks, participate in expert groups, sponsor policy debates, or even co-opt regulators, all in order to steer legislation such as the DSA and the DMA. The report maps a wide ecosystem of lobbying actors: platform giants, infrastructure providers, and policy organisations with close ties to big tech. Such lobbying raises concerns about regulatory integrity; it can lead to regulatory capture, where powerful companies influence or direct regulation in ways that benefit them rather than the public (Cohen, 2019).

Big tech and political elites have become even more intertwined in 2025. In the United States, a multibillion-dollar investment in AI infrastructure, led by OpenAI, SoftBank, and Oracle under the US$500 billion Stargate initiative, was championed by the Trump administration as a national priority. At the same time leading tech figures blurred the lines between corporate and state interests by financing significant political projects such as Trump's private renovation of the White House ballroom. In China, too, the relationship between tech leaders and the state is close; the state's firm role in governing the tech sector reflects this reality – as did the sudden disappearance of Alibaba's Jack Ma in 2020, after he criticised China's financial regulators, then his re-emergence into limited public view.

Finally, as Fabian Ferrari (2024) points out, while the state is often cast primarily as a regulator that imposes constraints on platforms, it also plays a more complex role in platform governance. States frequently act not only as *regulators* but also as market *facilitators*, major *customers* of platform services, and *producers* of infrastructure. These overlapping roles complicate states' ability to enforce regulation. In the case of AI, Ferrari shows how EU public investment and institutional collaboration with big tech can have the unintended effect of subsidising dominant platforms. Charis Papaevangelou and Eugenia Siapera (2025) offer a concrete example from Greece, where Microsoft has become a central partner in the digitalisation of the public sector: it constructs local data centres and delivers training programmes that promote digital skills, and these are, in practice, Microsoft-specific. According to all three authors, then, it is important to consider empirically the very diverse roles that states play at any one time in relation to market actors (e.g. platforms) and civil society. Junic Kim and Shanghe Ahn (2025: 1) observe a broader tension in state approaches to platform governance, as governments attempt to balance 'innovation encouragement with regulatory stringency'.

Evolving platform governance

The internal and external pressures that force platforms to adjust their governance mechanisms raise an important question: how can we observe and study these changes over time?

In our study on app store governance (Weltevrede et al., 2025), we analysed archived versions of developer policies for Apple's App Store and Google Play from 2008 to 2019; these versions were retrieved from the Internet Archive's Wayback Machine (IAWM). By tracking changes in length, structure, and content, we found that these documents became significantly more detailed, especially around the introduction of the GDPR in May 2018. Policy revisions reflected a combination of internal developments (e.g. expanding platform functionality), public concerns (e.g. about children's apps), and external regulatory pressures (e.g. notably from the GDPR and COPPA).

A similar strategy underpinned our study of Facebook's API governance (van der Vlist et al., 2022). We analysed more than 1 million archived documents from the portal Facebook for Developers (2006–2022) – developer blog posts, policy updates, and API reference materials – as well as their archived versions from the IAWM. This large-scale reconstruction allowed us to trace the way Facebook's treatment of third-party developers and data access changed over time. It also revealed that access to platform data and services was managed differently for general developers and advertising partners, exposing systematic disparities in transparency and raising concerns about privacy and algorithmic discrimination. These findings show the importance of archived developer resources when it comes to making governance practices legible and holding platforms accountable.

A recurring challenge in these studies was identifying the precise causes of policy changes. Direct causal claims are often difficult to make, yet platforms frequently leave behind traces that hint at internal and external pressures documented in changelogs, blog posts, documentation updates, and public announcements. These materials often reference legal requirements, reputational risks, or business incentives, providing valuable indicators about the forces behind platform governance.

To support systematic research on such changes, Christian Katzenbach et al. (2023) have created the Platform Governance Archive, a curated, publicly accessible dataset designed to study policy evolution over time. The archive has two components: a reconstructed archive of key governance documents from platforms such as Facebook, Instagram, Twitter, and YouTube (2005–2021), all retrieved via the IAWM; and a live scraping engine that monitors in real time and stores governance-related updates from seventeen platforms. These resources make it possible to trace governance evolution both within and across platforms, offering an important toolset for the study of changes in platform rules in response to technological, societal, and regulatory developments.

Summary

This chapter has shown that platforms are not neutral intermediaries but powerful private governors of digital life. Their governance operates across multiple layers – legal, technical, economic, and algorithmic – and is embedded in formal policies as well as in platform interfaces and architectures. Far from being mere facilitators, platforms actively create and enforce the rules that govern the activities of billions of users, developers, advertisers, content creators, gig workers, institutions, and others.

We have seen that platform governance operates in two main ways: through *internal* rule-making and enforcement (e.g. terms of service, developer policies, algorithmic enforcement systems), and through *external* regulation by states, regulators, and civil society. Governance is not applied uniformly and evenly. It is tiered, layered, and asymmetrical, meaning that different groups of users face different rules, enforcement mechanisms, and degrees of transparency. This results in a set of layered governance regimes that reflect platforms' multiple sides or facets, as stakeholder groups have different incentives and unequal access or privileges.

Platform governance is also material. Technical infrastructures such as APIs, app stores, algorithmic ranking systems, and data interfaces play regulatory roles alongside operational ones. They determine who can participate, what is visible, and how value flows. As argued throughout this book, platforms govern not only through written policies but also through infrastructure, an insight that aligns with the material, ecosystem-oriented approach introduced in chapter 2.

Platform governance is not only legal or technical; it has also become *geopolitical*. As platforms have grown into essential communication, commerce, and data infrastructures, they have attracted significant national and international regulatory attention. From the EU Digital Services Act through TikTok bans in the United States and India to China's platform regulations and AI rules, we are witnessing intensifying struggles over who governs the digital sphere. Platforms now sit at the heart of wider geopolitical contests over sovereignty, trade, data governance, privacy, and security.

Despite the growing significance of platforms, platform governance remains highly fragmented and reactive. It is best understood as a patchwork of legal regimes, corporate decisions, technical constraints, and informal norms that often change in response to crises or political and commercial pressures. Governing power is therefore *distributed*. It is not concentrated in platforms alone; it is shared and contested across a wider ecosystem that includes governments, advertisers, standards bodies, contractors, NGOs, and even end users themselves.

By looking at platforms as both *governing* and *governed*, this chapter has shown that governance and regulation are central to platform power. Combined with the political-economic analysis of chapter 3, this approach helps us to understand our thesis that platforms operate through rule-setting, infrastructure, and global negotiation.

The concluding chapter that follows builds on these ideas in order to reflect on what platform governance, power, and embeddedness mean for the field of platform studies.

It identifies key conceptual, methodological, and empirical directions for future research and practice and considers how scholars, institutions, and publics can engage more meaningfully with platform infrastructures, as these continue to evolve.

Discussion questions

- **Distinguishing governance and regulation** The chapter distinguishes governance *by* platforms (internal rules) from governance *over* platforms (external pressure, law). How do these two forms of control intersect or conflict? Discuss a recent example, such as the regulation of AI platforms, or labour disputes involving gig-work platforms such as Uber or Deliveroo.
- **Platforms as governing systems** The chapter argues that platforms are powerful governing systems. Discuss the implications of this statement. Should large platforms be regulated like public utilities or public institutions with stronger accountability requirements, rather than being treated as private companies under commercial and corporate law?
- **Geopolitics and platform governance** Global disputes around TikTok and the EU DSA highlight a struggle over national sovereignty and global regulation. How effective can regional regulations such as the DSA be in governing global platforms, and what challenges do platform–state relations pose for a unified global digital order?

Further reading

Gorwa, R. (2024) *The Politics of Platform Regulation: How Governments Shape Online Content Moderation.* Oxford University Press.

Flew, T. (2021) *Regulating Platforms.* Polity.

Klonick, K. (2018) The new governors: The people, rules, and processes governing online speech. *Harvard Law Review* 131(6): 1598–1670.

5
Conclusion and Outlook

Introduction

Our world runs on platforms, and platforms in turn shape the world around them.

From the spread of misinformation on X and the regulatory scrutiny of TikTok in Europe to the integration of AI tools from OpenAI, Google, and Anthropic in business, education, and healthcare, platforms influence not only digital interactions but entire sectors and societies. Farmers, military agencies, universities, content creators, and gig workers all experience the consequences of platform-mediated control, while energy-intensive data centres and AI infrastructures transform local environments and global resource flows. This book has shown that these developments are not isolated incidents but manifestations of the underlying dynamics of platform power.

Our book has offered a critical introduction to platforms and to the interdisciplinary field of platform studies, an area that has become essential to understanding the contemporary digital condition. Across three main chapters, we developed a conceptual and empirical framework for analysing platforms as powerful socio-technical systems under several aspects: as digital services used by billions; as parts of companies

– but parts that pursue strategic and economic objectives of their own; as technologies and infrastructures that underpin and structure online and offline life; and as ecosystem orchestrators that bring together and govern a great diversity of human and non-human actors.

Throughout the book, we have emphasised three cross-cutting dimensions or domains of analysis that underpin the power of platforms: political economy (profit and power), governance, and strategy. These dimensions are deeply interconnected and offer complementary entry points for examining the mechanisms and processes by which platforms expand, embed themselves in the social fabric across domains, and exert influence. Our approach has been both relational and material: we treat platforms not as simple digital services or interfaces (e.g. for social media) but as layered ecosystems that incorporate many interdependent actors – users, apps and services, policies, institutions – all orchestrated towards platform objectives.

Platform studies, we have argued, must be both critically grounded and empirically oriented. They need to pay attention to the mechanisms and materials through which platforms operate and to the broader societal transformations they mediate. In this concluding chapter, we revisit the book's core insights and outline key directions for future research. As the field continues to grow alongside the technologies and companies it studies, it should remain conceptually rigorous, methodologically inventive, and politically aware, so that it may be able to trace both entrenched formations and emergent platform phenomena.

We begin with a review of the book's central arguments and contributions, then offer an outlook on the future of platform studies.

Platforms: A brief review

This book began by situating platforms as dominant forces in the digital economy and in everyday life. We traced a small number of extraordinarily powerful companies, from the Magnificent Seven in the United States to BATX firms in China and super apps in other regions, that now structure markets and much more besides: infrastructures, institutions, and governance regimes. We argued that platforms are best understood as *powerful convenors and shapers*, entities that assemble a great variety of actors into complex ecosystems while orchestrating their interactions and structuring their environments through technical, organisational, and economic means.

We also historicised the field of platform studies, identifying three broad analytical waves: what is known as 'the early medium–oriented' studies of platforms (wave 1), that is, the early (late 2000s) study of platforms as cultural and communicative spaces (medium-oriented); the rise of digital methods and infrastructural analysis (wave 2); and the recent turn towards platformisation and the political economy of digital capitalism (wave 3). This trajectory provided the context for the analytical framework developed throughout the book.

Understanding platforms

Chapter 2 laid the conceptual foundations by approaching platforms as socio-technical systems: digital entities owned and operated by companies that enable and organise interactions, exchange, and creation among diverse actors. We argued that platforms operate simultaneously as online services used daily for communication, consumption, and coordination; as corporate actors pursuing strategic and economic objectives; and as technologies or infrastructures on which others build and come to rely or depend. In their design and operation, platforms function as powerful agents that bring together users, developers, businesses, and institutions and structure their interactions through interfaces, algorithms, and infrastructural and organisational arrangements.

The chapter showed that platforms share a set of core characteristics that must be understood as analytical dimensions: multisidedness, programmability, layering, and materiality. These vary across cases and must be analysed relationally. Platforms cultivate and govern ecosystems by positioning themselves as intermediaries and orchestrators between different user groups and by providing ecosystem resources and rules that structure participation and value creation. Their architectures, economic models, and governance mechanisms determine how actors interact, on what terms, and with what consequences.

We situated these insights within the wider field by comparing the conceptualisation of platforms in economics, computing, and media and communication respectively. Despite their differences, these three traditions share a core concern: understanding not only what platforms are, but the way they both influence and respond to the economic, cultural, and political environments in which they operate. Hence we introduced the platform ecosystem as a crucial analytical lens for tracing the methods by which platforms enrol, coordinate, and govern third parties worldwide – particularly through the resources and documentation that structure participation.

Across all platform types, be they social media, mobile, cloud, or new AI services, we identified three dimensions that underpin platform power in ecosystems: political economy, governance and regulation, and strategy. These dimensions throw light on features such as platform scaling, the embedding and integration of platforms across domains, the accumulation of influence, and the organisation of asymmetric relationships with the actors that rely on platforms.

Methodologically, the chapter advanced a technographic and empirical perspective, emphasising interfaces, artefacts, and documentation as key materials for analysis and visualisation. This complements other approaches, for example digital methods, which focus more on social media content. Platforms, we argued, operate as infrastructures of participation, control, and value, and this relational, material, and ecosystemic view provides the conceptual backbone for all chapters.

Understanding the power of platforms

In chapter 3 we examined platforms' accumulation of power through strategic, economic, and infrastructural means. We introduced four sets of interrelated mechanisms that determine platform power: datafication and surveillance, which involve turning user activity into monetisable data assets; platformisation and infrastructuralisation, which describe the embedding of platform logic across sectors; conglomeration and financialisation, which capture platforms' expansion through corporate strategy, their acquisitions, and their alignment with financial markets; and orchestration and evolution, which refer to the continuous management and adaptation of ecosystem relationships.

Drawing on critical scholarship and on our own research, we proposed a conceptual model of platform power as a cycle of convening, integration, and capture. Platforms invite participation, embed themselves in workflows and infrastructures, and generate lock-in through dependency and alignment. Empirically, we highlighted two strategies: follow the money (i.e. corporate and financial data) and follow the data (i.e. infrastructural and partner analysis). These strategies offer practical tools for those who wish to study platforms' creation of markets and cultivation of long-term dependencies both through their business models and strategies and through infrastructural integrations and control.

In chapter 4 we examined the governing power of platforms, manifest in their governing as well as in their being governed. Internally, platforms shape user behaviour and ecosystem interactions through rules, algorithms, monetisation policies, social media content moderation, and interface design. Externally, they are increasingly subject to oversight from states, supranational institutions, and civil society actors. Therefore, following the literature, we distinguished between governance *by* platforms (internal rules and enforcement) and governance *over* or regulation *of* platforms (external legal and political frameworks). Case studies showed that platform governance is often layered, reactive, and crisis-driven, producing tiered systems where users experience different levels of oversight, accountability, and access. In practice, platform governance forms a patchwork of legal requirements, corporate decisions, and infrastructural choices that rarely add up to a coherent or stable system. The chapter also discussed the different regulatory models across the United States (market-driven), Europe (rights-based), and China (state-directed) and pointed out that governance seems increasingly difficult to separate from broader questions of sovereignty, legitimacy, and infrastructural power.

Throughout these chapters we emphasised that platform power is relational, layered, and embedded. Platforms are not isolated actors; they operate within dynamic ecosystems that configure and are configured by political economy, governance, and strategy. These domains explain how it is that platforms accumulate influence, structure asymmetric dependencies, and exercise control across technological, economic, social, and institutional domains even as they face competition, resistance, and contestation from these domains. Together, political economy, governance, and strategy provide the analytical foundation for critical platform studies as presented in this book.

Platform studies outlook: Present, future, past

What comes next for platform studies?

Over the past two decades, online platforms and the scholarly efforts to study them have consistently imparted one core lesson: platforms are always changing, always in the making. They are not static entities but dynamic systems enmeshed in broader social, cultural, political, and economic transformations. Platforms produce visions of the future; they imagine how we will work, learn, communicate, shop, and govern. At the same time they embed these visions in the materiality of interfaces, code, infrastructures, and policies.

This process of making is not unidirectional. Platforms, their users, and their uses coevolve, often in unpredictable ways. Yet public recognition of the significance and conse-quences of platforms, be these about new tools, products, services, or acquisitions, often lags behind the initial rollout. Societies typically wake up to the risks, dependencies, and harms of platforms only after these systems are already deeply embedded into daily life, when their business models, technical infrastructures, and governance mechanisms can no longer be easily unravelled. Such delays generate waves of public concern, regulatory responses, and critical scrutiny, which are often too late to fundamentally alter the playing field.

As platforms become more deeply embedded in culture and society, they increasingly drive transformations across domains such as media, education, labour, health, mobility, governance, and defence. Their growing centrality has reshaped not only social institutions but also academic disciplines, creating new coalitions and shared concerns. In recent years, questions about platform power, accountability, and public values have become pressing in policy circles, civil society, journalism, and everyday life (van Dijck et al., 2018; van Dijck et al., 2025).

In this context, platform studies has emerged as a vibrant and generative field of interdisciplinary research, spanning communication and media studies, sociology, law, political economy, computer science, and science and technology studies (STS). This field has produced rich conceptual frameworks, critical vocabularies, empirical analyses, and methodological innovations. It is sustained by journals, conferences, networks, and research centres committed to analysing platforms as dynamic socio-technical systems that influence the conditions of contemporary life.

What lies ahead

Three intersecting trajectories define the future of platform studies as we see it. Each one builds on the concepts, case studies, and approaches introduced in this book and has the capacity to extend them.

First, there is an urgent need to critically examine the ongoing expansion and entrenchment of *dominant platform ecosystems*, particularly those based in the United States and China; and this trajectory focuses on the present. The companies involved in such ecosystems continue to consolidate infrastructural power, reorganise sectors, and influence the economic, social, and political fabric of everyday life. Future research should carry on mapping these developments; but it should also broaden to include non–social media, regional, and alternative or decentralised platforms – for example enterprise platforms, public-sector platforms, fin-tech, and platforms in the Global South. Such work is necessary for producing a more compendious global account of contemporary platform power.

Second, there is a need to study new and emerging platform formations; and this trajectory relates to the future. As new technological paradigms take shape, so too do new platform principles. Emerging AI platforms, large language and vision models, internet of things devices, augmented and mixed reality environments, super apps, and other cross-sectoral platform conglomerates are redesigning the digital landscape. These developments blur long-standing boundaries between software and hardware that have often been backgrounded in social media–focused platform studies. Future research should analyse how such formations are built, by whom, and with what social consequences; and it should interrogate the promises, assumptions, and exclusions they carry.

Finally, it is important to preserve and investigate platforms that are fading, being discontinued, or long gone; and this trajectory relates to the past. Understanding the present requires historicising the past. There is growing recognition of the need for critical platform histories. This means research that reconstructs the development of platforms, apps, and infrastructures over time, with an eye to the role of platforms as convenors and shapers (Helmond and van der Vlist, 2019; 2021). Such work could trace the coevolution of technical architectures, business models, regulatory frameworks, and user practices; it could throw light on moments of contestation, consolidation, and change. As platforms increasingly frame themselves as the future, historical analysis offers an essential corrective: it reminds us that other paths were possible – and still are.

Next we offer a more in-depth discussion of the opportunities and challenges associated with each of these three directions.

The present: Dominant platforms and ecosystems

Despite more than two decades of research, platform studies has largely concentrated on a familiar group of social media giants: Facebook, Instagram, YouTube, TikTok/ Douyin, WeChat, and Twitter/X. While these platforms warrant attention, such a narrow focus can obscure the wider range of systems and sectors affected, or even created, by platformisation. Much platform power operates through less visible layers, which target advertisers, developers, business partners, or enterprise users. As this book has argued, digital platforms are more than social media. They are economic actors, programmable infrastructures, and rulemakers that operate as powerful agents that bring together the strands of cultural, economic, and institutional life to modify or restructure them.

Studying platforms in their present forms requires us to extend our gaze beyond user and content cultures and examine platforms' response to technical innovation, regulatory intervention, and ecosystem competition. In 2025 Mark Zuckerberg, the CEO of Meta, declared to the US Federal Trade Commission that 'social media is over' (Chayka, 2025). This statement signalled a broader strategic pivot by Meta, away from interpersonal networking and towards a model based on algorithmically curated, increasingly AI-generated content, alongside messaging, immersive experiences, and generative AI assistants. Central to this shift is Zuckerberg's vision of AI chatbots that will replace not only search functions but also friends, therapists, and service workers: 'AI companions who know you like a friend' (Bobrowsky, 2025).

This reimagining of sociality is not merely rhetorical. Internal data cited by Meta suggest that interpersonal content now accounts for a shrinking share of user engagement. Instagram and Facebook increasingly resemble mass media environments: they prioritise viral video, influencer content, and AI-generated posts. As Meta redefines its services, it challenges the characterisation 'personal social networking services', used by the Federal Trade Commission (FTC) in antitrust investigations that followed Meta's acquisitions of Instagram in 2012 and WhatsApp in 2014. Meta now argues that platforms operate across a much broader competitive landscape, which includes TikTok, YouTube, and iMessage. The company's court win against the FTC in the fall of 2025 supports this position and points to a broader transformation: the platform model is shifting, consolidating, and expanding.

These changes are not confined to social media. Platforms increasingly organise services across sectors as varied as automotive, health, education, agriculture, defence, and advertising. Platformisation now extends to super apps, where messaging, transport, commerce, and payments are bundled together in unified environments, especially in parts of Asia, Africa, and Latin America. Studying the present therefore requires examining both the dominant players and the many platforms that operate beyond the social media core.

Beyond social media

Numerous platform types remain understudied despite their significance. In advertising, Google and Meta still operate as a dominant duopoly, but the rise of Amazon, ByteDance, and Alibaba means that the five companies together now capture more than half of global advertising revenues (Goldman, 2024). Through its demand-side platform (DSP), Amazon targets audiences across its own services and third-party apps, drawing on extensive data from e-commerce, streaming, and smart home devices. Adobe, once known primarily as a software firm, now operates a DSP for connected television and a customer data platform designed to build cross-channel audience profiles.

Meanwhile, thousands of lesser known intermediaries populate the programmatic advertising ecosystem. Trade Desk, Criteo, Adform, and others help with buying and selling ads, while data brokers like LiveRamp, Experian, and Epsilon offer key audience resolution services, stitching together user data across platforms. These intermediaries shape how people are profiled, categorised, and targeted, yet they receive relatively little scholarly attention despite their central role in surveillance capitalism and data-driven economies.

In agriculture, big ag companies like John Deere and IBM are rebranding themselves as data-driven platforms by offering precision farming tools and climate risk prediction via AI cloud platforms. These efforts reflect a vision of agriculture as optimisable through proprietary software and infrastructure – a vision supported by cloud giants such as AWS, Microsoft Azure, and Google Cloud. This entire problematic raises important critical questions about infrastructural dependency, environmental impact, techno-solutionism, and platform power in sectors not traditionally studied within media and communication research.

As Napoli and Caplan (2017) argue, the distinction between media and tech companies, which has long shaped regulatory approaches, is increasingly difficult to maintain. The field of communication and media studies is well positioned to analyse these shifts, particularly in dialogue with perspectives from law, design, political economy, and STS.

Global perspectives

Platform studies has often privileged US-based companies, which is understandable given their global dominance. Jin's (2015) notion of 'platform imperialism' highlights that American companies have come to dominate the platform landscape by holding asymmetric power over local economies and cultures. But platform ecosystems in Asia, Africa, Latin America, and Europe offer distinct models and merit deeper engagement. Steinberg (2019), Davis and Xiao (2021), Lin et al. (2025), and other scholars argue that the field must de-westernise and re-regionalise its analyses by recognising that platforms take shape differently according to culture, infrastructure, regulation, and political economy.

Regional platform diversity

Examples abound that illustrate this diversity. In Southeast Asia, apps like Grab and Gojek operate as super apps, bundling transport, delivery, finance, and messaging (Steinberg et al., 2022). In South Korea, Kakao is so central to everyday communication that a 2022 outage prompted the president to describe it as 'national infrastructure' (van der Vlist, Helmond, Dieter et al., 2025: 3332). In India, Jio and similar platforms have reshaped access to connectivity, digital payments, and service delivery by bundling mobile data plans with an expanding suite of apps for entertainment, messaging, and e-commerce.

In Africa, platform development is closely tied to telecommunications and financial services. This situation reflects the critical role of mobile network operators in building digital infrastructure in contexts in which broadband access is limited. In Kenya, M-Pesa, owned by Vodacom (Vodafone), enables users to send and receive money, pay merchants, and access services such as healthcare on a single mobile app. MTN Shortz is a short video platform operated by MTN, Africa's largest mobile operator. The super app Max It, developed by Orange, bundles telecommunications, financial services, e-commerce, content, and ticketing across its operations in Africa and the Middle East. Similarly, Gozem, active primarily in West and Central Africa, integrates transportation, delivery, e-commerce, and financial services in one app tailored to local needs and infrastructures.

In Latin America, two regionally rooted platforms warrant close examination. These are Rappi, a Colombian delivery app that has diversified into payments, financial services, and grocery shopping; and Cabify, a Spanish ride-hailing platform active in the region. Studying these alongside global incumbents such as Uber can illuminate the context-specific characteristics, operational rationales, and competitive strategies of platforms in different markets. Platform development outside the West reveals distinctive organisational forms and strategic principles. Further, given that 'the next billion users' of platforms (Arora, 2019) are primarily outside the West, these regions can be seen as key markets of growth and experimentation.

Localisation and differentiation

As will be further discussed in the next subsection, super apps frequently adapt their services locally, so as to accommodate regional conditions – regulatory, economic, and cultural; and they do so by offering, say, cash payments, integration with local retailers, or bespoke logistics models adapted to urban realities. Even globally ubiquitous apps like WhatsApp operate differently in different contexts. In the Netherlands it functions primarily as a messaging app among friends, family, and businesses. By contrast, in India, Singapore, and especially Brazil, WhatsApp also operates as a peer-to-peer payment platform. This illustrates the point that the same app can become infrastructurally and economically differentiated as a result of local adoption and platform strategy.

Chinese platforms have pursued what Kaye et al. (2021) call 'parallel platformisation': the development of similar platforms, which are then adapted to different user practices and regulatory contexts, as is the case with Douyin and TikTok. Such strategies enable expansion while navigating geopolitical tensions and compliance constraints. Understanding these dynamics is key if we want to analyse firms' balancing of global ambitions with local realities. For example, China's interrelated governmental Belt and Road Initiative (BRI) and Go Global strategy are encouraging its companies to embed themselves into African nations by offering essential telecommunications and platform infrastructure and thus making themselves indispensable to the local economies.

In Europe, key regional players remain relatively underexplored in platform studies. These include Adyen (payment infrastructure, Netherlands), Booking.com (travel, Netherlands), Zalando (retail and fashion, Germany), SAP (enterprise software and cloud, Germany), BlaBlaCar (ridesharing, France), Bolt (ridehailing, Estonia), and Nextcloud (cloud storage and collaboration, Germany). The rise of European AI platforms adds a new geopolitical dimension. Companies such as the French Mistral AI explicitly promote European-hosted AI, in alignment with digital sovereignty goals (Mistral AI, 2025). Helsing, a German defence company, offers AI-powered battlefield decision-making software that, as declared on its official website and in several press releases, is supposed to protect 'our' democracies – which raises critical questions about platformisation in military contexts. These examples command further attention from communication and media studies scholars, as well as cross-disciplinary collaboration and policy engagement.

Alternative and decentralised social media

Geopolitical tensions, commercial dominance, and surveillance concerns have also renewed the interest in alternative and decentralised social media. After Elon Musk acquired Twitter, the platforms Bluesky and Mastodon gained traction. During the threatened US ban of TikTok, many users migrated to Xiaohongshu (RedNote), an event that generated more than 5.5 million comments in one day under the hashtag 'TikTok refugee'.

The Fediverse, a constellation of decentralised platforms such as PeerTube, Pixelfed, and Mastodon, offers a notable alternative to centralised big tech ecosystems. These projects are driven by concerns about data privacy, digital autonomy, interoperability, and democratic oversight (Gehl 2025).

As van Dijck et al. (2025) argue, understanding both dominant and alternative platforms is essential. Only by recognising the full spectrum of actors and infrastructures – those that are visible and invisible, dominant and marginal, local and global – can platform studies develop research and governance frameworks that are attuned to real power dynamics, dependencies, and cultural diversity.

The future: Emerging platform formations

A second key direction for platform studies is the analysis of emergent platform formations such as AI infrastructures and super apps. As this book has shown, platforms are not static entities. They are continuously reconfigured through developing strategies, interfaces, partnerships, infrastructures, and use cases. Studying these transformations as they unfold, rather than after the fact, is essential for understanding the generation of digital futures.

One of the most urgent tasks for platform studies is therefore to analyse platforms in the making. This involves examining how discursive framings, business models, user practices, software development resources, and governance arrangements come together longitudinally. Such research must remain empirically grounded while being conceptually alert to the futures that platforms imagine, promote, and begin to implement – not least because platforms often do these things well before public debate, policy, or media coverage catch up. An anticipatory orientation is central to understanding platformisation – not only as a historical process but as an ongoing strategic and infrastructural project. In the context of AI, Bareis and Katzenbach (2022) describe this orientation as a way of 'talking AI into being', which highlights the fact that imaginaries and narratives influence technological trajectories (cf. Richter et al., 2023).

In what follows we highlight three domains in which these dynamics are particularly visible: immersive media such as metaverse environments and virtual reality; AI as a platform; and the rise of conglomerate infrastructures in the form of super apps. In each of these domains, platforms are actively reimagining and reorganising themselves as they pursue integration into services, sectors, and infrastructures and consolidate power and configure standards, interfaces, and user expectations.

Virtual reality and the metaverse

In 2021 Facebook rebranded as Meta and announced its intention to build the metaverse, which it presented as the next big step and the future of digital connection beyond the mobile internet. While it is easy to dismiss such statements as corporate hype, they often have material consequences. As Carter and Egliston (2024) show in their analysis of Meta's virtual reality initiatives, platform imaginaries are not just rhetorical. They have an effect on real investments, development priorities, tools, and infrastructures.

Meta's Horizon platform illustrates this dynamic. It provides a suite of tools for building and monetising virtual worlds. The virtual worlds are accessible through Quest VR headsets and, increasingly, on mobile devices. Horizon's virtual worlds–related initiative and others of the same ilk are backed by familiar orchestration strategies: offers of application programming interfaces (APIs), incentive programs such as the 50M Creator Fund, and extensive developer support intended to create early content, lock in developers, and establish long-term dependencies.

Although the metaverse discourse has cooled down and Meta has shifted its focus towards AI-powered glasses and wearables designed to 'weave AI and AR into everyday life' (Meta n.d.), the underlying infrastructural and economic arrangements of the spatial web continue to develop and mature. This reflects a broader pattern discussed throughout this book: strategic visions are performative. They help with the more important tasks of bringing technical development and investment flows in one place and influencing governance and policy agendas. The same performativity can now be observed in the rapid rise and expansion of AI platforms.

(Generative) AI as a new platform

One of the most consequential developments of the 2020s is the ongoing (generative) AI platform shift. More than a suite of tools or models, AI is emerging as a foundational infrastructure on which new services, applications, and business models are being built; and the platformisation of AI is also restructuring markets and creating deep infrastructural dependencies.

The societal transformations under way run much deeper than the success of any single application. AI is increasingly understood as a new systemic technology: a pervasive and foundational infrastructure that is deeply interrelated with other technologies and has a big impact on work, culture, and society at large (e.g. Prins et al., 2021). Platforms are not passive conduits for these changes; they orchestrate who participates in AI ecosystems, how resources are distributed, and how new services and applications are structured.

Platformisation and the industrialisation of AI

A key moment in this transformation was the launch of ChatGPT in late 2022, an event that triggered what van der Vlist, Helmond and Ferrari (2024) term the industrialisation of AI: a rapid commercialisation and integration of AI into everyday platforms and services, alongside massive investments in computing infrastructure and ecosystem resources – investments particularly driven by contemporary generative AI. Chatbots arguably became the first widely adopted killer apps in AI, but their significance lies in the fact that they prefigure a much broader shift across the ecosystem.

In this continuous process of the platformisation of AI (Burkhardt and Rieder, 2024; Luitse, 2024; Hind et al., 2025; van der Vlist, Helmond and Ferrari, 2024), major platforms – Microsoft, Meta, Google, Amazon, TikTok, OpenAI, and Adobe – are now embedding AI into their product lines and restructuring their offerings around it. Microsoft's integration of Copilot throughout its Microsoft 365 suite (Word, Excel, Outlook, and Teams) exemplifies this trend: Copilot is a cross-application assistant powered by different underlying large language models, and it functions as a connective layer within the company's broader software ecosystem. Similar integrations can be observed on other platforms. Google's Gemini on Workspace and Adobe's Firefly models on Creative Cloud are examples that signal a shift towards AI as an integrated and infrastructural service. By embedding AI in this fashion, platforms determine both the technological possibilities available and the economic and organisational relations within which AI is deployed.

The OpenAI GPT platform further illustrates what we call its convening and shaping role. By providing API access to its models, OpenAI allows developers to build new services or integrate its models without hosting them themselves. Features such as Custom GPTs enable paying subscribers to create specialised AI personae, which can then be distributed through the GPT Store, a marketplace for AI agents and assistants that mirrors the familiar logic of mobile app stores. With the launch of apps in ChatGPT and a public, app store–like directory of third-party tools that can be used within ChatGPT, OpenAI now fully embraces the platform model in order to orchestrate a broad ecosystem of actors, practices, and commercial opportunities.

The platformisation of AI is further amplified by cloud marketplaces. Microsoft Azure, Amazon AWS, and Google Cloud now act not only as infrastructure providers but also as distributors of third-party AI apps, models, and services. Hugging Face, meanwhile, has become a key hub for open-source models and tools. 'There's an AI for that' has become a new refrain, which echoes the earlier appification of the mobile internet (van der Vlist and Weltevrede, 2025: 12).[1] Across consumer and enterprise markets, platforms mediate the adoption, diffusion and deployment of AI everywhere, from healthcare, education, agriculture, and defence to content creation, advertising, and enterprise workflows. And in both these markets the adoption of AI is accelerating. Tools once built for general use, such as ChatGPT, are now being customised for education, health, content creation, travel planning, companionship, religion, and more. In early 2026, OpenAI launched ChatGPT Health with additional protections and controls for sensitive health data, while Microsoft's Azure Healthcare Bot promises regulation-compliant AI for clinical triage and information services. But these developments also raise concerns about data, reliability, bias, and accountability – particularly in sensitive domains.

Concentration, dependency, and infrastructural risk

These AI ecosystems are highly centralised. The 'big three' cloud providers – Amazon, Microsoft, and Google – control over 60 per cent of global cloud infrastructure; they are followed at a distance by Alibaba Cloud, Oracle, Salesforce, IBM Cloud, and Tencent (Richter, 2025). As observers have noted, a key challenge is to stop big tech from consolidating into 'big AI' (von Thun and Hanley, 2024; van der Vlist, Helmond and Ferrari, 2024). The risk is that the same structural dependencies and market concentrations that characterised earlier eras of platform capitalism would re-emerge, but this time at the level of a technology widely seen as essential to future economic and social development. Their dominance raises deep concerns about structural dependency, market power, and geopolitical vulnerability. Mayer and Lu (2025: 4) describe these firms as 'technopoles' with disproportionate technical and political power over markets, standards, and geopolitics.

While largely invisible or hidden, these dependencies are not abstract. A Google Cloud outage in June 2025 disrupted 'large swathes of the internet' (Zeff, 2025). The incident affected major cloud platforms such as Cloudflare and popular apps such as Spotify, Discord, Snapchat, and Character.AI. Similar failures have occurred before, as social media platforms have put their tentacles in millions of websites and apps, creating infrastructural dependencies: a Facebook social plugin error in 2011 took down hundreds of websites (including nytimes.com), and a routing issue in 2021 disconnected Facebook's entire infrastructure, including Instagram and WhatsApp. These cascading failures betray the increasing fragility of overly complex and centralised platform infrastructures.

Geographic expansion and extractive infrastructures
AI's platform dynamics extend far beyond Silicon Valley. Major platform companies are expanding aggressively into emerging markets, where large populations, linguistic and cultural diversity, and underserved segments present opportunities for both data extraction and market growth. These regions are often treated as a testing ground and 'a place to gather diverse data, refine models, and test AI use cases that could later scale across other emerging markets' (Singh, 2025). Google's 2025 partnership with Reliance Jio in India exemplifies this strategy. By providing free access to AI Pro

services for millions of Jio users, Google gains access to a vast and linguistically diverse user base that can improve model performance across multiple languages and cultural contexts. Such initiatives can be understood as part of a broader expansion strategy, grounded in intensive data collection and use.

Yet these extractive dynamics are not limited to data, as AI's power derives from other forms of extraction as well. As Crawford (2021) and others have shown, AI relies on extractive labour and resource infrastructures: data labelling performed by gig workers, rare-earth mining for hardware, and water and energy consumption significant enough to operate data centres. Platforms gather and orchestrate these labour and resource chains, embedding them in AI ecosystems. Studying AI as infrastructure therefore requires attention not only to technical systems but also to the environmental, labour, and political economic conditions that sustain them around the globe.

Super apps and new conglomerates

A third development is the rise of super apps or 'do-everything apps' discussed in chapter 3 as emerging forms of platform constellations (pp. 99–100). From WeChat and Grab to Amazon and Meta, these platforms combine messaging, payments, logistics, shopping, and entertainment under one roof. Their emergence reflects a broader trend of digital conglomeration, which involves horizontal expansion across services and vertical integration into infrastructure layers such as payments and identity systems (Steinberg et al., 2022; van der Vlist, Helmond, Dieter et al., 2025).

This logic is now extending to AI. Both super apps and AI-driven environments promise to transform users' mode of interacting with digital services by merging functionality, consolidating services, and unifying interface experiences. At its 2025 developer conference, Google introduced the AI Mode, an overhaul of its search engine into an AI-powered environment that integrates search, productivity, communication, and more. As Wong (2025) notes, this mode resembles 'an everything app: a single tool that will be able to do just about everything a person could possibly want to do online', or 'one app to rule them all'. Whether the Google

AI Mode will achieve this ambition remains uncertain, but its launch signals a convergence between AI and the super app paradigm.

Van der Vlist, Helmond, Dieter et al. (2025) describe this broader dynamic as a form of super appification: a shift from single-purpose apps and tools towards conglomerate platform ecosystems, following different models or strategies seen around the world. These formations are not uniform; they differ by country or region as a result of economic, cultural, and institutional variation (e.g. Athique, 2019; Chen et al., 2018; Mukherjee, 2019; Plantin and de Seta, 2019), echoing the earlier call for global perspectives. But they do share a common logic of enclosure and integration, as they embed users, services, and infrastructures under a single corporate umbrella and data infrastructure.

This growing convergence between AI and super apps demands closer conceptual attention. As Srnicek (2024: 1) notes, firms such as Google, Amazon, and Tencent increasingly function as 'new conglomerates': digital empires spanning multiple sectors, sustained by infrastructural power, cross-subsidisation, and data integration. In keeping with the framework developed in this book, understanding these conglomerates demands moving beyond interpretations of platforms as standalone services and towards an ecosystemic, infrastructural analysis of platform capitalism. It also requires rethinking what counts as a platform today, which now extends far beyond social media.

The past: Discontinued platforms and memory

Lastly, important research gaps and blind spots lie not only in the future but also in the past. A third vital direction for platform studies is the continued development of critical histories of platforms, apps, and AI systems, many of which are already fading, even though they continue to influence society. As platforms constantly update and change, they overwrite their own past by redesigning interfaces, replacing infrastructures, and deleting content. This produces a growing form of *platform amnesia*, such that even influential services and ecosystems leave behind only small traces.

This lack of historical visibility is a missed opportunity. It limits our ability to understand how and where platforms originated and evolved, to denaturalise the present by showing that other paths were possible, and to imagine alternatives. Reconstructing the development of past and present platforms and the decisions behind their evolution can help us bring to light forgotten infrastructures, failed standards, user practices, and alternative governance models that challenge the inevitability of today's platform arrangements.

Crucially, much of this reconstruction relies on what we have called ecosystem resources (p. 40): the technical, legal, and informational artefacts that platforms produce and strategically use to coordinate, govern, and enable participation within their ecosystems. When collected and preserved, these resources provide essential empirical footholds for tracing the work of platforms in the past or over time.

In the next subsection we highlight three key traditions or frameworks for tracing the histories of platforms, apps, and AI systems.

Platform archaeology and lost alternatives

Drawing on media archaeology, Apperley and Parikka (2018: 14) argue that platform studies must look 'beneath the interface'; consequently they turn to the hidden materiality, technical systems, and infrastructural underpinnings of digital platforms. They observe that the field risks becoming a history of winners, since scholarly reconstruction often relies on the availability of stable archives. Platforms that were commercially unsuccessful are easily overlooked, even if they had cultural or technical significance.

This is evident in the case of Hyves, a Dutch social network founded in 2004. At its peak, Hyves had 10 million users (roughly 60 per cent of the Dutch population at the time) and was deeply embedded in the national culture. It supported a high level of customisation with 'pimped' profiles and other playful design elements that fostered expressive user identities. Its significance extended to politics. In 2006 the Dutch prime minister joined the platform during the elections, and Hyves hosted the first national chat debate between party leaders.

Hyves also participated in OpenSocial, a Google-backed initiative launched in 2007 to support cross-platform social app development with the help of open APIs (Ymerce, 2007). Framed as an open alternative to Facebook's ecosystem, OpenSocial ultimately failed to gain traction, revealing an early and now largely forgotten push for platform interoperability. As Facebook gained dominance, Hyves declined, and in 2013 the service was discontinued and repurposed as an online gaming platform. Much of its cultural history has been lost; it survives only in part, through (rogue) archiving efforts by the Internet Archive and Archive Team.

Such cases remind us that reconstructing platform history involves attending to alternative paths: paths that were not taken but that often reveal design values and ecosystem logics very different from those that prevail today. They also show the importance of grassroots archival efforts when it comes to resisting digital erasure.

This historical lens is equally valuable in critical data(set) and AI research. Crawford and Paglen's (2019) project powerfully exemplifies an archaeological approach to datasets. It investigates widely used training corpora such as ImageNet in order to reveal the social assumptions, biases, and labour embedded in AI systems. The authors describe their method as 'digging through the material layers ... and analysing what normative patterns of life were assumed, supported, and reproduced' (2019).

Similar benchmark datasets, which provide standardised reference sets for training and evaluating models, exist in domains such as healthcare or autonomous driving and are often organised around formal 'challenges' and competitions. These events drive model development and industrial alignment while offering training opportunities for students and early-career researchers (Hind et al., 2024; Luitse et al., 2024).

Such analyses show that AI platforms are built on political and infrastructural foundations rather than on neutral data. These foundations include classification systems, labour hierarchies, and planetary extraction processes (Crawford, 2021). Tracing those layers helps towards exposing the ways in which the past continues to contour the present, both through technical residues (e.g. APIs, software development kits (SDKs), changelogs) and through conceptual legacies.

In this sense, building on the framework developed in this book, *platform archaeology* is not simply a method for studying past or obsolete technologies. It is a way to uncover the embedded, material substrates of both contemporary and legacy systems, from AI governance arrangements to ecosystem structures and business models.

Platform historiography: Tracing features and cultures

Historians of media and technology have developed methodologies to address the specific challenges of studying platforms as evolving socio-technical systems. Burgess and Baym (2020) propose a 'platform biography' approach that follows the life cycle of key features such as timelines, hashtags, or 'like' buttons. By tracing how these features were introduced, adapted, redesigned, or contested, researchers gain access to shifting user cultures, strategic priorities, and economic logics. Features, they argue, are socio-material objects that guide user behaviour and reflect the platform's economic logics. Studying them gives access to platforms' mechanisms of mediating social life and adapting over time.

In related work, we developed 'platform historiography', a methodology and practical guide for reconstructing histories from a platform perspective (see Helmond and van der Vlist 2019, 2021). This approach foregrounds the roles of developers, businesses, advertisers, and other ecosystem actors – not just end users – while accounting for platforms' dynamic architectures and limited archival visibility. It addresses the specific challenges of studying and archiving platforms. Social media generate highly dynamic and personalised feeds, which are difficult to capture with the help of traditional web crawlers used in web archiving; and their content is often loaded dynamically, hidden behind interactive elements, gated behind logins, or tailored to individual users. Yet even without full snapshots in web archives, archived resources such as technical documentation, developer portals, app listings, or changelogs offer essential empirical footholds for reconstructing past versions, interfaces and affordances, governance arrangements, discursive visions, and strategic priorities, all of which are necessary for writing platform histories.

Importantly, in line with our framework, platforms must be understood as entities operated by companies and as layered infrastructures, and not merely as services. Historical accounts that trace interfaces, APIs, SDKs, and ecosystem shifts explain to us how platforms expanded in scope and power and how their infrastructural back ends evolved in ways that users cannot see. These histories shed light also on broader shifts in governance, regulatory responses, and the uneven geographies of platformisation. Because such developments are at risk of being forgotten, documenting them is essential to a critical understanding of new platform formations and their emergence, consolidation, and embedding in cultures, economies, and institutions worldwide.

App and AI historiography: New objects, new methods
Today's mobile apps and AI systems pose even greater historiographical challenges. Operating outside the open web, they follow rapid release cycles and rely on proprietary components. Yet, like earlier platforms, they leave behind material traces in web archives. App store descriptions, changelogs, developer documentation, and software packages (e.g. APK files for Android) in app repositories can be used to reconstruct developing features, partnerships, and platform integrations. However, apps are generally poorly archived, particularly Chinese apps such as Douyin and WeChat, which have been preserved even less systematically than their US-based counterparts (e.g. Facebook or Instagram).

The archived traces of apps allow researchers to reconstruct not only technical features in motion but also shifting rhetorical positionings and cultural imaginaries. For example, early versions of Instagram's tagline and description heavily emphasised simplicity and casual sharing through phrases like 'a fun, fast, and simple way to share your life with friends'. Later versions moved towards highlighting professional content creation, following one's favourite creators and influencers, discovering brands, and shopping for products. This illustrates that platform narratives adapt in the long run to attract new user groups (e.g. creators, brands, small businesses) and reinforce their role as infrastructures of the creator economy.

Historical analysis of earlier (i.e. international and domestic) versions of TikTok and Douyin disclosed that their embedded tracking infrastructures progressed longitudinally as a result of regulatory changes (Helmond et al.,

2022). While TikTok relied on both US and Chinese trackers, Douyin focused on local infrastructures that grew steadily. A major change occurred in 2019, when TikTok removed its Chinese trackers after a regulatory fine from the US Federal Trade Commission. This example illustrates that governance responses are reflected in app architectures and ecosystems; it also highlights the importance of studying the 'nationality' of apps and the infrastructures they rely on.

AI systems present even more complex historiographical challenges as a result of their ephemeral and dynamic nature. Core components such as datasets, model weights, or inference APIs are rarely archived and are often treated as trade secrets. Still, important archived materials such as API changelogs, dataset descriptions, and developer documentation can support reconstruction. These materials can be paired with company blog posts and ethical guidelines if we wish to examine diachronically the framing, governance, and adaptation of AI systems.

Histories of AI must also attend to their own imaginaries: how companies invoke ideas of intelligence, safety, or neutrality to legitimise their systems and how these narratives change in response to market competition, regulation, or public criticism.

Altogether, the historiographical approaches discussed here – platform archaeology, platform biography, platform historiography, app and AI historiography – yield empirical and conceptual tools for preserving and reconstructing digital history. They reveal the power dynamics embedded in platforms and build resistance to a potential digital dark age. These histories matter for what they recover, but also because they create room for imagining that digital infrastructures could have evolved differently, and still can. Writing and preserving platform history is therefore not simply a retrospective exercise but a critical project for outlining future alternatives.

Final remarks

As platforms continue to grow and embed themselves more deeply into society, so too must the approaches we use to study them. The critical framework developed in this book is designed not to prescribe one single method, theory, or definition but to support a diverse interdisciplinary field that thrives on empirical curiosity, methodological innovation, and conceptual discussions.

A central aim of this book has been to render platform research more accessible and actionable. Whether you are a student, a researcher, a journalist, an NGO worker, a policymaker, or a cultural practitioner, meaningful contributions to this field do not necessarily require technical mastery. Platforms may be complex and often opaque, but they are also public-facing, material, and researchable systems. They leave traces – documents, policies, interfaces, developer resources, datasets, and behaviours – that can be studied using a wide range of tools and perspectives from the social sciences, humanities, law, computational fields, and beyond.

The framework developed in chapter 2 equips students, scholars, policymakers, and citizens to interrogate platform power. When a platform announces a policy change, you can ask: what political economic interests does this serve? Who benefits and who is disadvantaged? What governance mechanisms are involved? What strategic objectives are being advanced? When platforms claim neutrality, you can examine their material design, for instance the algorithms that curate visibility, the APIs that structure data access, the terms of service and community guidelines that regulate behaviour, and the monetisation policies that determine which kind of content their creators are allowed to monetise and which they are not. And when platforms seem inevitable, you can recall that they are systems designed by particular choices, pressures, and interests and that they could be designed differently, to reflect other values.

The study of platforms benefits not only from disciplinary expertise but also from openness to methodological experimentation. Across the field, scholars have combined digital methods, media analysis, ethnography, data science, sociology, and critical theory to make visible what platforms do: how they are built, how they govern, how they generate value, and how they impact everyday life. Much can be learned by studying the infrastructures, services, and policies that platforms produce, which shows that they are not only technical artefacts but also cultural and political texts.

Underlying this work is a deeper commitment: to take seriously the role of platforms *within* and *as* culture and society. This requires looking beyond platforms as neutral technologies or intermediaries and recognising them as powerful infrastructures that mould institutions, norms, imaginaries, and relationships. Platform studies must therefore attend to both the visible and the invisible; to what appears on screens and what lies beneath them; to the interfaces and the APIs, the partnerships, the algorithms that create user experience and infrastructural dependencies.

Looking ahead, the task for platform studies goes beyond keeping up with the rapid expansion, transformation, and evolution of platforms: it is to interrogate the values, visions, and power struggles that underpin them. Who benefits from platforms? Whose interests are encoded in their design? What forms of life and labour are made possible, or foreclosed, by their infrastructures? These are more than empirical questions, they are ethical and political ones.

As platforms continue to impose the terms of participation in digital society, the field must remain alert to subtle asymmetries in power, new sites of contestation, and the possibilities for reimagining how platforms could, and should, be organised. Our hope is that this book contributes to a growing field that is as empirical as it is imaginative, as critical as it is constructive. Platforms are now among the most powerful entities of our time. Understanding them is essential to critique what is and, even more importantly, to envision what could be.

Discussion questions

- **Dominant platforms and ecosystems**   Our vision of the future calls for expanding the research beyond dominant platforms, to include non–social media, regional, and public-sector platforms. How do political economy, governance, and strategy operate in non-social media and in regional or public-sector platforms, and what do these cases add to our understanding of platforms beyond American and Chinese tech giants?

- **Emerging platform formations** Our vision of the future highlights the (generative) AI platform shift. What unique infrastructural and ethical challenges emerge when large language and vision models become foundational layers and other services and sectors increasingly depend on them?
- **Platform histories** How can platform historiography and the study of discontinued or 'lost' alternative platforms – platform models that were abandoned or sidelined – inform the design of future platform models that would be more equitable, more accountable, and more open to different values or governance arrangements?

Further reading

van Dijck, J., van Es, K., Helmond, A., and van der Vlist, F. N. (2025) *Governing the Digital Society: Platforms, Artificial Intelligence, and Public Values.* Amsterdam University Press.

Steinberg, M., Mukherjee, R. and Punathambekar, A. (2022) Media power in digital Asia: Super apps and megacorps. *Media, Culture & Society* 44(8): 1405–1419. DOI: 10.1177/01634437221127805.

Helmond, A. and van der Vlist, F. N. (2019) Social media and platform historiography: Challenges and opportunities. *TMG: Journal for Media History* 22(1): 6–34. DOI: 10.18146/tmg.434.

Glossary

This book introduces a set of key concepts central to the field of (critical) platform studies. Here we define a selection of these concepts and contextualise them with reference to the chapter or section in which they are discussed. Where relevant, concepts and readings associated with the concept under discussion are cross-referenced.

API: application programming interface   A set of tools and protocols that allow developers to access a platform's data or functionality. APIs make platforms programmable and extensible, supporting third-party innovation while they maintain platform control. They are central to platformisation and function as governance mechanisms by regulating data access and creating dependencies across ecosystems.
Main discussion: pp. 146–7.
Cross-references: see also ecosystem; ecosystem resources.
Further reading: Bucher, 2013b; Helmond, 2015a; Puschmann and Burgess, 2014; van der Vlist et al., 2022.

Conglomeration   The process by which platform companies expand their operations across multiple sectors through acquisitions, diversification, or service bundling. This cross-sector expansion allows platforms to leverage shared data, infrastructure, and ecosystem resources so as to consolidate strategic control, which gives rise to new types of platform formations such as super apps and digital conglomerates.

Main discussion: pp. 99–100.

Cross-references: see also financialisation.

Further reading: Srnicek, 2016, 2024; van der Vlist, Helmond, Dieter et al., 2025.

Convening The strategic act of assembling diverse actors into a platform's ecosystem, around a shared vision or strategy. Platforms exercise convening power by setting the stage: they attract participation (from users, complementors) through influence, incentives, infrastructure, and strategic vision, drawing entire sectors into their orbit and prefiguring how futures are imagined and enacted.

Main discussion: pp. 114–15.

Cross-references: see also orchestration.

Further reading: Egliston and Carter, 2022; Helmond et al., 2019; van der Vlist, Helmond, Luitse et al., 2025.

Datafication The process by which a platform turns human behaviour, interactions, or processes into quantifiable digital data. Datafication underpins surveillance-based platform business models and enables predictive analytics, personalisation, and monetisation.

Main discussion: p. 88.

Further reading: Birch and Cochrane, 2021; Crain, 2021; van Dijck et al., 2018; van der Vlist and Helmond, 2021; Zuboff, 2019.

Ecosystem (platform ecosystem) A configuration of interdependent actors – users, developers, advertisers, partners, apps and services, infrastructures, and institutions – that co-evolve around a platform. This perspective emphasises relationality and mutual dependence. Technical ecosystems consist of apps and services built on top of a platform, while organisational ecosystems consist of the companies and organisations behind them. Platforms cultivate developer ecosystems to expand functionality, facilitate innovation, and embed themselves into domains. The ecosystem represents the platform's larger sphere of influence and the dependencies it cultivates.

Main discussion: pp. 34–7.

Cross-references: see also API; convening; ecosystem resources; evolution; platform; power.

Further reading: De Reuver et al., 2018; Jacobides et al., 2018; Tiwana, 2014; van der Vlist, 2022; van Dijck, 2013.

Ecosystem resources The technical, organisational, and financial tools that platforms provide to attract, support, and govern third-party actors. Building on the concept of platform boundary resources, ecosystem resources include APIs, SDKs, interfaces, policy guidelines, analytics dashboards, monetisation tools, developer forums, and partner programs. Ecosystem resources regulate access and structure external contributions in line with the platform's strategic goals.

Main discussion: pp. 40–1.

Cross-references: see also API; ecosystem.

Further reading: Ghazawneh and Henfridsson, 2013; Helmond and van der Vlist, 2019; Helmond et al., 2019; van der Vlist, 2022.

Evolution (platform evolution) The ongoing transformation of platforms as they adapt, expand, and reorganise diachronically. Platform evolution involves technical and design changes, strategic shifts, and entry into new domains; it is driven by both internal goals and external pressures. Platform evolution is typically incremental and can be empirically traced through (archived) ecosystem resources.

Main discussion: pp. 105–7.

Cross-references: see also ecosystem; ecosystem resources; platform.

Further reading: Helmond et al., 2019; Helmond and van der Vlist, 2019; Nieborg and Helmond, 2019.

Financialisation The growing influence of financial markets, actors, and motives on platform strategies; it involves venture capital dynamics, acquisitions, and speculative investments.

Main discussion: p. 101.

Cross-references: see also conglomeration.

Further reading: Jia and Winseck, 2018; Klinge et al., 2022.

Governance (platform governance) The manner in which platforms govern and the manner in which they are governed. Internal governance refers to platforms' designing and enforcing their own rules, for instance terms of service, content moderation, data access controls, and algorithmic systems. External governance through regulation refers to pressures from states, regulators, civil society, and other actors to steer platforms' operations. Platform governance is tiered, layered, and asymmetrical: different user groups face different rules, enforcement mechanisms, and transparency across the platform's multiple facets or sides.

Main discussion: chapter 4, passim.

Cross-references: see also political economy; power.

Further reading: Gillespie, 2018a; 2018b; Gorwa, 2019; 2024; Klonick, 2018.

Infrastructuralisation The process by which platforms evolve into the essential infrastructure upon which other actors, services, and sectors come to depend. It describes how platforms embed themselves as indispensable intermediaries, creating conditions of participation and imposing their technical, business, and governance models.

Main discussion: pp. 93–8.

Cross-references: see also platformisation.

Further reading: Helmond et al., 2019; Plantin et al., 2018; van Dijck et al., 2018.

Layered architecture The understanding of platforms as multilevel systems composed of interfaces, APIs, databases, and algorithms, each with distinct governance dynamics and power relations. It is a core characteristic of digital platforms.

Main discussion: pp. 30–1.

Cross-references: see also materiality; multisided platform; programmability.

Further reading: Helmond and van der Vlist, 2019; van Dijck, 2021.

Materiality (platform materiality) The technical and infrastructural components of platforms – interfaces, features, APIs, and algorithms – that shape access, interaction, and governance. Platform materiality is dual: it refers both to these tangible elements and to the institutional, economic, and organisational conditions under which they are developed and maintained. It is a core characteristic of digital platforms.

Main discussion: pp. 31–2, 37–43.

Cross-references: see also layered architecture; multisided platform; programmability; technography.

Further reading: Helmond and van der Vlist, 2019.

Multisided platform A platform facilitating interactions between two or more distinct user groups (e.g. buyers and sellers, riders and drivers). The value of the platform and of its broader ecosystem arises from cross-group network effects. Being multisided is a core characteristic of digital platforms.

Main discussion: pp. 30, 43–4.

Cross-references: see also layered architecture; materiality; programmability; user.

Further reading: Evans and Schmalensee, 2016; Rochet and Tirole, 2003.

Orchestration The strategic coordination of relationships, resources, and activities within a platform ecosystem. Platforms orchestrate through APIs, policies, and infrastructures to manage access and align third parties with their goals. This key mechanism of platform power enables scalability, integration, and the shaping of stakeholder behaviour.

Main discussion: pp. 103–4.

Cross-references: see also convening.

Further reading: Tiwana, 2014; van der Vlist et al., 2022.

Platform A programmable digital infrastructure that facilitates and governs interactions between different actors through code, policy, and design. Platforms are simultaneously services, companies, and technologies or infrastructures. They are not standalone entities but socio-technical systems embedded in broader ecosystems of users, services, and institutions. They are powerful convenors and shapers of online and offline life. Platform studies is the field that critically examines their role in culture and society.

Main discussion: chapter 1, passim.

Cross-references: see also ecosystem; evolution; platformisation; socio-technical system.

Further reading: Helmond and van der Vlist, 2019; Poell et al., 2021; Srnicek, 2016; van Dijck et al., 2018.

Platformisation   The process by which digital platforms expand and intregrate their infrastructural and economic logics into new domains. Platformisation refers to the fact that social, economic, cultural, and institutional practices become increasingly mediated and structured through platform mechanisms, fundamentally restructuring industries, institutions, and everyday life.
   Main discussion: p. 93.
   Cross-references: see also infrastructuralisation; platform.
   Further reading: Helmond, 2015a; Helmond and van der Vlist, 2024; Poell et al., 2021; van Dijck et al., 2018.

Political economy   An analytical approach that examines how economic systems, power relations, and political institutions are intertwined. In critical platform studies, it centres on how platforms generate, capture, and distribute value; how profit motives determine their design, strategies, and governance; and how power is accumulated and exercised across markets, infrastructures, and institutions.
   Main discussion: pp. 73–6.
   Cross-references: see also governance; power.
   Further reading: Hardy, 2014; Mosco, 2009 [1996]; Narayan, 2024; Poell et al., 2021; Srnicek, 2016.

Power (platform power)   A platform's capacity to shape and control interactions, access, and outcomes across its ecosystem. It is multidimensional, encompassing economic power (e.g. market dominance), infrastructural power (e.g. control over data and APIs), and governance power (e.g. rulemaking and enforcement). Platform power operates through technical design, interfaces, policies, and infrastructures. It is relational, shaped by the dependencies of those who rely on the platform.
   Main discussion: pp. 62–3, 76–8, 108–12.
   Cross-references: see also convening; ecosystem; governance; political economy.
   Further reading: Nieborg and Poell, 2025; Nielsen and Ganter, 2022; van der Vlist and Helmond, 2021.

Programmability   A platform's capacity to enable third parties to build applications and services through its technical architecture, typically using tools such as APIs and SDKs. It supports external innovation, enables expansion into new domains, and underpins the cultivation of ecosystems. Programmability is central to platformisation, as it drives platforms' extensibility, scalability, and integration into other domains. It is a core characteristic of digital platforms.

Main discussion: pp. 30–1, 46–7, 50–2.

Cross-references: see also API; ecosystem; layered architecture; materiality; multisided platform; platformisation.

Further reading: Bogost and Montfort, 2009; Helmond, 2015a; Gerlitz, Helmond, van der Vlist et al., 2019.

Socio-technical system   A system composed of social elements (people, norms, institutions) and technical parts (software, infrastructure, algorithms) that mutually co-constitute each other. Platforms operate as socio-technical systems that influence and are influenced by culture and society.

Main discussion: pp. 32–3.

Cross-references: see also platform.

Further reading: Bijker et al., 2012 [1987]; van Dijck, 2013; van der Vlist, 2022.

Technography   A methodological approach for studying platforms through the materials they produce: interfaces, platform documentation, policies, and APIs. It critically analyses how technical systems are configured, governed, and used.

Main discussion: pp. 41–2.

Cross-references: see also materiality.

Further reading: Bucher, 2012; Burkhardt and Rieder, 2024; Helmond and van der Vlist, 2019; Luitse, 2024; Mackenzie, 2018; van der Vlist et al., 2022; van der Vlist et al., 2024.

User   A general term for any actor in a platform ecosystem. In multisided platforms, users span different sides or facets – such as advertisers, developers, creators, and institutions. These are often called complementors. Each side interacts with the platform through specific interfaces, affordances, and rules. 'End user' refers to the consumer side. Attracting and managing different users or sides is central to platform strategy and evolution.

Main discussion: p. 35.

Cross-references: see also multisided platform.

Further reading: Evans and Schmalensee, 2016; Helmond and van der Vlist, 2019; Helmond et al., 2019.

Notes

Note to Chapter 2

1 While not all platforms are for profit – there are also public, non-profit, and cooperative initiatives – this book, like much of the existing literature, primarily focuses on commercial platforms. This is due to their dominant role for digital economies, infrastructures, and governance.

Notes to Chapter 3

1 This list focuses on publicly listed firms that are open to investment and tracked through major stock indices. There are also privately held platform companies such as xAI, Elon Musk's AI company (which now owns X), as well as firms that operate in more specialised or opaque domains, for example defence-focused technology companies like Palantir and Anduril. While some of these firms are publicly traded, their operations and finances often remain less transparent because of the nature of their clients, contracts, and security restrictions.
2 ByteDance, the parent company of TikTok, has recently emerged as a major player in China's digital landscape, effectively replacing Baidu as the 'B' in the once dominant BATX acronym.
3 Relevant European initiatives, resources, datasets, and research and visualisation tools include: (1) App Studies Initiative. ASI Resources. https://appstudies.org/asi-resources; (2) Digital Methods Initiative. Digital Methods Initiative Tool Archive.

https://tools.digitalmethods.net; (3) Public Data Lab. https://publicdatalab.org; (4) DensityDesign, Calibro, and Inmagik. RAWGraphs. https://www.rawgraphs.io; (5) Gephi: The Open Graph Viz Platform. https://gephi.org.

4 In classical economic terms, conglomerate often designates a firm that owns multiple subsidiary businesses that operate in distinct sectors; while these subsidiaries often maintain operational autonomy, they remain strategically and financially tethered to the parent company. By contrast, most of the major platform firms – for example Alphabet, Meta, or Amazon – operate as tightly managed, integrated corporate groups. However, following critical political economy and media industry studies, we use conglomeration more broadly, to capture the strategic expansion of platform firms across sectors and value chains, and their integration of diverse services, infrastructures, and data assets under a unified corporate and technical architecture. In this sense, conglomeration highlights how platforms consolidate control across multiple domains while maintaining the appearance of diverse, interconnected services and/or subsidiaries.

Note to Chapter 5

1 Apple's 2008 marketing slogan for the new iPhone – 'There's an app for that' – was used not only to promote the device but also to encourage the proliferation of iOS mobile apps and to attract developers into its ecosystem (Dieter et al., 2019). It thus offers a clear example of a convening strategy.

References

The references included in this book, listed below, are openly available in a public Zotero Group Library, at https://www.zotero .org/groups/5475737/platforms_polity.

Alaimo, C., Kallinikos, J., and Valderrama, E. (2020) Platforms as service ecosystems: Lessons from social media. *Journal of Information Technology* 35(1): 25–48. DOI: 10.1177/0268396219881462.

Airbnb (n.d.) Our community standards. https://www.airbnb.ie /help/article/3328.

AlignPay (n.d.) Home. https://alignpay.com.

Amazon News (2024) Amazon and the Digital Markets Act. Amazon, 7 March. https://www.aboutamazon.eu/news/policy /amazon-and-the-digital-markets-act.

Amazon Press Center (2002) Amazon.com launches Web Services – Developers can now incorporate Amazon.com content and features into their own web sites – Extends 'welcome mat' for developers. Amazon US Press Center, 16 July. https://press .aboutamazon.com/2002/7/amazon-com-launches-web-services -developers-can-now-incorporate-amazon-com-content-and -features-into-their-own-web-sites-extends-welcome-mat-for -developers.

Andreessen, M. (2007) The three kinds of platforms you meet on the internet. PMarchive, 16 September. https://pmarchive.com /three_kinds_of_platforms_you_meet_on_the_internet.html.

Andreessen, M. (2011) Why software 6is eating the world. *Wall Street Journal*, 20 August. https://www.wsj.com/articles/SB1000 14240531119034809045765122509156 29460.

Annabell, T., Aade, L., and Goanta, C. (2024) (Un)disclosed brand partnerships: How platform policies and interfaces shape commercial content for influencers. *Internet Policy Review* 13(4). DOI: 10.14763/2024.4.1814.

Apperley, T. and Parikka, J. (2018) Platform studies' epistemic threshold. *Games and Culture* 13(4): 349–69. DOI: 10.1177/1555412015616509.

Aradau, C. and Blanke, T. (2022) *Algorithmic Reason: The New Government of Self and Other*. Oxford University Press.

Archer, M., Ravn, L., and Thylstrup, N. B. (2025) The political economy of platformed silos: Theorizing data storage reconfigurations in the age of interoperability capitalism. *Big Data & Society* 12(2). DOI: 10.1177/20539517241303144.

Are, C. (2025) Flagging as a silencing tool: Exploring the relationship between de-platforming of sex and online abuse on Instagram and TikTok. *New Media & Society* 27(6): 3577–95. DOI: 10.1177/14614448241228544.

Arora, P. (2019) *The Next Billion Users: Digital Life beyond the West*. Harvard University Press.

Athique, A. (2019) Digital emporiums: Platform capitalism in India. *Media Industries Journal* 6(2): 67–87. DOI: 10.3998/mij.15031809.0006.205.

Baldwin, C. Y. and Woodard, C. J. (2009) The architecture of platforms: A unified view. In A. Gawer (ed.), *Platforms, Markets and Innovation*. Edward Elgar.

Bank, M., Duffy, F., Leyendecker, V. et al. (2021) *The Lobby Network: Big Tech's Web of Influence in the EU* [report]. Corporate Europe Observatory and LobbyControl.

Bareis, J. and Katzenbach, C. (2022) Talking AI into being: The narratives and imaginaries of national AI strategies and their performative politics. *Science, Technology, & Human Values* 47(5): 855–81. DOI: 10.1177/01622439211030007.

Bates, J., Lin Y.-W., and Goodale, P. (2016) Data journeys: Capturing the socio-material constitution of data objects and flows. *Big Data & Society* 3(2). DOI: 10.1177/2053951716654502.

Bijker, W. E., Hughes, T. P., and Pinch, T. J., eds (2012) *The Social Construction of Technological Systems: New Directions in the Sociology and History of Technology* (anniversary edn). MIT Press.

Bijker, W. E., and Law, J., eds (1994) *Shaping Technology/Building Society: Studies in Sociotechnical Change*. MIT Press.

Birch, K. (2023) *Data Enclaves*. Springer Nature.

Birch, K. and Cochrane, D. T. (2022) Big tech: Four emerging forms of digital rentiership. *Science as Culture* 31(1): 44–58. DOI: 10.1080/09505431.2021.1932794.

Blanke, T. and Pybus, J. (2020) The material conditions of platforms: Monopolization through decentralization. *Social Media + Society* 6(4). DOI: 10.1177/2056305120971632.

Bobrowsky, M. (2025) Zuckerberg's grand vision: Most of your friends will be AI. *Wall Street Journal*, 7 May. https://www.wsj.com/tech/ai/mark-zuckerberg-ai-digital-future-0bb04de7.

Bogost, I. and Montfort, N. (2009) Platform studies: Frequently questioned answers. In D. M. Chun, A. Silver, and C. Bazerman (eds), *Digital Arts and Culture 2009: After Media: Embodiment and context*. University of California, Irvine.

Borra, E. and Rieder, B. (2014) Programmed method: Developing a toolset for capturing and analyzing tweets. *Aslib Journal of Information Management* 66(3): 262–78. DOI: 10.1108/AJIM-09-2013-0094.

Bowker, G. C. and Star, S. L. (1999) *Sorting Things Out: Classification and Its Consequences*. MIT Press.

Bradford, A. (2023) *Digital Empires: The Global Battle to Regulate Technology*. Oxford University Press.

Brock, A. (2020) *Distributed Blackness: African American Cybercultures*. New York University Press.

Bruns, A. (2008) *Blogs, Wikipedia, Second Life, and Beyond: From Production to Produsage*. Peter Lang.

Bruns, A. (2019) After the 'APIcalypse': Social media platforms and their fight against critical scholarly research. *Information, Communication & Society* 22(11): 1544–66. DOI: 10.1080/1369118X.2019.1637447.

Bruns, A. and Burgess, J. (2015) Twitter hashtags from ad hoc to calculated publics. In N. Rambukkana (ed.), *Hashtag Publics: The Power and Politics of Discursive Networks*. Peter Lang.

Bucher, T. (2012) *Programmed Sociality: A Software Studies Perspective on Social Networking Sites*. PhD thesis, University of Copenhagen.

Bucher, T. (2013a) The friendship assemblage: Investigating programmed sociality on Facebook. *Television & New Media* 14(6): 479–93. DOI: 10.1177/1527476412452800.

Bucher, T. (2013b) Objects of intense feeling: The case of the Twitter API. *Computational Culture* (3), 16 November. http://computationalculture.net/objects-of-intense-feeling-the-case-of-the-twitter-api.

Bucher, T. and Helmond, A. (2017) The affordances of social media platforms. In J. Burgess, A. Marwick, and T. Poell (eds), *The SAGE Handbook of Social Media*, pp. 233–53. SAGE.

Burgess, J. (2021) Platform studies. In S. Cunningham and D. Craig (eds), *Creator Culture: An Introduction to Global Social Media Entertainment*, pp. 21–38. New York University Press.

Burgess, J. and Baym, N. K. (2020) *Twitter: A Biography*. New York University Press.

Burgess, J. and Green, J. (2018) *YouTube: Online Video and Participatory Culture* (2nd edn). Polity.

Burkhardt, S. and Rieder, B. (2024) Foundation models are platform models: Prompting and the political economy of AI. *Big Data & Society* 11(2). DOI: 10.1177/20539517241247839.

Çalışkan, K., MacKenzie, D., and Callon, M. (2025) Stacked economization: A research program for the study of platforms. *Journal of Cultural Economy* 18(2): 304–31. DOI: 10.1080/17530350.2024.2423687.

Callon, M. (2021) *Markets in the Making: Rethinking Competition, Goods, and Innovation*, translated by O. Custer. Zone Books.

Caplan, R. and Gillespie, T. (2020) Tiered governance and demonetization: The shifting terms of labor and compensation in the platform economy. *Social Media + Society* 6(2). DOI: 10.1177/2056305120936636.

Carter, M. and Egliston, B. (2024) *Fantasies of Virtual Reality: Untangling Fiction, Fact, and Threat*. MIT Press.

Chayka, K. (2025) Mark Zuckerberg says social media is over. *New Yorker*, 23 April. https://www.newyorker.com/culture/infinite -scroll/mark-zuckerberg-says-social-media-is-over.

Chen, J., van Doorn, N., Grohmann, R. et al. (2024) Introducing *Platforms & Society*. *Platforms & Society* 1. DOI: 10.1177/29768624241235492.

Chen, J. Y. (2020) Thrown under the bus and outrunning it! The logic of Didi and taxi drivers' labour and activism in the on-demand economy. *New Media & Society* 20(8): 2691–711. DOI: 10.1177/1461444817729149.

Chen, Y., Mao, Z., and Qiu, J. L. (2018) *Super-Sticky WeChat and Chinese Society*. Emerald.

Cohen, J. E. (2019) *Between Truth and Power: The Legal Constructions of Informational Capitalism*. Oxford University Press.

CompaniesMarketCap.com (n.d.) Companies ranked by market cap. https://companiesmarketcap.com.

Crain, M. (2021) *Profit Over Privacy: How Surveillance Advertising Conquered the Internet*. University of Minnesota Press.

Crawford, K. (2021) *Atlas of AI: Power, Politics, and the Planetary Costs of Artificial Intelligence*. Yale University Press.

Crawford, K. and Paglen, T. (2019) Excavating AI: The politics of images in machine learning training sets. https://excavating.ai. Republished in 2001 in *AI & Society* 36(2): 675–85.

Cusumano, M. A., Gawer, A., and Yoffie, D. B. (2019) *The Business of Platforms: Strategy in the Age of Digital Competition, Innovation, and Power*. Harper Business.

Davis, M. and Xiao, J. (2021) De-westernizing platform studies: History and logics of Chinese and US platforms. *International Journal of Communication* 15(0): 103–22.

de Reuver, M., Sørensen, C., and Basole, R. C. (2018) The digital platform: A research agenda. *Journal of Information Technology* 33(2): 124–35. DOI: 10.1057/s41265-016-0033-3.

Dieter, M., Gerlitz, C., Helmond, A., Tkacz, N., van der Vlist, F. N., and Weltevrede, E. (2019) Multi-situated app studies: Methods and propositions. *Social Media + Society* 5(2). DOI: 10.1177/2056305119846486.

Dieter, M., Helmond, A., Tkacz, N., van der Vlist, F. N., and Weltevrede, E. (2021) Pandemic platform governance: Mapping the global ecosystem of COVID-19 response apps. *Internet Policy Review* 10(3). DOI: 10.14763/2021.3.1568.

Dror, Y. (2015) 'We are not here for the money': Founders' manifestos. *New Media & Society* 17(4): 540–55. DOI: 10.1177/1461444813506974.

Duguay, S. (2019) You can't use this app for that: Exploring off-label use through an investigation of Tinder. *Information Society* 36(1): 30–42. DOI: 10.1080/01972243.2019.1685036.

Duguay, S., Burgess, J., and Suzor, N. (2020) Queer women's experiences of patchwork platform governance on Tinder, Instagram, and Vine. *Convergence* 26(2): 237–52. DOI: 10.1177/1354856518781530.

Duguay, S. and Gold-Apel, H. (2023) Stumbling blocks and alternative paths: Reconsidering the walkthrough method for analyzing apps. *Social Media + Society* 9(1): 1–10. DOI: 10.1177/20563051231158822.

Dyer-Witheford, N., Kjøsen, A. M., and Steinhoff, J. (2019) *Inhuman Power: Artificial Intelligence and the Future of Capitalism*. Pluto Press.

Egliston, B. and Carter, M. (2022) 'The metaverse and how we'll build it': The political economy of Meta's Reality Labs. *New Media & Society* 26(8): 4336–60. DOI: 10.1177/14614448221119785.

European Commission (2024) Commission opens formal proceedings against TikTok under DSA. https://ec.europa.eu/commission/presscorner/detail/en/ip_24_6487.

European Commission (2025) Commission finds Apple and Meta in breach of the Digital Markets Act. https://digital-strategy

.ec.europa.eu/en/news/commission-finds-apple-and-meta-breach -digital-markets-act.

Evans, D. S., Hagiu, A., and Schmalensee, R. (2006) *Invisible Engines: How Software Platforms Drive Innovation and Transform Industries*. MIT Press.

Evans, D. S. and Schmalensee, R. (2016) *Matchmakers: The New Economics of Multisided Platforms*. HBR Press.

Ferrari, F. (2024) State roles in platform governance: AI's regulatory geographies. *Competition & Change* 28(2): 340–58. DOI: 10.1177/10245294231218335.

Flensburg, S. and Lai, S. S. (2023) Follow the data! A strategy for tracing infrastructural power. *Media and Communication* 11(2): 319–29. DOI: 10.17645/mac.v11i2.6464.

Flew, T. (2021) *Regulating Platforms*. Polity.

FTC (2019) FTC imposes $5 billion penalty and sweeping new privacy restrictions on Facebook. *Federal Trade Commission*, 24 July. https://www.ftc.gov/news-events/news/press-releases /2019/07/ftc-imposes-5-billion-penalty-sweeping-new-privacy -restrictions-facebook.

Fuchs, C. (2021) *Social Media: A Critical Introduction* (3rd edn). SAGE.

Fuller, M., ed. (2008) *Software Studies: A Lexicon*. MIT Press.

Gab (n.d.) About Gab. https://gab.com/about.

Gawer, A. (2021) Digital platforms' boundaries: The interplay of firm scope, platform sides, and digital interfaces. *Long Range Planning* 54(5): 102045. DOI: 10.1016/j.lrp.2020.102045.

Gehl, R. W. (2025) *Move Slowly and Build Bridges: Mastodon, the Fediverse, and the Struggle for Democratic Social Media*. Oxford University Press.

Gerbrandy, A. and Phoa, P. (2022) The power of big tech corporations as modern bigness and a vocabulary for shaping competition law as counter-power. In H. Brouwer, M. Bennett, and A. Gerbrandy (eds), *Wealth and Power: Philosophical Perspectives*, pp. 166–85. Routledge.

Gerlitz, C. and Helmond, A. (2013) The like economy: Social buttons and the data-intensive Web. *New Media & Society* 15(8): 1348–65. DOI: 10.1177/1461444812472322.

Gerlitz, C., Helmond, A., Nieborg, D. B., and van der Vlist, F. N. (2019) Apps and infrastructures: A research agenda. *Computational Culture* (7). http://computationalculture.net/apps -and-infrastructures-a-research-agenda.

Gerlitz, C., Helmond, A., van der Vlist, F. N., and Weltevrede, E. (2019) Regramming the platform: infrastructural relations Between apps and social media. *Computational Culture* (7). http://computationalculture.net/regramming-the-platform.

Ghazawneh, A. and Henfridsson, O. (2013) Balancing platform control and external contribution in third-party development: The boundary resources model. *Information Systems Journal* 23(2): 173–92. DOI: 10.1111/j.1365-2575.2012.00406.x.

Gillespie, T. (2010) The politics of 'platforms'. *New Media & Society* 12(3): 347–64. DOI: 10.1177/1461444809342738.

Gillespie, T. (2018a) *Custodians of the Internet: Platforms, Content Moderation, and the Hidden Decisions That Shape Social Media.* Yale University Press.

Gillespie, T. (2018b) Regulation of and by platforms. In J. Burgess, A. Marwick, and T. Poell (eds), *The SAGE Handbook of Social Media,* pp. 254–78. SAGE.

Gillespie, T. (2024) Generative, A. I. and the politics of visibility. *Big Data & Society* 11(2). DOI: 10.1177/20539517241252131.

Gojek (n.d.) Gojek community guidelines. https://www.gojek.com/en-id/help/akun/panduan-layanan.

Goldman, J. (2024) Global ad spending to hit $1 trillion milestone in 2024, says GroupM forecast. *eMarketer,* 9 December. https://www.emarketer.com/content/global-ad-spending-hit-1-trillion-milestone-2024-says-groupm-forecast.

Gorwa, R. (2019) What is platform governance? *Information, Communication & Society* 22(6): 854–71. DOI: 10.1080/1369118X.2019.1573914.

Gorwa, R. (2024) *The Politics of Platform Regulation: How Governments Shape Online Content Moderation.* Oxford University Press.

Gorwa, R., Binns, R., and Katzenbach, C. (2020) Algorithmic content moderation: Technical and political challenges in the automation of platform governance. *Big Data & Society* 7(1). DOI: 10.1177/2053951719897945.

Grohmann, R., Pereira, G., Guerra, A. et al. (2022) Platform scams: Brazilian workers' experiences of dishonest and uncertain algorithmic management. *New Media & Society* 24(7): 1611–31. DOI: 10.1177/14614448221099225.

Gustavsson, N. (2019) Views from the cloud: A history of Spotify's journey to the cloud, Part 1. *Spotify Engineering,* 9 December. https://engineering.atspotify.com/2019/12/views-from-the-cloud-a-history-of-spotifys-journey-to-the-cloud-part-1-2.

Hardy, J. (2014) *Critical Political Economy of the Media: An Introduction.* Routledge.

Hartley, J. M., Petre, C., Bengtsson, M. et al. (2023) Autonomies and dependencies: Shifting configurations of power in the platformization of news. *Digital Journalism* 11(8): 1375–90. DOI: 10.1080/21670811.2023.2257759.

Helmond, A. (2015a) The platformization of the web: Making web data platform ready. *Social Media + Society* 1(2). DOI: 10.1177/2056305115603080.

Helmond, A. (2015b) *The Web as Platform: Data Flows in Social Media*. PhD thesis, University of Amsterdam. https://hdl.handle.net/11245/1.485895.

Helmond, A., Nieborg, D. B., and van der Vlist, F. N. (2019) Facebook's evolution: development of a platform-as-infrastructure. *Internet Histories* 3(2): 123–46. DOI: 10.1080/24701475.2019.1593667.

Helmond, A. and van der Vlist, F. N. (2019) Social media and platform historiography: Challenges and opportunities. *TMG: Journal for Media History* 22(1): 6–34. DOI: 10.18146/tmg.434.

Helmond, A. and van der Vlist, F. N. (2021) Platform and app histories: Assessing source availability in web archives and app repositories. In D. Gomes et al. (eds), *The Past Web: Exploring Web Archives*, pp. 203–14. Springer International.

Helmond, A. and van der Vlist, F. N. (2023) Situating the marketization of data. In K. van Es and N. Verhoeff (eds), *Situating Data: Inquiries in Algorithmic Culture*, pp. 279–86. Amsterdam University Press.

Helmond, A. and van der Vlist, F. N. (2024) Platform: A tapestry of meanings and metaphors. In J. Farkas and M. Maloney (eds), *Routledge Anthology of Digital Media Metaphors*, pp. 24–38. Routledge.

Helmond, A., van der Vlist, F. N., Weltevrede E., et al. (2019) App (Store) Policy Histories. DMI Wiki, 12 July. https://wiki.digitalmethods.net/Dmi/SummerSchool2019AppStorePolicyHistories

Helmond, A., Weltevrede, E., Dieter, M. et al. (2022) (Super) apps evolution. DMI Wiki, 31 January. https://www.digitalmethods.net/Dmi/WinterSchool2022MobileAppsAndTheirPlatformDependenciesEvolutionSuperApps.

Highfield, T. (2022) How to select appropriate online methodologies. In K. Miltner (ed.), *Doing Research Online*, n.p. SAGE.

Hind, S., Kanderske, M., and van der Vlist, F. N. (2022) Making the car 'platform ready': How Big Tech is driving the platformisation of automobility. *Social Media + Society* 8(2). DOI: 10.1177/20563051221098697.

Hind, S., van der Vlist, F. N., and Kanderske, M. (2025) Challenges as catalysts: How Waymo's Open Dataset Challenges shape AI development. *AI & Society* 40: 1667–83. DOI: 10.1007/s00146-024-01927-x.

Hoijtink, M. and Planqué-van Hardeveld, A. (2022) Machine

learning and the platformization of the military: A study of Google's machine learning platform TensorFlow. *International Political Sociology* 16(2). DOI: 10.1093/ips/olab036.

Jacobides, M. G., Cennamo, C., and Gawer, A. (2018) Towards a theory of ecosystems. *Strategic Management Journal* 39(8): 2255–76. DOI: 10.1002/smj.2904.

Jia, L. and Winseck, D. (2018) The political economy of Chinese internet companies: Financialization, concentration, and capitalization. *International Communication Gazette* 80(1): 30–59. DOI: 10.1177/1748048517742783.

Jin, D. Y. (2015) Digital Platforms, Imperialism and Political Culture. Routledge.

Joseph, D. and Bishop, S. (2024) Advertising as governance: The digital commodity audience and platform advertising dependency. *Media, Culture & Society* 46(6): 1269–86. DOI: 10.1177/01634437241237935.

Katzenbach, C., Kopps, A., Magalhães, J. C. et al. (2023) The platform governance archive v1 [dataset paper]. University of Bremen. https://media.suub.uni-bremen.de/handle/elib/7010.

Kaye, D. B. V., Chen, X., and Zeng, J. (2021) The co-evolution of two Chinese mobile short video apps: Parallel platformization of Douyin and TikTok. *Mobile Media & Communication* 9(2): 229–53. DOI: 10.1177/2050157920952120.

Kenney, M. and Zysman, J. (2020) The platform economy: Restructuring the space of capitalist accumulation. *Cambridge Journal of Regions, Economy and Society* 13(1): 55–76. DOI: 10.1093/cjres/rsaa001.

Kerssens, N. (2024) (Micro)soft power in Dutch public education: Making classrooms platform-ready through partner work. *Critical Studies in Education*. DOI: 10.1080/17508487.2024.2428808.

Kerssens, N. and van Dijck, J. (2021) The platformization of primary education in The Netherlands. *Learning, Media and Technology* 46(3): 250–63. DOI: 10.1080/17439884.2021.1876725.

Kim, J. and Ahn, S. (2025) The platform policy matrix: Promotion and regulation. *Policy & Internet* 17(1). DOI: 10.1002/poi3.414.

Kirschenbaum, M. G. (2007) *Mechanisms: New Media and the Forensic Imagination*. MIT Press.

Klinge, T. J., Hendrikse, R., Fernandez, R. et al. (2023) Augmenting digital monopolies: A corporate financialization perspective on the rise of Big Tech. *Competition & Change* 27(2): 332–53. DOI: 10.1177/10245294221105573.

Klonick, K. (2018) The new governors: The people, rules, and processes governing online speech. *Harvard Law Review* 131(6): 1598–670.

Kwok, D. and Murdoch, S. (2023) Beijing's regulatory crackdown wipes $1.1 trillion off Chinese big tech. *Reuters*, 12 July. https://www.reuters.com/technology/beijings-regulatory-crackdown-wipes-11-trln-off-chinese-big-tech-2023-07-12.

Langlois, G. and Elmer, G. (2013). The research politics of social media platforms. *Culture Machine* 14: 1–17.

Langlois, G. McKelvey, F. Elmer, G. et al. (2009). Mapping commercial web 2.0 worlds: Towards a new critical ontogenesis. *Fibreculture* 14. http://fourteen.fibreculturejournal.org/fcj-095-mapping-commercial-web-2-0-worlds-towards-a-new-critical-ontogenesis.

Latour, B. (2007) *Reassembling the Social: An Introduction to Actor–Network Theory*. Oxford University Press.

Leerssen, P. (2021) Platform research access in Article 31 of the Digital Services Act. In H. Sichtertraub, M. Straub, and E. Tuchtfeld (eds), *To Break Up or Regulate Big Tech? Avenues to Constrain Private Power in the DSA/DMA Package*, pp. 55–61. Max Planck Institute for Innovation and Competition.

Leerssen, P. (2023) An end to shadow banning? Transparency rights in the Digital Services Act between content moderation and curation. *Computer Law & Security Review* 48: 105790. DOI: 10.1016/j.clsr.2023.105790.

Light, B., Burgess, J., and Duguay, S. (2016) The walkthrough method: An approach to the study of apps. *New Media & Society* 20(3): 881–900. DOI: 10.1177/1461444816675438.

Lin, J., Yang Wang, W., and Sun, P. (2025). *Chinese Platforms: A Critical Introduction*. Polity.

Luitse, D. (2024) Platform power in AI: The evolution of cloud infrastructures in the political economy of artificial intelligence. *Internet Policy Review* 13(2). DOI: 10.14763/2024.2.1768.

Luitse, D., Blanke, T., and Poell, T. (2024) AI competitions as infrastructures of power in medical imaging. *Information, Communication & Society* 28(10): 1735–56. DOI: 10.1080/1369118x.2024.2334393.

Mac, R., Barnes, B., and Hsu, T. (2023) Advertisers flee X as outcry over Musk's endorsement of antisemitic post grows. *New York Times*, 17 November. https://www.nytimes.com/2023/11/17/technology/elon-musk-twitter-x-advertisers.html.

Mackenzie, A. (2018) From API to AI: Platforms and their opacities. *Information, Communication & Society* 22(13): 1989–2006. DOI: 10.1080/1369118X.2018.1476569.

MacKenzie, D. (2018) 'Making', 'taking' and the material political economy of algorithmic trading. *Economy and Society* 47(4): 501–23. DOI: 10.1080/03085147.2018.1528076.

MacKenzie, D. and Çalışkan, K. (2025) *Inside Digital Advertising: Platforms, Power, and Material Politics.* Polity.

MacKenzie, D. and Wajcman, J. eds (1999) *The Social Shaping of Technology* (2nd edn). Open University Press.

Manovich, L. (2001) *The Language of New Media.* MIT Press.

Mayer, M. and Lu, Y.-C. (2025) Global structures of digital dependence and the rise of technopoles. *New Political Economy* 30(5): 755–74. DOI: 10.1080/13563467.2025.2497766.

McGuigan, L. (2023) *Selling the American People: Advertising, Optimization, and the Origins of Adtech.* MIT Press.

McLuhan, M. (1994) *Understanding Media: The Extensions of Man.* MIT Press.

Merrill, J. B. (2020) Does Facebook still sell discriminatory ads? *The Markup*, 25 August. https://themarkup.org/the-breakdown/2020/08/25/does-facebook-still-sell-discriminatory-ads.

Meta (n.d.) The future of wearables. https://www.meta.com/emerging-tech/orion.

Meta Newsroom (2024) Meta's progress implementing the Digital Services Act. *Meta Newsroom*, 28 November. https://about.fb.com/news/2024/11/metas-progress-implementing-the-digital-services-act.

Mistral AI (2025) Mistral Compute. Mistral AI, 11 June. https://mistral.ai/news/mistral-compute.

Montfort, N. and Bogost, I. (2009) *Racing the Beam: The Atari Video Computer System.* MIT Press.

Morris, J. W. and Murray, S. eds (2018) *Appified: Culture in the Age of Apps.* University of Michigan Press.

Mosco, V. (2009) *The Political Economy of Communication* (2nd edn). SAGE.

Mukherjee, R. (2019) Jio sparks Disruption 2.0: Infrastructural imaginaries and platform ecosystems in 'Digital India'. *Media, Culture & Society* 41(2): 175–95. DOI: 10.1177/0163443718818383.

Myers West, S. (2019) Data capitalism: Redefining the logics of surveillance and privacy. *Business & Society* 58(1): 20–41. DOI: 10.1177/0007650317718185.

Napoli, P. and Caplan, R. (2017) Why media companies insist they're not media companies, why they're wrong, and why it matters. *First Monday* 22(5). DOI: 10.5210/fm.v22i5.7051.

Narayan, D. (2022) Platform capitalism and cloud infrastructure: Theorizing a hyper-scalable computing regime. *Environment and Planning A: Economy and Space* 54(5): 911–29. https://doi.org/10.1177/0308518X221094028.

Narayan, D. (2024) The political economy of digital

platforms: Key directions. *Platforms & Society* 1. DOI: 10.1177/29768624241263071.

Nieborg, D. B. and Helmond, A. (2019) The political economy of Facebook's platformization in the mobile ecosystem: Facebook Messenger as a platform instance. *Media, Culture & Society* 41(2): 196–218. DOI: 10.1177/0163443718818384.

Nieborg, D. B. and Poell, T. (2025) Analyzing institutional platform power: Evolving relations of dependence in the mobile digital advertising ecosystem. *New Media & Society* 27(4): 1909–27. DOI: 10.1177/14614448251314405.

Nieborg, D., Poell, T., Caplan, R. et al. (2024) Introduction to the special issue on Locating and theorising platform power. *Internet Policy Review* 13(2). DOI: 10.1177/14614448251314405.

Nielsen, R. K. and Ganter, S. A. (2022) *The Power of Platforms: Shaping Media and Society*. Oxford University Press.

Ó Fathaigh, R., Hoboken, J. van, and Eijk, N. van (2019) Mobile privacy and business-to-platform dependencies: An analysis of SEC disclosures. *Journal of Business & Technology Law* 14(1): 49–105.

O'Reilly, T. (2005) What is Web 2.0. O'Reilly Media, 30 September. https://www.oreilly.com/pub/a//web2/archive/what-is-web-20.html.

Ovide, S. (2021) How big tech won the pandemic. *New York Times*, 30 April. https://www.nytimes.com/2021/04/30/technology/big-tech-pandemic.html.

Papaevangelou, C. and Siapera, E. (2025) State, platform capitalism and infrastructural power: Microsoft's data centres in Greece 2.0. *Platforms & Society* 2. DOI: 10.1177/29768624251323325.

Parker, G. G., van Alstyne, M. W., and Choudary, S. P. (2016) *Platform Revolution*. W. W. Norton.

Partin, W. C. (2020) Bit by (Twitch) bit: "platform capture" and the evolution of digital platforms. *Social Media + Society* 6(3). DOI: 10.1177/2056305120933981.

Plantin, J.-C. and de Seta, G. (2019) WeChat as infrastructure: The techno-nationalist shaping of Chinese digital platforms. *Chinese Journal of Communication* 12(3): 257–73. DOI: 10.1080/17544750.2019.1572633.

Plantin, J.-C., Lagoze, C., Edwards, P. N. et al. (2018) Infrastructure studies meet platform studies in the age of Google and Facebook. *New Media & Society* 20(1): 293–310. DOI: 10.1177/1461444816661553.

Poell, T., Nieborg, D. B., and Duffy, B. E. (2021) *Platforms and Cultural Production*. Polity.

Poell, T., Nieborg, D. B., and Duffy, B. E. (2022) Spaces of negotiation:

Analyzing platform power in the news industry. *Digital Journalism* 11(8): 1391–409. DOI: 10.1080/21670811.2022.2103011.

Popiel, P. and Vasudevan, K. (2024) Platform frictions, platform power, and the politics of platformization. *Information, Communication & Society* 27(10): 1867–83. DOI: 10.1080/1369118X.2024.2361095.

Prey, R. (2020) Locating power in platformization: Music streaming playlists and curatorial power. *Social Media + Society* 6(2). DOI: 10.1177/2056305120933291.

Prins, C., Sheikh, H., Schrijvers, E. K. et al. (2021) *Opgave AI: De nieuwe systeemtechnologie* [Mission AI: The new system technolgy] [policy report]. Scientific Council for Government Policy, 11 November. https://www.wrr.nl/publicaties/rapporten /2021/11/11/opgave-ai-de-nieuwe-systeemtechnologie.

Puschmann, C. and Burgess, J. (2014) The politics of Twitter data. In K. Weller et al. (eds), *Twitter and Society*, pp. 43–54. Peter Lang.

Pybus, J. and Coté, M. (2024) Super SDKs: Tracking personal data and platform monopolies in the mobile. *Big Data & Society* 11(1). DOI: 10.1177/20539517241231270.

Richter, F. (2025) Infographic: Amazon and Microsoft stay ahead in global cloud market. *Statista Daily Data*, 27 February. https://www.statista.com/chart/18819/worldwide-market-share -of-leading-cloud-infrastructure-service-providers.

Richter, V., Katzenbach, C. and Schäfer, M. S. (2023) Imaginaries of artificial intelligence. In S. Lindgren (ed.), *Handbook of Critical Studies of Artificial Intelligence*, pp. 209–23. Edward Elgar.

Rikap, C. (2024) Dynamics of corporate governance beyond ownership in AI. *Common Wealth*, 15 May. https://www .common-wealth.org/publications/dynamics-of-corporate -governance-beyond-ownership-in-ai.

Rikap, C. (2026) *The Rulers: Corporate Power in the Age of AI and the Cloud*. Verso.

Roberts, S. T. (2019) *Behind the Screen: Content Moderation in the Shadows of Social Media*. Yale University Press.

Rochet, J.-C. and Tirole, J. (2003) Platform competition in two-sided markets. *Journal of the European Economic Association* 1(4): 990–1029. DOI: 10.1162/154247603322493212.

Rogers, R. (2013) *Digital Methods*. MIT Press.

Rogers, R. (2020) Deplatforming: Following extreme internet celebrities to Telegram and alternative social media. *European Journal of Communication* 35(3): 213–29. DOI: 10.1177/0267323120922066.

Rogers, R. (2023a) Algorithmic probing: Prompting offensive

Google results and their moderation. *Big Data & Society* 10(1). DOI: 10.1177/20539517231176228.

Rogers, R. (ed.), (2023b) *The Propagation of Misinformation in Social Media: A Cross-Platform Analysis*. Amsterdam University Press.

Rogers, R. (2024) *Doing Digital Methods* (2nd edn). SAGE.

Rosenblat, A. and Stark, L. (2016) Algorithmic labor and information asymmetries: A case study of Uber's drivers. *International Journal of Communication* 10: 3758–84.

Rumble (n.d.) Rumble: The freedom-first technology platform™. https://corp.rumble.com.

Sandberg, S. (2019) Doing more to protect against discrimination in housing, employment and credit advertising. *Meta Newsroom*, 19 March. https://about.fb.com/news/2019/03/protecting-against -discrimination-in-ads.

Scharlach, R., Hallinan, B., and Shifman, L. (2023) Governing principles: Articulating values in social media platform policies. *New Media & Society* 26(11): 6658–77. DOI: 10.1177/14614448231156580.

Schreieck, M., Hein, A., Wiesche, M. et al. (2018) The challenge of governing digital platform ecosystems. In C. Linnhoff-Popien, R. Schneider, and M. Zaddach (eds), *Digital Marketplaces Unleashed*, pp. 527–38. Springer Nature.

Silva, M., van Teeffelen, J., and Çavuş, Ç. (2025) Big Tech acquires a new company every 11 days. Centre for Research on Multinational Corporations (SOMO), 15 April. https://www .somo.nl/big-tech-acquires-a-new-company-every-11-days.

Simon, F. M. (2022) Uneasy bedfellows: AI in the news, platform companies and the issue of journalistic autonomy. *Digital Journalism* 10(10): 1832–54. DOI: 10.1080/21670811.2022.2063150.

Singh, J. (2025) Google partners with Ambani's Reliance to offer free AI Pro access to millions of Jio users in India. *TechCrunch*, 30 October. https://techcrunch.com/2025/10/30/google-partners -with-ambanis-reliance-to-offer-free-ai-pro-access-to-millions-of -jio-users-in-india.

Smialek, J. and Satariano, A. (2025) Trump wants Europe to stop regulating Big Tech: Will it bend? *New York Times*, 26 August. https://www.nytimes.com/2025/08/26/business/trump -technology-european-union-tariffs.html.

Smythe, D. W. (2012) On the audience commodity and its work. In M. G. Durham and D. Kellner (eds), *Media and Cultural Studies: Keyworks* (2nd edn), pp. 320–56. Wiley Blackwell.

Srnicek, N. (2016) *Platform Capitalism*. Polity.

Srnicek, N. (2024) The new conglomerates. *Platforms & Society* 1. DOI: 10.1177/29768624241255309.

Steinberg, M. (2019) *The Platform Economy: How Japan Transformed the Consumer Internet*. University of Minnesota Press.

Steinberg, M. (2021) From automobile capitalism to platform capitalism: Toyotism as a prehistory of digital platforms. *Organization Studies* 43(7): 1069–90. DOI: 10.1177/01708406211030681.

Steinberg, M., Mukherjee, R., and Punathambekar, A. (2022) Media power in digital Asia: Super apps and megacorps. *Media, Culture & Society* 44(8): 1405–19. DOI: 10.1177/01634437221127805.

Thompson, B. (2017) Defining aggregators. Stratechery, 26 September. https://stratechery.com/2017/defining-aggregators.

TikTok (2023) Onze naleving van de Digital Services Act [Our compliance with the Digital Services Act] [press release]. TikTok Newsroom, 23 August. https://newsroom.tiktok.com/dsa-update.

Tiwana, A. (2014) *Platform Ecosystems: Aligning Architecture, Governance, and Strategy*. Morgan Kaufmann.

Uber (n.d.) Uber's community guidelines. https://www.uber.com/us/en/safety/uber-community-guidelines.

van der Vlist, F. N. (2017) Counter-mapping surveillance: A critical cartography of mass surveillance technology after Snowden. *Surveillance & Society* 15(1): 137–57. DOI: 10.24908/ss.v15i1.5307.

van der Vlist, F. N. (2022) *The Platform as Ecosystem: Configurations and Dynamics of Governance and Power*. PhD thesis, Utrecht University. DOI: 10.33540/1284.

van der Vlist, F. N. and Helmond, A. (2021) How partners mediate platform power: Mapping business and data partnerships in the social media ecosystem. *Big Data & Society* 8(1). DOI: 10.1177/20539517211025061.

van der Vlist, F. N., Helmond, A., Burkhardt, M. and Seitz, T. (2022) API governance: The case of Facebook's evolution. *Social Media + Society* 8(2). DOI: 10.1177/20563051221086228.

van der Vlist, F. N., Helmond, A., Dieter, M., and Weltevrede, E. (2025) Super-appification: Conglomeration in the global digital economy. *New Media & Society* 27(6): 3314–37. DOI: 10.1177/14614448231223419.

van der Vlist, F. N., Helmond, A., and Ferrari, F. (2024) Big AI: Cloud infrastructure dependence and the industrialisation of artificial intelligence. *Big Data & Society* 11(1). DOI: 10.1177/20539517241232630.

van der Vlist, F. N., Helmond, A., Luitse, D. et al. (2025) The political economy of AI as platform: Infrastructures, power, and the AI industry. In *Proceedings of AoIR 2024: Selected Papers of Internet Research (SPIR)*. DOI: 10.5210/spir.v2024i0.14088.

van der Vlist, F. N. and Weltevrede, E., eds (2025) *Appification in the Age of AI: Exploring AI App Cultures and Economies* [ASI Sprint Report]. App Studies Initiative. DOI: 10.17605/osf.io /hv34x.

van Dijck, J. (2013) *The Culture of Connectivity: A Critical History of Social Media*. Oxford University Press.

van Dijck, J. (2021) Seeing the forest for the trees: Visualizing platformization and its governance. *New Media & Society* 23(9): 2801–19. DOI: 10.1177/1461444820940293.

van Dijck, J., de Winkel, T., and Schäfer, M. T. (2021) Deplatformization and the governance of the platform ecosystem. *New Media & Society* 25(12): 3438–54. DOI: 10.1177/14614448211045662.

van Dijck, J., Nieborg, D., and Poell, T. (2019) Reframing platform power. *Internet Policy Review* 8(2). DOI: 10.14763/2019.2.1414.

van Dijck, J., Poell, T. and de Waal, M. (2018) *The Platform Society*. Oxford University Press.

van Dijck, J., van Es, K., Helmond, A., and van der Vlist, F. N., eds (2025) *Governing the Digital Society: Platforms, Artificial Intelligence, and Public Values*. Amsterdam University Press.

van Doorn, N. and Badger, A. (2020) Platform capitalism's hidden abode: Producing data assets in the gig economy. *Antipode* 52(5): 1475–95. DOI: 10.1111/anti.12641.

van Doorn, N., Mos, E., and Bosma, J. (2021) Actually existing platformization: Embedding platforms in urban spaces through partnerships. *South Atlantic Quarterly* 120(4): 715–31. DOI: 10.1215/00382876-9443280.

van Doorn, N. and Shapiro, A. (2023) Studying the gig economy 'beyond the gig': A research agenda. Social Science Research Network. DOI: https://doi.org/10.2139/ssrn.4583329.

Venturini, T. and Munk, A. K. (2022) *Controversy Mapping: A Field Guide*. Polity.

Venturini, T. and Rogers, R. (2019) 'API-based research' or how can digital sociology and journalism studies learn from the Facebook and Cambridge Analytica data breach. *Digital Journalism* 7(4): 532–40. DOI: 10.1080/21670811.2019.1591927.

Von Thun, M. and Hanley, D. A. (2024) *Stopping Big Tech from Becoming Big AI* [policy report]. Open Markets Institute and Mozilla Foundation, 17 October.

Walker Rettberg, J. (2014) *Blogging*. 2nd ed. Polity.

Weller, K., Bruns, A., Burgess, J. et al., eds (2013) *Twitter and Society*. Peter Lang.

Weltevrede, E. and Helmond, A. (2012) Where do bloggers blog? Platform transitions within the historical Dutch blogosphere. *First Monday* 17(2). DOI: 10.5210/fm.v17i2.3775.

Weltevrede, E., Helmond, A., van der Vlist, F. N. et al. (2025) Gatekeepers of the mobile ecosystem: Understanding app store moderation. *SSRN*. DOI: https://doi.org/10.2139/ssrn.5292303.

Weltevrede, E. and Jansen, F. (2019) Infrastructures of intimate data: Mapping the inbound and outbound data flows of dating apps. *Computational Culture* (7).

Wong, M. (2025) Big Tech's AI endgame is coming into focus. *The Atlantic*, 3 June. https://www.theatlantic.com/technology/archive/2025/06/everything-app-big-tech-ai-endgame/683024.

Ymerce (2007) Hyves gaat OpenSocial [Hyves is going OpenSocial]. Ymerce blogsite, 31 October. http://www.yme.nl/ymerce/2007/10/31/hyves-gaat-opensocial.

Zeff, M. (2024) Spotify cuts developer access to several of its recommendation features. *TechCrunch*, 27 November. https://techcrunch.com/2024/11/27/spotify-cuts-developer-access-to-several-of-its-recommendation-features.

Zeff, M. (2025) Google Cloud outage brings down a lot of the internet. *TechCrunch*, 12 June. https://techcrunch.com/2025/06/12/google-cloud-outage-brings-down-a-lot-of-the-internet.

Zuboff, S. (2019) *The Age of Surveillance Capitalism*. Profile Books / Public Affairs.

Index